Praise for Rivermouth

"A timely book by a translator at America's southern border, *Rivermouth* is one of the most thoughtful meditations on our nation's immigration policy in recent memory. Oliva's Kafkaesque portrayal of her work retelling the traumatic stories of migrants in English for asylum applications will linger long after you're done reading." **—*The Boston Globe***

"Amazing . . . a beautiful conversation about what immigration and migration looks like but also how we come to understand it, whose stories we get to hear, and how." **—Traci Thomas, NPR's *Here & Now***

"Oliva's excellent debut recounts her experiences volunteering as a Spanish-English translator in an immigration detention center at the U.S.–Mexico border beginning in 2016 . . . With uncut rage and breathtaking prose, Oliva edifies, infuriates, and moves readers all at once. This is required reading." **—*Publishers Weekly*, starred review**

"A graceful meditation on the unresolved traumas of life in a land where one is often not welcome . . . Evenhandedly and without sentimentality, Oliva urges that we can stand to be both more understanding and more generous." **—*Kirkus Reviews*, starred review**

"Undeterred by complexity, Oliva presents an accessible narrative electrified by transcripts of official exchanges, raw with emotion, that lay bare the tragic inadequacy of a sterile bureaucratic setting to ever do justice to petitioners in any 'credible threat interview'." **—Sara Martinez, *Booklist***

"Mexican-American translator and immigrant justice activist Alejandra Oliva is particularly situated to tell the stories of immigration at the U.S.–

southern border. She has seen the suffering, the space, and the struggles of the people firsthand as she interprets their words for them and now, their experiences for us." **—Karla J. Strand, *Ms. Magazine***

"Angela Juarez's delivery is fully engaging, and by the end of this important and timely audiobook—devastating . . . [*Rivermouth*] is an invaluable listen, particularly for those who are only passively aware of the larger political conditions that sustain our immigration crisis."

—*AudioFile Magazine*

"I am fascinated by translation both in theory and practice and it is translation that serves as the foundation of this excellent book that is about borders and migration, and how migration experiences can be so different. It's part memoir of growing up as the child of immigrants while working with migrants seeking asylum and harbor in the U.S. Oliva has prescient and deeply intelligent ideas throughout. It's always a pleasure to see an excellent mind at work."

—Roxane Gay, The Audacious Book Club July 2023 selection

"Subtle, personal, and deeply informative, this is one of those books that catapult you to a place you have never been. Translation is the author's vocation as well as a metaphor for the in-between spaces that her personal and professional identities compel her to traverse. Alejandra Oliva stands at a literal border and contemplates the metaphorical borderlines language creates, in terms of both the immigrant crisis and her own identity as a bilingual Mexican-American. Driven by a fierce sense of social justice, she is also an exquisitely controlled journalist. Her candid, intimate voice is irresistible."

—2022 Whiting Creative Nonfiction Grant judges's comments

"Alejandra Oliva's *Rivermouth* is a document of witness and grace told with devastating clarity and beauty. A beautiful and important book."

—**Kate Zambreno, author of *The Light Room***

"*Rivermouth* is a great gift in a time when migrants are demonized on the shores and borders of wealthy western countries, none uglier than the scar that is the U.S.–Mexico border that was forged through U.S. invasion and annexation, powered by societal white supremacy. Alejandra Oliva has not only written a poetic, gripping, and magnificent book, she is there, on the border, assisting the migrants in their attempts to escape hunger, deadly gangs, and dysfunctional governments, often due to U.S. coups, invasions, occupations, and economic sanctions."

—**Roxanne Dunbar Ortiz, author of *Not "A Nation of Immigrants"***

"*Rivermouth* is a supremely intelligent account of a translator's journey into the Kafkaesque machinery of U.S. immigration and asylum policy. Alejandra Oliva writes with great lucidity and empathy about the fractures at the U.S.–Mexico border and the human drama that plays out there." —**Héctor Tobar, author of *Translation Nation***

"Alejandra Oliva is a brilliant new voice of her generation, who is a writer of resistance with echoes of Simone Weil; her attention to immigration justice reaches us as a prayer. Translation in her hands becomes a deeper type of storytelling where bearing witness to injustices of immigration becomes not only a path of political reform but spiritual transformation. *Rivermouth* is a rich delta of braided essays where we are invited into spaces that break our hearts and carry us to a place of healing grace."

—**Terry Tempest Williams, author of *Erosion: Essays of Undoing***

Rivermouth

A Chronicle of Language, Faith, and Migration

Alejandra Oliva

ASTRA HOUSE ∧ NEW YORK

For my parents, Rogelio and Susana, with all my love

Permissions acknowledgments:
"God Bless Our Dead Marines"
Written by Thierry Amar, Beckie Foon, Scott Levine Gilmore,
Ian Michael Ilavsky, Efrim Menuck, Jessica T Moss, and Sophie Trudeau
Published by Rough Trade Publishing.

For information about permission to reproduce selections from this book,
please contact permissions@astrahouse.com.

Astra House
A Division of Astra Publishing House
astrahouse.com
Printed in the United States of America

Library of Congress Cataloging-in-Publication Data

Names: Oliva, Alejandra, author.
Title: Rivermouth : a chronicle of language, faith, and migration / Alejandra Oliva.
Description: First edition. | New York : Astra House, [2023] | Includes bibliographical references. |
Summary: "Rivermouth is a polemic arguing for porous borders, a decriminalization of immigration,
a more open sense of what we owe one another, and a willingness to extend radical
empathy"-- Provided by publisher.
Identifiers: LCCN 2022057997 (print) | LCCN 2022057998 (ebook) |
ISBN 9781662601699 (hardcover) | ISBN 9781662601705 (ebook)
Subjects: LCSH: Immigrants--United States--Social conditions. |
Political refugees--Legal status, laws, etc.--United States. | Spanish Americans
(Latin America)--United States. | Translating and interpreting. | United States--Emigration and
immigration--Government policy. | United States--Emigration and immigration--Political aspects. |
Classification: LCC JV6475 .O45 2023 (print) | LCC JV6475 (ebook) |
DDC 305.9069120973--dc23/eng20221222
LC record available at https://lccn.loc.gov/2022057997
LC ebook record available at https://lccn.loc.gov/2022057998

ISBN: 9781662602672 (pb)

First paperback edition, 2024
10 9 8 7 6 5 4 3 2 1

Designed by Richard Oriolo
The text is set in Adobe Garamond Pro.
The titles are set in Denver-Serial.

Contents

Preface: The River, The Table, The Wall
1

PART I
Caminante No Hay Camino
11

PART II
Sobremesa
113

PART III
El Azote
201

Afterword
281

Endnotes
287

Discussion Questions
299

Q&A with Alejandra
301

National Resources
308

Acknowledgments
309

About the Author
311

Preface:
The River, The Table, The Wall

I AM SITTING IN A church basement just off Washington Square Park, across the table from a woman who's only been in the United States for three weeks. Between us sits an I-589 form, the Application for Asylum and for Withholding of Removal, and we're surrounded by a handful of other people, pens poised, hands hovering over their keyboards, ready to take notes on our conversation.

"¿Lista?" I ask. She nods. "We're ready," I tell the group, and we dive in.

It's the last day of January 2017. Eleven days earlier, Donald Trump was sworn into office, and in the next four years, the United States immigration system, especially the asylum system, will be systematically dismantled, rule and regulation by rule and regulation. One attorney general after another will step in to review and reverse the Board of Immigration

Appeal's rulings, restricting asylum categories one by one; entire nationalities and religions will be banned from entering the United States; the Federal Register will become cluttered with proposed rules limiting asylum, raising fees for application processing, cutting off immigration; the various tentacle branches of the Department of Homeland Security—Immigrations and Customs Enforcement, Customs and Border Protection, the Border Patrol—will grow and extend into quasi-paramilitaries at the president's beck and call, deployed into too-welcoming sanctuary cities; the premise of birthright citizenship will be questioned; parents will be separated from their children; tent cities to house migrants will be erected in the desert and then eventually pushed back across the border into Mexico; miles upon miles of a "big, beautiful border wall" will actually be built up across parklands and ground sacred to the indigenous.

But at this table, at the beginning of 2017, none of that has happened yet. Today, I'm sitting across from a woman—Mayra, let's call her—and we're filling out an application so she can stay in the United States. The question of where Mayra will be allowed to call home is so critical because the answer is a matter of life or death. Back in Honduras, where she had lived her whole life up until a few weeks ago, her brother was shot in front of her, and the guy who did it told her that she would be next. This asylum application is her best shot at convincing the U.S. government that her survival is dependent on staying in the country.

Even though we are all here around this table, ready to fill out this application together, all of us wish we did not have to be. I, and the team of volunteers around me, wish that Mayra's presence in this country was not, to some extent, contingent on the strength of my translation for this application, on the tear-jerkiness or trauma of Mayra's story. The U.S. government appears to wish Mayra was not here at all. Mayra wishes that this translation we are working on was unnecessary. She would rather her life had continued in its familiar way—her brother alive, her family together—

in Honduras. And yet, here we all are: Mayra, a tableful of volunteers and the U.S. government, collaborators on this translation that no one really wants.

While the task at hand may seem simple, linear even—figuring out how to best explain to the United States government that Mayra is afraid to return to Honduras because her life is at risk there—trauma often complicates the telling of a story like Mayra's. If you've experienced deep grief, if you've lived through any kind of event with an aftermath, you know the way that time fractures and splinters, the way true things take on the sheen of unreality while dreams feel vivid and visceral. You also know how talking about any of it can sometimes feel like reliving it, your pulse thundering in your ears, time shattering all over again, your breath stuttering out of you. My job, sitting across the table from Mayra, is to let her talk, to ask clarifying questions and see if, through the interview, new information can be shaken loose, placed in a chronological order to form a cohesive narrative with cause and effect. My job is also to take her words and carry them across, from the Spanish she has spoken her entire life, into English, the language spoken by most people in the United States, and the language spoken by the government officials at the United States Citizenship and Immigration Services that will read and judge her application.

Mayra is just one of thousands of Spanish-speaking immigrants who have come to the United States from the entire spread of nations to the south, often fleeing the results of American intervention: gang members deported from overpoliced, under-resourced communities in Los Angeles full of refugees fleeing the dirty wars in Honduras, Guatemala, and El Salvador that were in turn caused by CIA destabilization of the region, Chilean and Argentine asylees fleeing U.S.-installed dictators, Mexican farm and factory laborers left hungry after the U.S.'s extortionary trade agreements. There are Tejano families in South Texas that never moved, just had the border pass over them until their language was the wrong one.

Spanish speakers of the United States have little in common as a group—they are of different races, religions, nationalities, political alignments, economic classes, immigration statuses. The things they do have in common are a shared language and the shared misfortune of proximity to a world superpower. And all many of their U.S. born-children have in common is often not even a language, just a vague and uneasy sense of cultural alliance to something incomplete, full of holes and misunderstandings that at its best feels empty and superficial and at its worst feels harmful and hegemonic. I wrote this book because our shared language reminded me that the stories we tell are a foundation for change.

I REFER TO the thing I did for Mayra, the way I helped her fill out the form, the conversation we had that evening, as "translation." It both is and isn't that—it's a constellation of many different acts, one of which is translation, yes, but also includes interpretation, or the verbal translation of someone's speech for an audience, interviewing, advocacy, diplomacy, care. All different skills, all different ways of trying your best to understand someone, and to help make them understood. I talk about the work I do with immigrants in a variety of different ways, but most often as a translator because it was through translation theory that I began to understand the work and the context I did it in differently. Translation theory—learned in classrooms and through texts by authors as various as ancient saints and nineties Quebecois feminists—helped illuminate the space I was occupying as a translator, helped me clarify my conflicting allegiances and emotions, provided a framework within which my experiences might rattle the bars, carve out escape routes.

The written word that a translator engages with is static and fixed, however much the prolonged stare translation requires makes it feel as if it is dancing under your eyes. Working with people is different—they change their words, walk things back and then send them out again, have tone, inflection, nervous tics and take calming breaths. When you're interpreting with someone, you're engaged not in a one-way transportation of their words, but in a repeating feedback loop that requires consideration and care in both directions. When I talk about translation, know that while I'm taking the theories of people who wrote about translating the Bible or a novel, what I'm most often talking about is this constellation of other activities that, for me, is a part of translating, that comes along with the territory of engaging with the texts and talks of someone else.

THIS BOOK IS unapologetically bilingual. It is written for an audience of largely English speakers because that is where the power and the fault in much of our immigration system lies. If you are a monolingual English-speaker, you may come across longer sections of untranslated, unexplained Spanish than you're used to. That doesn't mean this book isn't for you—it is—but it does mean I'm trusting you to figure it out, the same way so many immigrants do with English.

I know that in writing this book I might be speaking for a cause other than my own, eclipsing the voices of those directly affected by dangerous and deadly immigration policies. I hope that publishing this book will open the door to others like it—that reading this book will help someone make sense of a life lived between two languages. I hope that this book will awaken someone to the politics and the ethics of being in-between, help them find strength in the middle places. I hope that in these pages I show how common cause can be drawn from the points of intersection in our stories. While I believe that my proximity to the people who are the subject of this book doesn't authorize me to speak over them, I also believe that proximity has enabled me to listen more closely.

Living between languages allows me to do the work of the translator: that is, to meet people where they are, on either side, and bring their meanings to meet in the middle. This book acts as chronicle and testament of a life between these languages at a moment in time when their meanings, and the meaning of living in and within both, is being contested on stages both intimate and public. It's an archive of the things I've seen and experienced as someone who became a part of the immigration system without actually going through it myself.

I have never gone through the immigration system. Because I want to center and reflect the experiences of people who have, this book is structured not according to the chronological order of my own journey, but in the order that someone applying for asylum or attempting to defend themselves from deportation might experience each of these steps: the border, the legal clinic, the courtroom, and the detention center. I've spent time in each of these places, usually as an advocate or interpreter, but sometimes as an observer, as accompaniment to someone worried about going through it alone.

In the same way that the theory of translation gives us a variety of useful metaphors to understand the role and task of the translator—bridge, spy, traitor, general, diplomat, hostage negotiator, ambassador—the whole dizzying, byzantine span of immigration into the United States might also be better understood through metaphor. This book is divided into three parts, each one organized around a central metaphor, and largely taking place in one "zone" of the immigration system: a river and the border, a dinner table and an asylum application clinic, the wall and an immigration courtroom.

PART 1, "CAMINANTE No Hay Camino," takes as its metaphor a river—the Rio Grande, the Styx, the river of meanings translators are said to bridge in their work. Largely set in Tijuana in January of 2019 in the aftermath of the migrant caravan, this section is focused on the idea of border crossing. I contrast my parents' immigration stories, the people in Tijuana attempting to present themselves to ask for asylum who face bureaucratic violence, and the crossing between two languages and ways of being required of all immigrants.

Part 2, "Sobremesa," is set around a table. My family dinner table, a table in a church basement where people are filling out asylum applications, an imaginary table of everyone who has contributed to the translation of that application. The experiences are based largely around the *pro se* asylum workshop where I met Mayra, run by the New Sanctuary Coalition in New York City where I volunteered in 2016. This section will lay out some of the utopian promises of translation, even under the abridged, violent setting of the I-589 form needed to apply for asylum, and the ways in which actual translation often falls short. I'll also be using the table to think about the ways that immigration and the exploitation of people and resources are intertwined with our foodways: from the journey of an avocado in a grocery store on Super Bowl Sunday, to the ways in which the migrant farm worker movement began a lot of what we consider contemporary immigrant rights today.

Part 3, "El Azote," is about walls—the border wall, the walls of a detention center or a jail cell, and the ways in which the carceral system interacts with the immigration system. The central scenes are the two sides of the detention coin: a Boston immigration courtroom where I did accompaniment work in early 2019, watching one person after another defend themselves against deportation on trial via video screen, their translator's voices piped in via speakerphone; and the detention center in Mississippi I visited later that year with a cohort of civil rights attorneys, surrounded by cotton fields and full of recently arrived immigrants. I discuss the fundamental injustices inherent in the immigration detention system, and about the criminalization of legal asylum seeking that has been going on since the Clinton years and before. Based on a bilingual joke my father likes to tell, "El Azote" is also about finding limits—to understanding, to language, to the aid one can provide. But this is a book about bearing witness and learning how to create change from within those limits.

TO BE AN immigrant is to belong to two worlds while also belonging to neither. Solid land is hard to come by and what is left to the immigrant is the watery dreamworld of the river, which sweeps them along in ways you can only half understand. Language anchors you to home and allows you to cast about for a way to the other side of the river. Language helps you identify your people in a new place, it fills your ears with familiar warmth. Working in two languages is a way to claim this both-and-neither identity for yourself, a way that parents pass it down to children, a way to call down the ages of a lineage and root it in a new place. Let this book serve as an invitation to step into the river with me.

Rivermouth

PART I

Caminante No Hay Camino

Tijuana, January 2019

1

GENERATIONS OF MYSTICS AND MONKS have described the desert as the place to find God. The closest I've come to finding God is in rivers.

You'll hear it before you see it: the raucous chatter of birds, the burbling of the river as it rushes past. Follow the noise until you crest a hill, round a corner, and there it is, shocking in its lush emerald after so much dusty, scorched orange and brown. As you get closer, you'll smell it too—that particular riverine odor of wet mud and green shoots. Flycatchers swoop low over the waters, dragonflies hover and hum in the air, cottonwood leaves flash their pale undersides in the bright sun.

Rivers are life-bringers, life-creators, the deepest point of the map to which all other things flow.

The water of the Rio Grande winds its way down from its headwaters up in Colorado, south through New Mexico, then cuts east across Big

Bend National Park. It flows on to the vast, flat scrublands between Texas and Mexico. By the time it finally reaches the sea, only about a fifth of its volume remains to marry the Atlantic. At every point in its winding journey, water is diverted away from the Grande to irrigate American fields and American farms along the way. This siphoning makes the river too shallow for boats, and so the Rio Grande has two functions only: to feed the land and to cut across it as a border.

Even this border river, conceived of as immovable when it was set as one end point of the United States in the treaty of Guadalupe Hidalgo in 1848, has changed its path dozens of times since then. Artist Nicole Antebi created a meander map for the Rio Grande, showing the ways in which the riverbed has changed and shifted from 1827 to 1960. She charts oxbows and islands of contested territory. These ebbs and floods are not only natural, but political: the volume determined by dams farther up the river, the flow determining whether or not people feel safe in crossing. Antebi's hypothesis in creating her meander map rings true: "To me, the story of the river of two names has always belied the idea that two neighboring countries can ever really be fully separated— much less that the passage of people in between them can be controlled."

No one can agree on the Rio Grande's name. In the United States, its name means "the large river," sounding it out as an unbridgeable chasm, so far from the rest of the country as to be in an entirely different language. On the Mexican side, the Rio Grande is known as the Rio Bravo. "Bravo," when applied to a body of water, means white caps, waves, danger. It is the same word you use to describe an angry bull, or someone courageous or, like a bull, so angry they're brave. Thanks to agriculture, the Rio Bravo is no longer that—but it still represents a danger, the beginning of a wild new land, a possibility to be braved.

These two rivers that are the same river—the Rio Grande and the Rio Bravo—are not allowed to meet in the middle. Instead, they paint a wide, savage line across the brushland, the distance from one shore to another only a fraction of the distance between the countries on either side.

2

MY FAMILY ON MY FATHER'S side has a similar relationship to this river, and thus the border, as a planet does to the sun: We orbit around it in generationally wider circles, crossing and returning to the places we came from, time and again.

My grandmother, Dolores Ann Pue, was born in the border-straddling town of Brownsville at the mouth of the Rio Grande. Dolores was the first-born child to Señora Peggy, a firecracker of a German-Irish lady, and Mr. Wilson, part Welsh-English and part Mexican, from a family that proudly counted itself back to Spanish nobility. Dolores spent her first eight years in Brownsville, on the Texas side, before her family crossed over for an opportunity in Mexico.

Señora Peggy, born Doris Lorrain Agnew in West Virginia to a family with Appalachian roots at least three generations deep, had moved to Texas with her family as a child, following her father's new job in the Texas oil boom. Mr. Wilson, actually Wilson Henry Pue, came from a family that had been in Texas for generations—his forebears settled in San Antonio when Texas was still a newly minted state, buying up vast tracts of land for cattle ranching. Since then, Mr. Wilson's family crisscrossed the border, members born in Mexico and dying in Texas, and vice versa, since the Civil War.

And so, I am rivermouthed for generations. My parents born on one side of the river, I on the other, our languages flying back and forth between them.

THE BORDER, FOR those who live near it, is porous in this way. Sometimes you cross for a day job, and sometimes you cross for keeps—love, and life, and work can be found on either side.

Still, there was something different about my great-grandparents, Peggy and Wilson, moving their entire family into Mexico. They struck out further into Mexico than Wilson's family had for generations, settling not near the border but some 300 miles south of it in San Luis Potosí. Theirs wasn't the usual immigration story—neither culturally, in terms of direction, nor for my family, in terms of its seeming permanence.

Still, it's important that in one telling of my family story, Mexico was the promised land. It matters that when she was a girl my grandmother lived in a forest in Mexico she now describes as enchanted, full of deer that would eat from her hand, and caves that were also ballrooms, and dragonflies that could be kept on a string. It's important that my family's story has wound across the river both ways, that people I am descended from have stood on both banks of this river and wondered what promise might lie on the other side.

This border river not only runs through the history of my family, but through the history of this country—from the earliest colonizers to the people attempting to cross into safety in the United States today.

3

I SPEND THE SECOND WEEK of 2019 on the border between the United States and Mexico. Or rather, I spend the nights of that week in San Diego. Then every morning, as the sun rises over parking lots and outlet malls and border fences, I walk across the footbridge at PedWest, the U.S. Customs and Border Protection's pedestrian entrance at the San Ysidro Port of Entry. 7-Eleven coffee in hand, I flash my American passport at a Mexican border guard and send my backpack through the X-ray machine. By the third day, the guard recognizes me and waves me through without looking up.

San Ysidro is the largest land-border crossing in the world. It is estimated that ninety thousand people pass through this port daily, on foot and in cars. As I navigate the maze of passageways, I pass a steady stream of bleary-eyed commuters—nannies, gardeners, cleaners—on their way to their jobs on the U.S. side of the border. They are part of a whole informal workforce of daily border crossers that have sprung up in cities like Tijuana. We see this daily migration in twinned cities all along our southern border: San Diego/Tijuana, El Paso/Juárez, Brownsville/Matamoros. Entire communities full of people good enough to work in the United States, to provide cheap labor cleaning houses or watching children, but not good enough to be sponsored for visas or to be paid a living wage as defined on the U.S. side of the border.

I climb down a maze of concrete ramps that look like a diagram of Dante's hell, past a security guard with an AK-47 strapped to his front and his head bowed over his phone and exit the turnstile into a plaza. Ahead of me, taxis idle next to a sign with 15-foot-high letters that reads, in red, white, and green: Mexico Tijuana.

Tijuana is some 700 miles west of where the Rio Grande takes on the responsibility of acting as the U.S.–Mexico border. But here too, a line runs through the earth: a visibly rusting behemoth, parallel to the highway, shaped to the contours of the ridge it sits on, stretching all the way out to the shore and then into the sea. I am here as a volunteer, part of a temporary reverse migration of volunteers converging in Tijuana to try to meet the needs of the caravan of Central Americans—mostly from Honduras, Guatemala, and El Salvador. They have walked northward from their countries of origin and are now awaiting their turn to seek asylum on the U.S. side of the border.

Even though I was in the middle of divinity school at the time, surrounded by people who had God-given purpose, the desire to go to Tijuana was as close as I'd ever felt to a calling. When, after months of obsessively following the news about the caravan, I learned that an organization I had worked with in New York was setting up a temporary center there, the idea of traveling to Tijuana chimed through me like a bell. In the following weeks, I talked my way into a reimbursement grant from the divinity school for "experiential learning," put the plane tickets and my hotel room on a credit card, and made sure my dwindling checking account still held enough to cover food and endless cups of 7-Eleven coffee.

Before I arrived I knew my fluency in Spanish would be an anomaly in our group. The organizers' excitement when I listed that I was bilingual on my intake survey had tipped me off. But that excitement, in turn, signified something else to me: I would be useful, I would be necessary, I would be able to help.

4

———

"TRANSLATION" COMES FROM THE LATIN, translatus, to carry across. The word itself implies an edge, a dividing line. To translate means to carry across languages, across borders, across cultures.

Translation is something we do with our bodies, something that lives in our blood: We move through our mother tongue into new homes, we sense what the right word or phrase is not with our minds, necessarily, but with some kind of bodily intuition where shades of meaning dwell. Our bodies remember the specific flavor of words in two languages, the flavor of the edge between two ways of saying. As the word implies, we also use our bodies to carry meaning from one language to another. I've done all kinds of translation: the kind that involves sitting across from someone, knee to knee, and feeding their words back to them in a different language;

translation of books, of essays and articles for teenagers, of Know Your Rights pamphlets and legal documents; of someone's words well after they've spoken them.

It is impossible not to feel what I am translating inside my body, impossible not to carry it with me from a church basement or a plaza or after I hang up the phone, damp and hot from being pressed next to my ear for an hour.

In my translations for asylum seekers, this goes double. Their stories are often ones of violence against their bodies, stories that pass through me as they pass through language. I can catalog on my own body the places where people have shown me their scars as I've translated their stories, turning me into a mirror. Cigarette burns on the back of a carefully manicured hand. The aftermath of a surgery that was itself the aftermath of a stabbing, someone's chest and the softness of their belly crisscrossed with ropes of scar and the puncta of stitches on either side. Old, old bullet scars running cleanly through both ankles. An unset broken leg, and the weight on my shoulder of the man who used me as a crutch for a short walk. I don't know in my body what it is like to be hurt in these ways, but I carry a record with me anyways because it's impossible not to.

So much of translation and interpretation requires me to pass someone else's language through the first person. Their "I" becomes my own, their injuries and experiences enter a language that, for all that I am trying to render faithfully as theirs, is in reality only mine.

This line of self-and-not-self is like chalk on a blackboard. From far away, the line looks crisp, stark, easy to understand but, as you approach it, as your nose bumps the dusty slate, you understand that the line is not exactly unbroken, that no matter how much you erase, the particles of the chalk that were that line still float through the air.

Walter Benjamin describes a good translation as one that is transparent; so that it "does not cover up the original, does not block its light, but allows the pure language . . . to shine upon the original all the more." He gestures not only at the pure language of Babel and the Bible, but to the threshold space that translation occupies, the way it needs to both exist and not.

In a sense, as translator, I do not exist on the page. When I take up the weight of someone else's story by translating it, the thing I carry is a ghost, and the teller is no lighter for my carrying the story alongside them. It's in feeling the weight of the story that I can transmit it to you also, which is why I try. And why I try to erase myself in the process, so that you might read someone's words that I have translated and be reminded of your mother or aunt or sister, your neighbors and friends, forgetting the step in the middle.

I aim to become invisible because then this asylum seeker is speaking directly to you, and you have no choice but to listen.

5

BEFORE ARRIVING, I THOUGHT I knew what I'd find in Tijuana. I was prepared to be useful, prepared to bear witness because that was what you did when the world broke down, or rather, when it pointed at its own brokenness. I'd spent the prior year of divinity school talking endlessly about witnessing in the abstract, about not looking away, about the difference between action and prayer. And so, while this trip wasn't about faith in that it wasn't about God, it was a little bit about having faith in myself as an agent of change, as a comforting presence, as someone helpful.

I know now that this belief in my own usefulness was tied to an expectation that I'd be given concrete tasks to complete. I thought I'd be helping people prepare for their Credible Fear Interviews or working with those who had "passed" their interviews to begin the actual paperwork of applying for asylum. The work I had trained for in New York was helping people fill out that actual paperwork, and I knew the contours of the interview and the form, of what they asked applicants to prove.

The Credible Fear Interview, or CFI, is the all-important and only step to being admitted into the United States without a visa or special status acquired before arrival. It is administered shortly after an asylum seeker arrives in the U.S. The interview determines whether they will be immediately deported or allowed to stay in the country and given some time to build their case for remaining.

The central question this interview seeks to answer is a simple one: Do you have a credible fear that, if you return to your country, you will be tortured or killed? The only way to "pass" this test, to be admitted to the U.S. as an asylum seeker, is if that question can be answered, "yes," and more critically, if an asylum officer believes that "yes."

The Credible Fear Interview doesn't necessarily require evidence—that part comes later, during the actual asylum application, but it does place the burden on a traumatized person to recall, in order, the events that led to their trauma while sitting alone in a cold office with a law enforcement officer scrutinizing their every inflection.

I came to California with experience helping people apply for asylum; I had helped dozens of people fill out application forms in a church basement. On my first day in San Diego, I trained specifically to do CFI prep, role-playing with other volunteers. These experiences and the trainings, both in New York and San Diego, the day before crossing the border into Tijuana, taught me both how to stay warm and sympathetic—to not rush anyone or cut them off or dissolve under the weight of their stories. I learned the best ways to interview asylum seekers without retraumatizing them, knew how to create enough space for the worst things to be said, and did my best to help them be brave enough to tell an officer what had happened to them. The trick of it, which like most tricks is easier said than done, lies in making someone feel comfortable, and safe—expressing sympathy but not judgment, explaining the process and each question as you come to it, getting consent every step of the way.

Because of my work in the asylum application clinic in New York, I knew the kinds of stories people were carrying with them on their long walks to the United States. I had watched women take deep breaths to muster the bravery to give testimony, had laughed with boys barely out of their teens cracking wise to get through the telling. I knew without a doubt that every single person I had talked to deserved safety, deserved the chance to start over after an irrevocable harm. In assisting with these applications, I was able to help them take the first steps towards claiming that right. With my work in the clinic, I could enumerate the help I gave, could count the number of applications filled, quantify the good I had done that day.

When I felt that bell of a calling chime in me, it was at least in part because I thought Tijuana would be the same kind of experience as that asylum application clinic. It was another opportunity to break out of the quotidian feeling of not knowing whether I was right or wrong, helping or harming, and instead turn myself into someone doing unmistakable good.

Because that's the messy truth of it: I went to Tijuana for myself. I went because I wanted to be the kind of person who had moved towards those in need, who showed up. I went because I wanted to prove, to myself, my own goodness.

6

THE DAY I ARRIVE IN Tijuana, I follow directions to the morning meeting, held in a run-down hostel near the border crossing. Assembled on a variety of couches is the group of volunteers from our organization, from those that had been in Mexico since November to the batch of people that arrived in my training group. I see glimpses of myself in many of the other volunteers, especially those who had been in Tijuana the longest. They're young, many of them also in graduate school, many of them women, mostly white, several of them not. I also recognize the first-timers from my training the day before—Katie, a woman a little older than me with a shy smile who I immediately liked; Rachel and Libby, professors of immigration history, here on a trip that like most of their work was half research, half activism; Hilary, a retired attorney with a sudden laugh who had driven me from our hotel to the crossing that morning. Rounding out our group of the newly arrived is a family of Quakers from New England, a college student in town because he wanted to "see it for himself," and the same kind of socialist elders I know so well from the clinics I had gone to in New York.

Of the people who have been there the longest, it is Kayla I will get to know the best. She's from New York—lives I think down the street from one of my friends—but has been here since early November. I find out later she's pushed back her departure at least twice since then, going back home feels impossible in the face of all this. This morning, though, she introduces herself as the team leader of the Chaparral team, those who wander around the plaza answering questions and observing the proceedings. She's tall and looks much more regal than someone who has been staying in a hostel for almost two months has any right to. This is mostly because of her scarf and headwrap, what she grinningly calls "her textiles," which she's picked up from street vendors around Tijuana. Her face is warm and welcoming as she tells the newbies assigned to her team, including me, to huddle up with her after this meeting for a quick orientation.

As the leaders explain our responsibilities, it becomes apparent that we are there, yes, to offer information, to give Know Your Rights talks, to explain the Credible Fear Interview. But the real work lives somewhere underneath what they are saying: We are there to accompany people as they prepare to cross the border.

In the coming week, I will discover that this real work looks very different than what I expected. My job is to play with kids, to hand out tamales and Styrofoam cups of coffee. I am there to listen to someone's story, not because there is a form between us or an end goal in mind, but because they need to tell someone, anyone, what they have lived through. I am there to reassure them that they have made the right choices, that they are keeping their kids safe, that I can see how hard they are working for the

people they love, that they are making the best decisions, and that any decision they make from now on will be a good one too. I am there to see
scars, to see tears, to see immigration officials shouting, and to serve as a
warning that they are being observed; to be a warm hand on a back, a tissue held out quietly, a body between a person and someone else with a
clipboard and a megaphone. I am there to gossip or to commiserate about
the cold or the rain. I am there to answer questions, scan documents, lend
a telephone, write names and numbers on arms in permanent marker. What
this all means is that I am there, in the plaza every morning, for the calling
of the numbers and the names.

EL CHAPARRAL, THE plaza next to the port of entry on the Mexican side
of the border, is the central hub for most asylum seekers in Tijuana and
where I will spend the next week. Even as the border itself is liminal, El
Chaparral is a temporary space nestled within it: a few thousand square
feet of barren concrete sandwiched between a port of entry, its parking lot,
an overpass, and the border fence itself. It takes up this land because nothing else will. There are no businesses, no stores, not even any real buildings
adjoining the plaza, other than the ramp that drops you into El Chaparral
from the port of entry.

Over the course of the early morning, the space transforms from a
place devoid of humanity into a community gathering spot. A canopy tent
is set up on the far side of the plaza near the highway, beneath tall, white-
barked trees. Some men then set out traffic cones and rig caution tape in a
ring around it, before settling into folding chairs and pulling out a cheap,
beat-up notebook with crooked wire spiral binding.

This notebook holds "la lista," the name of every migrant in Tijuana
who has declared they want to cross the border "the right way"—which is
to say: to cross, get detained for an indefinite period of time, and, during
that detention, ask for, demand, insist on a Credible Fear Interview.

Crossing "the right way" is a kind of right-wing/nativist catchphrase: Sitting atop a veritable mountain of xenophobic laws, rules, and regulations, they claim they'd be fine with all these immigrants if only they followed the rules, if they waited their turn "just like everyone else." You can almost see their mental image: An army of highly employable yet fundamentally dangerous people thumbing their noses at American laws by jumping border fences or crossing deserts, swimming across rivers. Their argument is that if someone is willing to break the law to come into the country, God knows what other laws they might break.

Never mind that most people who do "jump the fence" do so not because it is fun, or easy, or they have a natural disdain for the law, but because they're desperate: chased down by hunger or violence. Never mind that seeking asylum is one of many "right ways" to enter—it's an internationally sanctioned right, enshrined in the United Nation's Universal Declaration of Human Rights, and in the United States' own laws. Never mind that under our current asylum system we actively punish those asking for safety. Never mind that we imprison them for weeks and months under horrifying conditions, separate them from their children, place them under a dehumanizing system intended to strip them of even more agency than they had lost by living under constant threat of violence, just so they can prove that violence is real. And so, people line up at the border, waiting to get a number, waiting for that number to be called.

Once we are huddled up outside, Kayla explains the system to us. Each name on the list is assigned a number, ten names to a number, and every morning, some of these numbers, and the names beneath them, are called out. The quantity of numbers called day by day varies. She says that some days, they don't call anyone, leaving the milling crowds at the plaza dissatisfied and restless. On other days, like one last week, she says, they run through sixty numbers, six hundred people, in quick succession, only a handful of them making it to the tent or the vans, across the border.

As we watch the first numbers be called, we witness the system at work. When someone's number comes up, they have a few minutes to run up to the tent and present a form of identification. Their names then get crossed off the list, and they are told when to come back to be processed. Kayla tells us that there are usually two crossings a day: one right after the numbers are called that morning, another a few hours later. When you saw pictures on the news of children with their sleeves pulled up to show numbers scrawled on their forearms in permanent marker, she explains, those were the numbers of la lista, mothers ensuring that their children wouldn't miss the calling of their numbers or names.

As we listen, it becomes clear that not every name called is present at El Chaparral that morning. Given the months of waiting, some people give up on this ad-hoc system and choose to cross on their own. Kayla calls this "jumping the fence," even though in reality it often means days of trekking through an unforgiving desert or swimming for miles along the Pacific coast, hoping to make it far enough north that there aren't Border Patrol agents waiting on the shore.

Some people simply miss their name being called—maybe they are sick and stayed back at El Barretal, the concert venue repurposed into a shelter a 45-minute drive away, or they didn't think their number would be called that day, so they decided to save the bus fare. Regardless of the reasoning, missing your name means beginning the long wait again. They have to get back in line, get another number, spend another month or two at El Chaparral until they are given the chance to cross again.

Because of the importance of the list, of the random, arbitrary nature of it, entire networks of communications spring up around this process. The final number of the day circulating and forwarded along branching paths throughout El Barretal and our volunteer's phones through Whats App, the preferred method of communication for many migrants. For a while, there was a website that a lot of the volunteers used, which was updated every morning with the latest from la lista. The legal aid organization Al Otro Lado posts the last number called that day on the door outside their office.

No one wants to miss their number being called, no one wants to be stuck in a Mexico that has made it absolutely plain it does not want them there, no one wants to return to the dismal El Barretal where armed guards reportedly don't let people carry in cleaning supplies for the bathrooms shared by hundreds. Everyone in that spiral-bound notebook has something waiting on the other side—a job, a spouse, a child, a long-awaited reunion with a parent, safety from whatever chased them across a continent. And every day they spend here in Tijuana for their one arbitrary number out of thousands to be called is yet another day waiting for their lives to resume.

But the harm of la lista is not only in the lives it puts on pause. Because of the rapid changes in the U.S. and Mexico's immigration policy, someone's number on la lista—and thus, the timing of their crossing—can have a huge impact on their fate.

The scale of the list is hard to comprehend. The week I'm in Tijuana, the numbers, each of which represents ten people stuck in limbo, tick up past the year of my birth—1989, 1990, 1991, 1992, 1993—then turn the corner of the millennium. Then 2019 is called, and the numbers roll forward into future years unimagined.

7

NO ONE QUITE KNOWS WHO manages the list, or how.

Despite reading endless articles on la lista, none of the sources I find seem to agree on the details of what it is and when it started. It's either a year old or four, either an official policy of the U.S. government or migrants' best attempt at building their own orderly system to cross, legitimate or not. The importance of the list, the meaning of the list, whether the list is cruel or just a fact of life all spring from this initial question: Who is responsible?

I guess at the easy answer to this question as I watch the calling of the names for the first time. Under a cordoned-off tent, a small group surrounded by men in orange windbreakers begin the day's proceedings. They look like every other person in the plaza that day except for one key difference: They hold the notebook. One person holds the list itself while another looks on calling the numbers and names slowly out to the crowd through a megaphone. Beside them, a few others sit at a folding card table checking the documents of those whose numbers are called and directing a flow of new arrivals to sign up for their numbers. The handlers of the notebook are clearly the people in charge of who and how many get to cross the border each day.

The reason that the people under the tent are not readily distinguishable from any other migrant in the plaza is because they are migrants themselves. Which means that, every so often, the people under the tent's awning will change. On any given morning, someone new may be holding the megaphone or checking documents because whoever had been calling out numbers the day before came across their own, gathered their things and their family, and climbed into the vans.

This suspicion is backed up by the level of power it seems these migrants have over who is allowed to cross. Sometimes, but not always, the people guarding the list can be bargained with, asked to consider extenuating circumstances or someone's humanity, something you might not expect to see if the organizers were just government bureaucrats.

Later that week, I will meet a mother whose children had almost been kidnapped the night before. Tijuana migrant accommodations are notoriously unsafe, circled by narcos and creeps and kidnappers and all manner of people looking to take advantage of the desperate. The mother is sobbing and anxious, her head whipping around wildly every time her son, still boisterous and unbothered, tumbles out of view. The next morning, with the help of some other migrants, she manages to get herself and her son and daughter called in the next round, even though they were dozens of numbers away.

And isn't that authority the gift of this list being self-organized? If migrants organize the list themselves, then whatever harm happens to the people who are waiting to cross is just incidental, the sad luck of having to travel through an inhospitable place on the long road to a better life. It means the months of waiting and desperation are just the result of the system these migrants have worked out for themselves, occasioning a shrug from government bureaucrats on both sides of the border—it's their own business how they present for asylum, isn't it?

Of course, the answer can't be this simple. Because there are still the men in the orange windbreakers milling around the outskirts of the tent. These are members of Grupos Beta, theoretically a humanitarian aid organization and a branch of the National Institute of Migration of Mexico. When Grupos Beta first grew from a local Tijuana-based institution to the national level in 2001, it was the subject of elegiac newspaper articles accompanied by photos of its orange-polo clad members rescuing passed-out migrants from the desert and handing out water bottles to small children. Their job is supposedly to protect migrating Mexican nationals as they move northward toward the U.S. However, as the demographics of who exactly is crossing Mexico in search of asylum has shifted, Grupos Beta has become more hostile towards those that don't claim Mexican citizenship.

The stories of how Grupos Beta interferes with crossing are endless: They have been known to reject people's identity documents for no reason, call the more punitive branches of Mexico's immigration services to deport groups of migrants, and extort individual migrants themselves. Most mornings in the plaza, Grupos Beta is represented not just by the guys in windbreakers, but by another man, also in orange, with a thick salt-and-pepper mustache. He stands by the readers of the list with his arms crossed, impassive, or circulates through the plaza, eyeing people as he goes. He emanates an air of authority, and is most often the one who will chastise migrants or briskly shepherd them towards a different part of the plaza. There's no name embroidered onto his jacket, no way of tracing him back to a personnel website somewhere, so he remains the man with the mustache. He is usually the migrants' last point of contact on this side of the border, armed with a clipboard and brisk impatience. Still, even he, with his gruff authority, isn't really the one in charge here.

The organization that is actually responsible for the list, of course, is the government of the United States. First-hand accounts from some of the migrants who have run the list in the past mention meeting with Customs and Border Protection officials to discuss the number of people called across each day. They said that the U.S. officials promise but never actually allow more people to cross to alleviate the number waiting on the Mexico side of the border. This is also part of the reason Grupos Beta and la lista are looked at with such skepticism by so many—if they're collaborating with the feds on the U.S. side, can they really be looking out for the migrants?

The United States government's involvement is also the reason the list feels so overwhelming and arbitrary and unknowable—it is designed to be. Like every other part of our immigration system, this process is designed to keep people uncertain, on their toes, prepared for the unexpected to rear its head at highly charged moments. This opaqueness also means that when something bad happens—when someone is extorted for a better place on the list, or when someone is frustrated because they haven't been able to cross, or when someone dies while waiting for their number to be called—the fault has to be peeled back, layer by layer, before getting to the actual culprits, insulating the United States government from blame.

IT IS ALSO important to note that the list itself is illegal. When volunteers from Al Otro Lado, a legal defense organization made up of mostly American lawyers with offices in Tijuana, speak amongst each other, they call it "the illegal list." This is more than a little ironic: "Illegal" is, of course, the preferred pejorative in some circles for someone who has crossed the border without a visa, a work permit, a job, or $100,000 in a savings account.

Policies, on the other hand, no matter how informally structured, could never violate the law—they *are* the law, or at the very least, tradition.

The effect that la lista makes real is known as metering. The battered notebook with its endless row of names printed carefully in ballpoint pen ensures that those coming into the country are just a slow trickle, while pools of people out of options gather and wait and eddy on the other side of the border. Historically, metering was implemented at moments of high traffic to ensure that the bottleneck of getting through the border doesn't happen at a border agent's desk. However, as the Trump administration has attempted to end immigration, metering has been a useful tool in restricting the number of people able to cross. Informally, it's become a forever policy, reinforcing the need for itself as more and more people arrive, spreading east along the border.

This is why metering is illegal. Let's say an asylum seeker tried to cross into the U.S. the same way I do, by walking the half-mile from El Chaparral to the barred revolving doors flanked by Customs and Border Protection officials. If, when called up to the desk by the unsmiling border guard, they do not hold out a valid passport stamped with a visa but instead ask for asylum, they would simply be turned around and shooed back into Mexico. This refusal is against U.S. asylum law, which states that "any alien physically present in the United States . . . may apply for asylum." Somewhere on the walk to the CBP officer's desk, this asylum seeker has crossed the brass line embedded in the concrete walkway that demarcates the beginning of the United States. By the time he is asking for asylum, he is present in the country, has been for some hundred feet, and has the legal right to have his case considered. Nevertheless, border guards have the ability to more or less act with impunity—what recourse does an asylum seeker have, after all?

The CBP agent, behind his desk, has all the power. Migrants fear that if they talk back or try to reason with the agent, it will be a black mark on their case. The people claiming asylum by coming in through a port of entry instead of simply jumping the fence have already taken pains to ensure that they're doing everything "the right way." Most don't want to risk upsetting an already opaque and unfriendly system.

There are, of course, people who will still try to ask for asylum without risking the long wait of la lista—those in desperate need of medical attention or actively pursued by cartel members, LGBTQ+ youth whose lives are directly and increasingly at risk—and they too get turned back at the door by CBP agents.

Others will still bank on crossing the border first—fence jumping—and only then, when they're apprehended by Border Patrol agents, ask for asylum. These people can then be prosecuted for "illegal entry," even as they plead for asylum. It is these prosecutions, which ramped up during the Trump administration's Zero Tolerance policy, that allowed immigration officials to use their discretion to charge nearly all parents crossing the border with children. Adults under criminal investigation nearly always have children in their custody removed from them, and can have a harder time obtaining asylum. These prosecutions essentially criminalize asking for asylum without going through metering first.

So yes, the list is illegal, and yes, there are people—mainly lawyers at huge nonprofits with the resources to assemble years-long, expensive class action suits—fighting against it. But for now, la lista remains, if not as law, then as unofficial policy. These unofficial policies, quick to institute and slow to remove, are how the majority of immigrant rights have been chipped away during the last several decades. It's rarely something as big as an act of Congress, too small to rally people to organize or call in about that has made the difference in whether or not someone is allowed in. Instead, it's a policy memo, a federal rule, an internal invisible shift at a time. Measures that are only contestable through extended court battles that drag on for years at a time, trailing paused and damaged lives in their wake. While the court battles and the challenges wind through the system, in order to cross into the United States, an asylum seeker needs to go through the byzantine process of getting assigned a number, waiting for that number to be called, being shoved into a van with their belongings, and then finally, finally being allowed to cross that border.

Metering ensures a humanitarian crisis on the Mexican side, as people who are passing through but unable to actually pass attempt to survive. Mexican shelters run out of beds. People sleep on the streets and take poverty-wage jobs to try and hold on until their numbers are called, or give money to people who promise to get them a better number before disappearing into the night, or they are kidnapped and violated and extorted. Metering leaves people isolated, poor, and vulnerable in a city already overcrowded with those affected by the wall.

Metering also helps hide the thousands of people, kept in desperate conditions, seeking asylum in the United States. Where Mediterranean countries have offshore refugee camps like Lesbos and Lampedusa, and Australia has Nauru and Christmas Island as convenient ways to store their refugee camps out of sight and out of mind, the United States, which receives more migration over land than by sea, hides the people it will not let in across the border. American narcissism is such that we cannot—or will not—see clearly what happens just beyond the ends of our country, and so after the outcry of Zero Tolerance and Family Separation, the Trump administration ratcheted up the use of metering, hiding away all the mothers and children that were, yes, still together, but no, not safe.

A week after I left Tijuana in January 2019, the campaign for migrant invisibility was compounded by the Remain in Mexico policy, bizarrely known as the "Migrant Protection Protocols." Instead of allowing asylum seekers to wait for their asylum hearings in the United States, as had previously been the law, MPP forced them to wait in Mexico for years, without work permits or a permanent way of making a life.

On January 29, 2019, the day the first person was turned back as part of MPP, his photo is published in the paper. You can see him, squinting into the throng of reporters in a baseball cap and a big tan windbreaker, holding his backpack down by his side. Carlos is in his fifties, with a sun-lined face—I imagine him as a farmer back in Honduras. In the photo, he still has his belt and shoelaces, items that will be taken from later groups of returnees after their brief stays in American detention centers to be processed. Almost as soon as his picture is taken and he tells journalists who he is, he's whisked away into a van by Mexican officials. No other mention of him exists in the media.

Out of sight, out of mind.

8

THE CARAVAN ARRIVED IN TIJUANA in November of 2018, a few months before I did. As the U.S. president talked and tweeted endlessly about the convoy in the months prior to its arrival at the border, the headlines started: This group of initially around one thousand people had set out from Honduras and was heading to the United States. Some outlets claimed that the caravan was full of Al-Qaeda members and criminals, that these people walking northward were on their way to overtake the United States with all the inexorable force of an army or a flood. A group of people on the move as an annihilating force.

But as the news media was whipped into a frenzy, the president also served as an unintentional publicist for this mass migration. His incessant tweeting ensured the story stayed in the headlines for months. As the caravan progressed, people would hear about its movement from the news and join as it passed through their communities. At its peak, the caravan was around 7,000 members strong, including an estimated 2,300 children.

In reality, many of the people who made up the caravan were those fleeing the same gangs and violence Trump so loudly decried. Others were trying to outrun the droughts that accompany climate change, dispossession from their lands, lack of opportunity, and an inability to care for their families in economies devastated by U.S. extractionism.

These circumstances, writ large across a nation, across governments too weakened and destabilized by U.S. intervention to take action—are what made people pack up their homes, sell off their belongings, and start walking across a continent. These circumstances, and what waits on the other side: the opportunity to breathe free, to build something, to live lives outside of threats and danger and late-night knocks on the door.

And so, they walked.

WHEN WE COMPARE the stories of the members of the caravan to the stories we've historically told ourselves about immigrants and refugees, there's a will behind the walking that feels like something new.

Many of our most dramatic stories of immigration and people seeking refuge involve taking to the sea. The Mediterranean is crossed in plastic dinghies by families escaping famine and economic and political hardship in North Africa. The U.S.–Cuban immigration policy was for many years known as "wet foot, dry foot," in deference to that first step onto some South Florida beach after a ninety-mile ocean crossing away from the evils of communism, usually on a leaking raft. Eight hundred thousand refugees worldwide, recently in danger of being deported from the United States, are known as "boat people" due to their rapid, seaborne escape from the American bombs falling on Vietnam. The myth of the founding of our nation is itself based on a group of people climbing aboard a boat and crossing waters in search of a better life and religious freedom.

The caravan is fundamentally different from these stories, an unfamiliar form of resettlement. For starters, these modern migrants are not fleeing a tyrant king but more diffuse forms of violence. They flee the accumulation of drought years and starvation caused by climate change, the theft of their traditional lands by developers, the poverty in countries repeatedly exploited for what they can give.

However, we primarily hear a single story about what the caravan is fleeing. This narrative comes, yes, from right-wing politicians, but also from those across the political spectrum who are unwilling to see the responsibility the United States has for global warming, for the rapacious exploitation of natural resources in other countries, for the weakening of governments. That single story is about migrants fleeing the threat of gang violence and narcos, or the kind of machismo that means a man can beat his wife without repercussions, or a gay man can be assaulted simply for existing. These forces are described as part of a culture that is morally weak, incapable of self-governance.

Where one side of the discourse vilifies migrants, the other side tends to view them as children or victims. While the violence people are fleeing is unimaginable, while the consequences for saying "no" to gang recruitment or speaking up to the police, or any of it are high, they're also choices that people have made, as part of their own complex political and personal realities. Choosing to leave land that has been in your family for generations, choosing to leave a partner with whom you've had a child, choosing to come to an entirely new place are difficult decisions, not instinctual impulses for survival.

While reporters were busy either showing aerial shots of the caravan "horde" crossing rivers or interviewing individual mothers and their children as they made camp, the caravan—which had self-organized into a variety of groups and committees—was putting out press releases with political demands, working with nonprofits to have their voices amplified, and operating as savvy movers on the geopolitical stage they occupied.

A few weeks before they reached the border, the Mexican government forced the caravan to take a more dangerous route through cartel-ridden Veracruz. In response, they released a consensus statement: "We hold the state government of Veracruz and federal authorities responsible for every person who is wounded, falls ill, faces extortion, is kidnapped, forcibly disappeared, trafficked, or murdered on this route that we are being forced to take." Two days after the U.S. government teargassed migrants who attempted to cross the border on New Year's Day 2019, caravan leaders put out another statement: "We don't want to go back to violence. It has not been easy to leave our countries, leave part of our families, expose our children and walk through unknown places to have a chance at living in the United States. We want our children to have access to an education, to health care and to a life without threats."

Allowing the members of the caravan this kind of voice and power before they cross the border violates the idea of migrants as solely a political subject, never acting, always acted upon. By acknowledging these documents, we would be acknowledging and magnifying their collective power and agency instead of removing it or ignoring it. These statements, which argue for the right to safe passage, the right to free migration, the right to a better life, disrupt every narrative we want to tell ourselves about asylum seekers.

This agency, this willingness to disrupt the narratives put upon them is what makes the caravan threatening, what makes those that walk across the continent incomprehensible to a public that has only heard the single story of what the caravan is. Members of the caravan are seen as equally morally suspect as the society they're fleeing. They are looked on as importers of violence into the United States, the fact that they are arriving by land marks them as foreign not just in identity but in approach.

There's a poem, dating back to the Spanish Civil War, by Antonio

Machado, a poet who had been exiled from the lands where he was born by the looming threat of fascism. He wrote, "Caminante, no hay camino, Se hace camino al andar."

The caravan put one foot in front of the other and made their own way forward. They walked down roads and up mountains, along rivers and across deserts. Taking to the sea is understandable because it requires just the single decision, a leap off of shore. But walking across a continent for days, weeks, months, miles at a time, is incomprehensible. The sheer repetition, the reiteration of every day, every step, making the same decision to walk away from home over and over again. The willpower and determination that keeps someone going beyond exhaustion and danger and difficulty. What kind of fear could make someone leave everything they've ever known like this? Why give yourself over to aching, to calluses, to blisters, to skin rubbed raw? Why endure these throbbing muscles, carrying your child on your back for hundreds of miles, across a border into a new life?

9

ON MY FIRST DAY IN Tijuana, sitting on the floor of the concrete shelter our group was using as an office, I meet Sara. She is sitting on the floor, legs crossed, next to her partner, holding her baby in her arms. All three of them are beautiful. Sara has tilted, laughing eyes and perfectly done nails, a mass of curly hair heaped on her head; her partner is a serious-looking and quiet man with dark skin and a neat beard, who seemed unable to look away from his daughter, the roundest and most cheerful baby I have ever seen, all rolls of baby fat and deep dimples and a little wrinkle on the bridge of her nose when she laughs, which is often.

Sara is from Mexico, and her partner has a more complicated immigration story: He's spent time in a lot of countries, but where he's from is never made clear. They met here, in Tijuana, over a year ago, after they had both fled their homes for different reasons. Their baby, Sara told me, had almost died a few months ago. She was born prematurely, with a heart condition. As the little girl reaches for her bottle with both hands, Sara talks about the miracle that is watching her baby eat. "She's got some catching up to do," she says. "She was just so little when she was born."

Sara and her baby and her partner become regular fixtures at the shelter, coming every morning after the numbers are called. She is the kind of person that is bad at sitting still, so when we start passing out lunches, she'll hand her baby to her partner, or leave her under his watchful eye on a blanket in the corner, and come to help—distributing pasta salad; sometimes miming extravagantly at the French speakers to see if they want tamales or more coffee; trying to tell Katie, who doesn't really speak Spanish but is willing to work with that, what to do; bringing people to one of the volunteers when she realizes they have an unanswered question or an unmet need.

She always knows when someone needs some light, distracting patter—I hear about her manicures, her former job as a dental hygienist, the way her diet has changed from heavy Mexican masa to the lighter vegetable-based Caribbean food her partner prefers (Ay Dios, cómo bajé de peso! Pero extraño mis taquitos, eso sí.). She also knows when someone needs quietness, just a hand on their back, or when someone needs tough love, to be told to straighten up and figure it out, that nothing will be solved by them sitting here crying. She is a natural, just like some of my classmates on the chaplaincy track are, social and warm and careful, intuitive about people's emotional states. We love having her in the office: Volunteers swap Sara stories at our closing meetings in the evenings. Seeing her and her partner staking out some corner of our shelter—heads leaning together, grinning baby between them—is a tiny moment of serenity amid everything else.

10

———

A RIVER IS, OF COURSE, not only water: It is an edge, a border, a boundary, a threshold, or a space between, a road, a route, a path to freedom. The Nile after the first plague and the Israelites escaping along its banks. The River Jordan, one last river to cross before reaching the Promised Land. People escaping slavery by following the water spilling from the Drinking Gourd's North Star into the Mississippi and Missouri Rivers and northward. The Styx and the Nile, rivers separating the land of the living from that of the dead in ancient Greek and Egyptian cosmologies. All that time spent along and in and across the river, splashing in it to throw off the dogs, is time spent in between.

Translation works like this too. In the middle of translating something, I feel like I'm waist-deep in some river, meanings flash by me on opposite banks, and it's my job to arrange and orchestrate them. Translators often speak of translation loss—those places where some cleverness in the original is rendered flatly in the new language, where a shade of meaning becomes so subtle as to be imperceptible. There are also moments, standing mid-river, where it feels as if, rather than slipping out of my fingers, the meanings build up, swell, orchestrate themselves into a bridge between the two sides, where instead of one or the other, you get to have and keep both. This is a fleeting illusion, though. Because after all, language has edges, so does the country, and so does the river you're in, and not everyone is willing to wade in.

POET AND THEORIST Gloria Anzaldúa famously described the Mexico-U.S. border as "*una herida abierta* where the Third World grates against the first and bleeds."

The border between Mexico and the United States *has* been an open wound, a river of blood since its inception: A war was fought over it, border crossings and land disputes in lands newly held by the U.S. led to lynchings in the 1800s. Today, Border Patrol agents destroy water stations left for border crossers in the desert so people die daily in the crossing; they become bodies lost to the ravages of the dry winds and scavenging animals of the desert. Parents are separated from their months-old children. Detention centers, known by migrants as hieleras/iceboxes or perreras/kennels—as much for their frigid temperatures and animalistic architecture as for the agency that runs them—are scattered along the border: Karnes, Dilley, Eloy, Torrance County, Otay Mesa, Cibola. It isn't uncommon for people to choose a so-called "voluntary departure" when threatened with an extended stay in a hielera or a kennel. The whole process seems to force an answer to the question: What are you more afraid of: What we are capable of, or what you left behind? For many people, detention in these facilities is also the first step to getting a Credible Fear Interview, to being able to stay in the country.

Despite—or because of—its bloody past, Anzaldúa describes the border as the site of the creation of a new language: "Change, *evolución, enriquecimiento de palabras nuevas por invención o adopción* have created variants of Chicano Spanish, *un nuevo lenguaje. Un lenguaje que corresponde a un modo de vivir.*" Blood as wound-blood, but also as life-blood. While I didn't grow up in Anzaldúa's Rio Grande valley, a similar Chicano Spanish, Spanglish, Tex Mex, bubbled up in me, the way it will when there's a border between home and school. When I was a kid finding footing in two languages, my mother used to scold me, "No hables así, todo pocho."

Pocho is a difficult word to translate. In some cases, it means people like me: Mexican-American. You can also use it to tell someone you feel sick, ("ando medio pocho") or that the fruit you meant to eat is now over-ripe ("ese mango ya está pocho"). To me, it has always sounded like a pot-hole of a word, something mundane that will wreck your transmission. Much like talking pocho, the word itself is overripe, sticky, spilling over with meanings, a pothole in the properness of "good" Spanish. It carries with it what Anzaldúa calls "the slant-ways" of the border-dweller, the threat of impurity and illness contaminating a pure tongue. It also holds in it the joy of cobbling together. *"Un lenguaje que corresponde a un modo de vivir."*

THREE YEARS AFTER MY PARENTS were married but a little bit before I was born, my father was admitted to a PhD program in Boston. Both of them had lived in Mexico nearly their entire lives, had only left the country for a year at most, always with a return in sight.

When they got to Boston, English wasn't exactly their first language, but it wasn't completely foreign to them either. My dad was nearly fluent—he knew English from his Texan grandmother and mother, from a year spent in Ohio in middle school with friends of friends of relatives, and from his master's program in the UK. My mom had gone to American schools for most of her grade schooling, taught by gringo expats who mispronounced her name. She knew enough English to get by, but it wasn't a comfortable language for her. Still, the change of Boston was something of a shock to the system.

I don't know much about the logistics of their early lives in the States, the shape of their days. My imagination is limited by the myopia of childhood, unable to comprehend the shape of my parents' lives before my own arrival. I've learned enough from family lore to describe some of it: their tiny apartment in student housing, my dad's classes in a building visible from their windows, my mom watching *Sesame Street* and *Good Morning America* to get the sound of English ringing in her ears before she walked across the street to her job at the Au Bon Pain that's still there, at the corner of Main and Hayward. The way they've described their building makes it sound like the melting pot of America that they had been promised. Their neighbors were from Japan and Kenya and France—and California and Alabama, which felt similarly foreign to my parents.

A year or so after they arrived, I was born.

My parents spoke to me mostly in Spanish as a baby, trusting that the rest of the world around us would teach me English. My mom still watched *Sesame Street*, but this time with me alongside her. When my little sister was born, I was two and a half and my mom's English came more easily, both of us learning language alongside each other. Our present-day family vocabulary is littered with the kind of malapropisms common to little kids learning to talk in two languages at once: los perros que barkean, calling my dad's desk an escritoire as if I was a miniature antiques dealer. My parents also had a community—they had friends to babysit us, a church we attended every week, complete with Bible studies and outings to go apple picking. There are photos from day trips to see the leaves change in New Hampshire, potluck dinners, trips to the zoo. Spanish was still the main language at home, the language we lived in for most of every day, but English was no longer simply the language of classes or of talking to the cashier at the grocery store, it was the language for worshipping God, for friendship, for being part of a community.

By the time my dad graduated from his PhD program, my parents had decided they wouldn't go back to Mexico. In the photos from my dad's graduation day, my mom is already pregnant with my sibling, her belly ballooning in a sundress.

Shortly after my father's graduation, we moved to Chile. I was four and started going to preschool "in Spanish." This meant making friends in Spanish, learning songs and telling stories and counting and naming colors in Spanish. Chile was never meant to be a permanent move, so the language roles reversed, and English became the language of home and family. I don't think the return to Spanish came as a relief to my parents—Chilean Spanish had different vocabulary for basic words, different pronunciation, weird conjugations. Their language still marked them as being "from elsewhere," a rarity in a fairly insular country.

We moved back to the States when my sibling was a year old and I was five, just starting kindergarten. I brought English home with me every day, this once unfamiliar language suddenly seeming easier and easier to me, the first thing that came when I reached for a word. It wasn't that my Spanish was slipping away, it was just that there was so much more I could *do* in English, so many more people I could be.

This was when my parents' eternal refrain of "En Español!" picked up. More often than not, my siblings and I played in English, fought in English, bossed and sassed each other in English. My sibling grew up in a house that was not just bilingual, but filled with spangled, brilliant Spanglish. To this day, I'm the one most comfortable in Spanish—I fall back on borrowed words less often, am a little better at code-switching, while my sibling and sister's understanding of Spanish was never just as my parent's language, but also mine. By the time the three of us could talk easily with one another, it seemed impossible that there was ever any less language in our house, that there had ever been any narrower a range of ways to talk to each other.

12

AS A SMALL CHILD, I understood Mexico as the place where my parents were from. Even on my dad's graduate school stipend, we would visit every year. My first passport shows me as a near newborn baby, months old, with a shock of dark hair sticking straight up. When we lived in New England, Mexico was accessible to us only by plane. I relished sitting by the window, getting to unwrap cellophane trays of plane food, ordering usually forbidden sodas, watching movies on the headrest in front of me.

What I don't remember from those early visits is the bureaucracy of customs, the sense of kinship my parents must have felt with the other people on the plane heading home. We'd fly from Boston to Houston or Dallas or Atlanta, from there to Mexico City, and finally on to Tampico to find my grandmother idling at the arrivals curb beside her long black Cadillac DeVille with cherry red leather seats and a little koala bear on the sun visor. My siblings and I would be plied with Dramamine, so bitter our tongues would burn, to ensure that we'd doze off for the hour and a half to my grandmother's house.

This was what Mexico was: sleepovers with my cousins, riding around in the back of my grandfather's pickup truck, long afternoons spent swimming at my cousins' other grandmother's house, trips to cascades and sinkholes and natural caverns and pools, late night (8 p.m.) trips to El Güero Mendiola, a taco stand where the beef for the tacos de bistec was chopped so fine it almost caramelized on the griddle, eating sweet, cold raspas de cajeta.

At that time, the border was something we literally flew over and the place that waited on the other side was a paradise of vacation and late bedtimes and extended family. While Mexico was sometimes out of reach because of the simple cost of five international plane tickets, the border was always ephemeral and slight, the difference between Massachusetts and Mexico a matter of a few hours' air travel, family on either side.

It wasn't until we moved to Texas the year I turned 11, following my dad to a new job and a house closer to his family, that we started crossing like many others do—by car. The drive from our home in Texas to my grandmother's took twelve hours: six in the U.S. and another six through Mexico, assuming there was no traffic on the bridge between the two (there was always traffic on the bridge). Encountering the border this way felt different—the product of a full day of driving, the aftermath of a slow-moving line. This new mode of crossing turned the border solid, into something real and substantive in my mind, an actual piece of geography that we physically encountered, that could stop us short. It was no longer an imaginary line flown over without a thought but something real, given shape by solid layers of bureaucracy and long, long lines, protected by German shepherds and men with guns. It was clear, even then, that it was meant to be easier for someone to travel in one direction and not the other.

. . .

AT FIRST GLANCE, there is no difference between El Chaparral and any other plaza on a busy morning: people chatting over coffee, vendors selling tacos and smoothies, people bustling to and fro. But amongst this familiar morning chorus, volunteers in hiking backpacks and sensible shoes float between family groups and explain the manita.

They pass out fliers. "Tu Asilo Está En Tus Manos," it says, reminding asylum seekers that in the midst of their Credible Fear Interviews, they should look down at their hands to remember (one for each finger) to tell the asylum officer WHAT happened, WHO did it, WHY they think it happened, whether they went to the POLICE, and whether they had tried to just move SOMEWHERE ELSE within the country they hold citizenship. "Your Asylum Is in Your Hands," is a cute but ultimately hollow slogan. Nothing about this process is really in your control, of course, but being able to look down at the mnemonic device of your own hands is better than having to meet the eyes of the asylum officer asking those questions.

When I arrived in Tijuana, I hadn't expected the extent to which El Chaparral would feel like a kind of bordertown international arrivals terminal. Like maybe every other American, I was aware that there was a caravan moving northward from Central America and, thus, that a few of the migrants it held were likely to be Mexican themselves. Yes, the vast majority of people waiting to cross at El Chaparral are Spanish-speaking, but there are also francophone Haitians and Cameroonians in large numbers; a family of adults from Georgia; a tall, blonde Russian mother with her two tow-headed little girls, all their hair neatly braided; a group of men who had cycled from Ecuador to Tijuana, originally from Eritrea. Everyone is sprawled near their luggage, sipping food-stand coffee, and watching kids as they run shrieking through the maze of legs. Everyone is waiting to hear their number, waiting to be given the green light to cross the border into the promise of California.

They are all here, in this waiting room of a city, the last possible place to prepare for what's coming. The hubbub in the plaza comes also from people packing and re-packing their luggage, trying to figure out how to carry ID documents on their persons, folding papers into tiny squares to be shoved into socks, calling family members and sponsors in the States to let them know they're about to cross and to get the spare rooms ready.

EVERY MORNING, THE plaza is chaos until the megaphone comes out. Then, everyone clusters toward the tent, hushes, strains, leans in close.

The calling always starts with the number, then the ten names underneath it. The crowd self-organizes into concentric rings, those whose number was called congregate closest to the center, their faces tense and documents in hand. Further out are those who are pretty sure they won't be called until tomorrow or even next week. Some people start showing up days before they expect their number to be called: better to hang around the plaza than risk missing it and have to begin the waiting process again.

As the circles widen, the atmosphere is more relaxed. The outermost circle is full of people who know they won't be called that day, who are here to otherwise break up a monotonous day or week or month. They treat the calling like a social occasion, laughing and gossiping. I hang back, too, make small talk with people who won't be crossing for a while, watch the proceedings and make sure everyone knows about the free lunches we serve at our offices down the street.

Some of the people in these outer circles are well settled into Tijuana. They work under-the-table jobs cleaning houses, rent apartments, have routines that sometimes include spending a morning at the plaza to watch the numbers be called. I understand the impetus behind this—after months of moving, of propulsion, they are suddenly frozen in place, unable to do anything but wait as the slow wheels of bureaucracy turn. The same energy that attracts them to the plaza is what propelled them across a continent to get here in the first place. They're eager to witness the process, to feel part of a moment, to be with other people who know what they've been through.

I know this because of the way people at El Chaparral ask me questions. Sometimes they'll just ask logistical questions—which line is the one to get the numbers? What number did they just call? How long will I be detained? What's the process like once you cross? But most often I receive a story disguised as questions, an avalanche of narrative. They don't expect me to have an answer, they just need someone who will listen.

One morning, I end up chatting with a woman who shares a first name with my own mother. She is also a mother, her three-year-old daughter clinging to her cloud-print fleece pajama pants. The woman's eyebrows are tattooed on but not filled in, so she looks perpetually surprised, even though she has the long, slow blinks of someone still half asleep. She tells me her number on la lista, a few dozen away from what is being called that morning and says she's just here to check and see how many they get through, what the process is like. She waves at a car idling across the plaza where her husband is napping with their six-month old daughter. She asks me where I'm from and I tell her Boston.

"Oh! That's where I'm going," she says. "Well, close by, really." She names a suburb an hour outside of the city. "My husband's brother is there, and they say they've got a place waiting for us there, until we get on our feet."

Not many people here are headed to Boston. Mostly, I hear Los Angeles, Chicago, New York. Thinking I might be able to help her family in a more real way, I tell her about a few organizations in Boston doing immigration justice work that I could put her in touch with. When she accepts, I program my number into her phone and tell her to call me, that I'll try to figure out how I can help them get through the gap between their arrival and their ability to apply for a work permit, maybe find someone to accompany them to their court hearings.

"So, how did you get here?" she asks, gesturing at the metal gates to the port of entry.

"Oh, I flew. I'll be heading back in a week or so."

"And here, to Tijuana?"

"I'm staying in San Diego, so I walked over the bridge this morning."

"And for home tonight?"

"I'll walk back across to the hotel."

"¿Así na'más?"

I nodded, aware of my passport in the outer pocket of my backpack. It lives there while I work, hovering 6 inches out from the edge of my body, encasing me in a protective halo like an amulet or saint's medal for nearly supernatural protection. I try to ignore my impulse to check on it during the day, keep my hand from compulsively snaking up to make sure it's still there.

I feel something a door down from guilt, almost as if I required forgiveness for the passport. There is nothing I have done to deserve this ease of crossing, nothing she has done not to.

The next morning, she finds me in the plaza again, her eyebrows filled in and looking better rested. She waves, we chat a bit about what number they're calling, what her plans for the day were. Later, when I had already returned to Boston without seeing her again, I make it a habit to check the volunteer group chat for what number la lista has gotten to. On the day her family's number is called, I do impossible calculations to figure out how long a family with two small kids might spend in detention. Months later, even after I have waited that imperfectly calculated length of time over and over again, I answer every call from an unknown number.

13

———

AS I CHAT WITH OTHER volunteers or people waiting to cross in El Chaparral, I sometimes get mistaken for a migrant. Volunteers stop to ask me "si usted conoce sus derechos" in heavily accented Spanish, migrants ask me how long I'd been there, what my number is, and on one occasion, the most aggressive member of Grupos Beta, the man with the mustache, tells me to get my kids—someone else's, that I was watching over while she unpacked and repacked her bags—in order and get back in line.

And sometimes, with the magnetic power a name has, I mistake *myself* for a name on the list. I'll be talking to someone, explaining the mechanics of the asylum-seeking process or passing along a helpful phone number, when suddenly, out of the megaphone's crackly static, I'll hear my own first name. It pulls me up out of the conversational stream, turns my head, makes me pause, only to dissolve into a stranger's middle and last names. Sometimes they are accompanied by a sudden upstretched hand, clutching papers, moving towards the tent. Over that week, I hear my own name, both first and last, my mother's name, my father and brother's name, my sister's name. My whole family is accounted for over the week I'm there and, every time, the sound catches me up.

MY NAME, ALEJANDRA, is an old name. It first traveled from the Greek—alexo, "I defend" and andros, "man." Defender of men. My name is the Spanish version of it, with the connotation and cognate of "alejar."

My last name also travels: The earliest I've seen a mention of my family name was in an exhibit. The Olivas were a family of cartographers in medieval Catalunya, some of the first to plot the eastern coast of the Americas onto a map. Funny, considering where we ended up. What my last name *means*, though, is the hundred-year-old gnarled branches of an olive tree reaching towards the sky, farmers keeping watch over their groves for generations. In other words, a symbol of an attachment to a land and further, a call to watch over and guard peace where it grows. And if you lay my first and last names next to each other, like tarot cards you need to build a future from, you get a little of both.

My name is also just my name. It's particular to me—given to me because it "sounded strong"—and the ways I've chosen to live inside it. I've never done it myself, but I have to imagine that naming a child involves a best attempt at casting a protective spell or articulating a hope.

Waiting in the plaza, I hear the names of poets, of singers, of apostles and saints. I hear children's names that echo those of the parents, and names that have been left behind in favor of more fitting ones listed everywhere but on identification documents. I hear names that have always been traveling names, and names that have only recently become traveling names. Names in Spanish and French, and Haitian Creole and Arabic and Russian and Portuguese. Names that call down some kind of future, names called to carry someone forward into survival.

AFTER NAMES ARE called from la lista, and identification papers are checked, the people who will cross that day are led away from the plaza; they go around the corner to line up against the fenced-in parking lot where the vans wait. This waiting area is a little strip of land, no wider than the sidewalk, sheltered away from the hubbub of El Chaparral and down a dead-end road. The entrance to the parking lot is at the end of the sidewalk, and this is where the first person is lined up, everyone else trailing behind them towards the plaza. You can see the vans that will take people to the other side through the bollards, across a small strip of Bermuda grass and jungle geraniums.

Volunteers are allowed to be here for this part, so we do our best to make the time pass easily. We play tiring games of running and jumping with little kids, lend out phones to make last-minute calls, or just chitchat, telling jokes and commenting on the weather. The atmosphere is always tense and expectant: So much work and money and time and sheer bodily effort has been expended to get people to this point, but all careful plans come unraveled against this border fence.

Even though the wait at this point is never long—thirty minutes, an hour maybe—it's all their waiting of the last few months condensed into a tight package. It is the moment when crossing the border goes from a longed-for abstraction into a real thing: They'll be getting into *those* vans that will take them, finally, across *this* stretch of border, *these* clothes they put on that morning will be the ones taken from them by Border Patrol agents. Crossing the Mexico–U.S. border is going into a tunnel where an uncertain future is on the other side, and this line is the moment when the black mouth of the tunnel is yawning towards you.

· · · ·

ONE OF THE mornings, I look down the line from where I'm standing towards the ragged sounds of a man unmistakably in the middle of a panic attack. I have no idea what to do, so I stand there, watching, the end of a jump rope dangling from my hand while a six-year-old looks at me expectantly. Hilary, the retired lawyer who has been giving me rides from my hotel to PedWest every morning, moves to stand close by him, puts a hand softly on his arm. She asks what's wrong, even though it's obvious, and the man says the obvious thing, that he doesn't want to go to jail, he just wants to be safe. I'm not the only one looking over at them at this point, but Hilary, in her slow, gringa Spanish, is completely focused on this man who she's helped to the ground, his back leaning against a fence, head hanging between his knees.

"¿Qué lo hace sentir mejor? ¿Cúales son las cosas que le gustan?" she asks him.

The man keeps breathing hard, on the edge of sobs.

"Mira el sol," she says, pointing up at a weak January sun. "Imagine que está recibiendo todo el calor del sol. Cada vez que tenga frío en la hielera, puede imaginar el sol, calentándolo."

She rubs one of his arms a little, as if warming him right then, the other hand still pointing upwards. The man follows her finger, closes his eyes, the pace of his breath slowing as tears roll down his face.

"¿Le gusta la música?" Hilary asks.

The man nods, eyes still closed.

"¿Si está muy triste, hay una canción que le guste cantar?"

The man nods, starts singing a hymn in a thin voice, his breathing back down to a normal pace, his voice still breaking every now and then.

"Así es," she says.

Hilary stays with him until he gets in the van, glaring at the man with the mustache when he motions to try to get her to step away. The man steps in last, with a shaky breath, and the van door slams shut behind him.

I have his faltering hymn, a song I half-recognize, stuck in my head for the rest of the day, the image of Hilary pointing at a wide-open sky and knowing that its existence was the most comfort she could offer to someone about to be hurt.

THE LINE WAITING for this bus is like a church and a beauty salon and a departures gate all in one. Couples get married in this line, kiss each other goodbye in this line, cry, recite over and over again to themselves the answers they have prepared for their Credible Fear Interviews like litanies. Mothers Sharpie phone numbers onto their children's bellies—the family separations have allegedly stopped at this point, but nobody wants to take any chances. Sometimes there is a white-collared priest or a pastor among the volunteers, and they ask if anyone wants prayers. Sometimes I translate, a huddle of us holding hands. There are little moments of comfort: A woman passes a huge jar of Vaseline to a single man waiting in line next to her so he can use it to cover scrapes and bumps on his legs, a woman re-braids the hair of someone else's daughter eye-wateringly tight to prevent the lice that is said to run rampant at the detention centers and the hopelessly tangled hair that results from not being able to brush or bathe adequately for days. "Hay que estar bien arregladita," the woman says, snapping an elastic band onto the end of a wispy little braid.

"Estar arregladita" is a kind of ward against mistreatment—it was one of the lessons my mother repeated over and over again, especially after we had moved to Texas. Being arregladita—having clean, neat clothes, well-combed hair, shined shoes, tasteful makeup, well-done nails—was a way to signal your worth, a way to demand respect in situations where it wasn't always forthcoming. This was the rule wherever we went—grocery store, school, restaurants, doctor's office. Even more so as you were heading into a detention center in a new country. The same kind of protection as the perfect outfit for the first day of school, this was a perfect presentation for the first day of a new life, but with the limitations of months on the road.

And then, just as the last baby hair has been brushed into submission, as clothes are straightened out and crumbs and dirt are brushed off, the man with the mustache from Grupos Beta starts calling out names again, checking things off on a clipboard, sending people around the concrete bars that make up the fence and into waiting vans with metal grates across the windows. Up until this point, everything has felt ad hoc, somewhat informal and loose, or at least negotiable, but with that clipboard, and that line, there's an order put in place, the knowledge of some kind of authority standing over it all, a knowledge that disobedience comes with consequences.

Sometimes, especially when there are mothers with young children, a volunteer or two are allowed to cross behind the fence, helping them carry their suitcases and bags and bundles, or holding the hands of children to make sure they don't wander off. When we are allowed, we try to linger as much as possible, shaking hands and hugging as they're divided into separate vans, following people all the way to the end of the sidewalk. If we aren't allowed to cross into the parking lot, we'll stand and reach our hands through the bollards, sometimes squeezing fingers over the stretch of Bermuda grass if we're able, waving madly through the bars if we're not. Sometimes the Grupos Beta guy yells at us, tells us all to get back, this group of histrionic gringos making his job harder, motions us away from the fence, but still, we make noise loud enough for everyone to hear us.

Two times each day, once in the morning and again in the afternoon, we watch this familiar procession. Those who'd heard their number called that morning load whatever luggage they have into the back of the van, pass children into the cabin, and then climb up its steep steps themselves, disappearing behind windows with bars over them, like a prison van. The man with the mustache shuts the door and the grates close over.

Then, as the vans slowly pull out of the lot, we stand there yelling: "Vayan con Dios! Adiós! Adiós!" "Buena suerte!" You can barely see their hands waving back out of the windows, their faces peering back out of the glass as the vans hurtle down the street, turning a corner and falling off the face of the earth. This happens every day, twice a day, for as long as we are there. Some version of it is still happening now.

THROUGHOUT THOSE LONG days, as we prepared people to cross over, we listened to them talk about "el otro lado" with burning intensity, even as they could only give vague answers about what it would look like and feel like, what they would do when they got there, and what would happen next. We prayed over people, blessing their journeys. I helped translate the prayers of clergy from English to Spanish: "Que Dios les bendiga, que les vaya bien, que Dios los cuide." We offered a few small comforts before they left—but all with the forced cheerfulness of a wake that's trying to be a party.

Our language was that of crossing a border, but it was also the language of death.

14

MIDWAY THROUGH MY TIME IN Tijuana, Sara's partner's number is called and he gathers up their little girl in his arms. The two of them get in line for the van, and Sara stands with the rest of the volunteers, arms stretched through the whitewashed concrete bollards as they board.

I am not there that morning—I had taken a group of people over to another center for consultations with attorneys, but I hear about it when I get back to the shelter, the news of it whispered from volunteer to volunteer. I don't understand why someone would do that, why Sara hadn't traveled across with her partner and their baby, can't imagine why she had spent so much time here, in Tijuana, if not to cross over with her infant daughter.

There is, of course, a carefully considered reason. Men who cross with children aren't detained as long as they would be if they crossed alone, usually a week at most, because only a few detention centers have the infrastructure to house both men and children. There are also fewer women's detention centers, so Sara's stay will hopefully also be shorter.

Sara and her partner would still be separated if they crossed together, this time by the United States government instead of by their own choice. By letting her partner cross with the baby now, as wrenching as it is, they are hedging their bets that he will be out of detention quickly, instead of the weeks or months it generally takes for men crossing the border alone. They'll be reunited sooner than if they had tried to cross together.

While much of this logic is conjecture, based on anecdotal information from others waiting at El Chaparral who have had family and neighbors cross ahead of them, it's also the only strategy they have to protect themselves from the cruelty that is coming.

As Kayla and I unlock the doors to the office the next morning, Sara returns. Surprised to see her, we pause when we notice her walk through the door. Her usually flawless makeup is replaced by red and puffy eyes, still damp cheeks, a runny nose. I didn't expect her to return until her own number was called, not wanting to face the last place she had been with her partner and daughter. Every morning, people make the same kinds of decisions Sara had made, every van full of asylum seekers would be a reminder of her family's absence. Kayla asked what she was doing here, if she wouldn't rather go home.

"No pude dormir anoche," Sara said. "Ni modo quedarme yo sola ahí nada más en mi casa sin nada que hacer, mejor aquí con ustedes." She sniffed. "¿Con qué puedo ayudarles?"

After a sleepless night, faced with the prospect of a long day stretching out before her in her depressingly empty apartment, she had come here, to the shelter, ready to help.

And she does. In the days that follow, she hands out the tamales we buy in bulk, makes countless cups of watery instant coffee, plays with kids, and fiercely advocates for other migrants against Grupos Beta in the plaza. She also helps give charlas, our Know Your Rights presentations, which she has picked up from listening to one or two a day—every once in a while there is a question she can't answer, so she waves over a volunteer, but most of the time she barrels ahead, telling people about their rights, what lies ahead. Her talks prepare people in a way none of us volunteers can, with our passports glowing dimly in our back pockets and the knowledge there is always someone there to get us out of a scrape.

When we gave charlas, we often replicated the ways we were taught to speak during school and trainings: reading off a bulleted list of points, telling people that something was "muy importante," as if flagging it for someone taking written notes. Sara, instead, leaned forward like she was gossiping.

"Mira," she'd say. "They're going to ask you, are you here to work, y no te dejes! You have to say no, that you're here because you're afraid, because if you don't . . . ." She dusted her hands. "Se acabó. You can still get a job, but that's not the *reason* you came, right?"

I watched her with other moms, contemplating the same choices she had made, tucked away in a corner of the shelter, one eye always on the kids squelching playdough into the floorboards or carefully stacking blocks. We all knew that she wouldn't hear from her family until they were on the other side of the system. Every morning as she came in, there was the unspoken question, every morning answered "no."

15

WHEN I SPEAK SPANISH, I'M speaking the language of Hernán Cortés and la Malintzin, Sor Juana and Gioconda Belli, Cervantes and Márquez. It's also my own language—the words taught to me by my mother when I was learning to ask for what I wanted, the made-up in-between language of mine and my siblings as we were learning to talk, the borrowed words from English, the patterns of sentences and 1980s slang I unknowingly absorbed from my parents' ways of speaking and made my own.

This language is the water I stand in, the well I draw from. There are tributaries feeding my spot in the river, both above and below the earth. This same river, a little further upstream, is the one the 17th-century poet and nun Sor Juana Inés de la Cruz drew from, and when I say the word "mujer," or the word "fe," these are words that have been fundamentally altered by her having written about them some three hundred years ago. The Spanish she wrote, in turn, was as influenced by her time in the Viceroy's court as a lady-in-waiting as it was by the Nahuatl she learned from her mother's household staff as a child; as influenced by the Spanish of Hernán Cortés who had first come to Mexico just 129 years before her birth, and by the language of Malintzin, the enslaved Nahua woman who served as his interpreter and the mother of one of his children. This was the water Sor Juana drew from, and what she returned to the river was forever altered by having passed through her hands.

When I speak or write, my words flow out from my own little eddy to rejoin the wider stream—my turns of phrase become part of the Spanish that exists in the world, just as Sor Juana's did, able to be picked up and passed around, drawn up to drink from and to be appropriated by another wader.

In this way, language is made up of the personal and the cumulative—each of us standing in our own space, absorbing the words around us, and contributing to the greater stream. Like the waters of the river, it's an inevitable, inseparable commingling of the collective and the individual. Language would not work if we could not share it, but the individual impressions we leave and the baggage we bring with us on each word we say matters too.

IN TIJUANA, I'M not translating so much as speaking, existing, working in Spanish. This is a little disorienting at first—the times in my life that have just been navigated in Spanish are few and far between, and mostly wrapped up in family, where the odd Spanglish insertion, the individual oddities of my way of speaking are shared with my family.

During my first few days at El Chaparral, I don't want to admit when someone uses a word or a turn of phrase I don't recognize. I ask around it, try to get context, try to pretend I'm not at sea. I worry I'll be seen as a fraud, as someone who speaks Spanish, sure, but hasn't lived in the language. I fear being seen as a gringa, a maleducada, someone who has no business here, someone who's not actually capable of helping at all.

This is how I always feel when I'm in a mostly Spanish-language space—like someone is going to catch me out, make fun of me for my old-fashioned and slightly formal way of speaking, for my inability to code-switch comfortably. Or worse yet, that I'll come off as snobby and pedantic and uptight.

It doesn't take long for this strategy to fall apart though—I'm talking to a lady in the plaza and she laughs and says, "¿Ay, pero tú no sabes lo que es tortillera, verdad?" The confusion must have been evident on my face when she told me she had been run out of her hometown for, apparently, making tortillas. "Es que soy lesbiana," she says. "Me gustan las mujeres." We both end up laughing, even though mine is tinged with shame, and after this, I start asking people for clarification.

"Ay no," I say. "Es que mi Español está medio agringado, medio Mexicano. ¿Eso qué es?" I hope that blaming my lack of understanding on the geographies between us—Honduran or Salvadoran and Mexican/American—makes my lack of understanding forgivable.

Language is something we construct together—across a continent and centuries as much as within communities and conversations. There is no expression, no understanding without the other, to express or to understand. With the other also comes uncertainties, comes gaps and expectations, comes the spaces where language can slip through your fingers into misunderstanding. But this is the thing you have to risk to make yourself understood, to understand another. By widening your language, you widen your community, make eye contact with someone downstream and wave.

SOMETIMES, WHILE I am chatting with someone waiting to cross at El Chaparral, another volunteer will come by, say my name, wave me over urgently. She is almost always a woman because most volunteers here are, usually older than me, always white. Our training over and over emphasized flexibility, emphasized being ready to jump in, help out, so I make my apologies to whomever I'm talking to and walk over.

"I don't speak much Spanish," she says, looking at me a little apologetically and gesturing at whomever she's standing next to. "Can you tell them that I want to wish them luck?" "Can you ask them if I can hold their baby?" "Can you tell her that I'm sorry I don't speak Spanish?"

I smile and nod and translate. Sometimes I find that there *is* a question, *is* an urgent need here that I can fill. But no matter the situation, the woman who waved me over is at my elbow, speaking over the questions I'm trying to understand with her own frantic interruptions: "What are they saying? Does she need help?"

More often, though, I convey the luck she wanted to wish them. Maybe some stickers or a toy are handed over, or a baby carried, or an apology made. Then the polite, quiet smiles of the people waiting in line let me know that we are being humored.

The first day this happens, I tell myself that these interruptions are easier than the alternative. I feel awkward, unsure, unsuited to the task at hand. How am I meant to bring comfort or stability in a situation that is so utterly broken? I don't believe I can be as unflappable as Hilary singing to a man on the edge of a breakdown, that I can summon a reserve of calmness to offer someone else when my own mind feels so jittery and anxious. The women who call me over are also there with a church group, some of them religious leaders themselves, and I assume that they're somehow better at this than me, that they know more about how to step into a breach and offer comfort.

And so, accepting this role as a go-between is a form of protection. Being a medium for other's words and blessings and feelings actually insulates me from the responsibility of coming up with words of comfort on my own. It allows me to feel like I'm helping while keeping myself a little shielded from the horror of it all. I am unsure of how much of myself I want to give up, selfishly worried that there would not even be enough of me to fill the relentless need we're facing. But the nights after I am called over, my brain wrung out from connecting English to Spanish and back again, I feel worn down, like maybe I had spent the day catering to the wrong people's needs.

One of these nights, exhausted and cranky, I spill all of this out to Katie over beers at her Airbnb and then immediately feel bad. I don't know if "guilt" is the right word, or "shame," but it strikes me that what I've just done to Katie is make my problem, in some sense, hers, which is, more or less, what people have been doing to me all day. Katie, who doesn't speak Spanish herself, has waved me over a couple times, but it's almost always to answer the question of someone she's struck up a purely gestural friendliness with, not to act as her conversational assistant. For all my upset, for all the exhaustion she must have also been feeling, she listens carefully to me now and suggests kindly, that I simply . . . stop. Stop acting as an interpreter, and instead prioritize the conversations and connections I'm in the midst of instead of running to attend to someone else's. "You're not here to make their experience of Tijuana better," she tells me. "You're here to fill a bigger need."

BUT THEN THERE is the larger question of whether or not I am, ultimately, catering to anyone's needs but my own. Sometimes I feel good and helpful, and other times, I wonder how much I have in common with some of the people in Tijuana who are there to help, but actually seem like they want to see something for themselves. It seems sometimes that volunteering at the border is almost a fad for the kinds of people who show up at sites of injustice to see, to document, to help, but also to star in the helping. Any given morning, there are a number of people live streaming from

El Chaparral, panning their cameras to show the waiting crowds and earnestly asking their followers for donations.

There are also smaller, quieter kinds of self-centering at work. A duo of non-Spanish-speaking retired ladies, who ask me if I am triggered by experiencing so many traumatic stories so similar to my own (needless to say, they did not know "my immigration story"), complain that they haven't seen any "action," and have instead spent two days assigned to chopping vegetables in the kitchen that distributed food to shelters. The next day, they are assigned to join us at El Chaparral, where I pretend not to notice whenever they wave me over.

On another day, next to the line for the vans, I watch a girl in high-heeled boots with a film camera slung around her neck smoke cigarette after cigarette as people climb into the vans. As the vans drive down the street, she says, over and over, "Isn't this just *so* bittersweet?"

She's not wrong—no one here really is. It *is* bittersweet, the people here *do* need donations, I *am* facing down some kind of secondhand trauma that isn't related to my story or my family's story except for the ways in which it is, a relationship so complicated I've written a book to explore it. I don't know that I can actually explain what's different from what these people were doing in Tijuana to what I thought I was doing, what I think I did now that I look back on it. I don't mean to say that you *need* the language to be helpful, that anything as small and simple as words in a shared language is enough to make any of what is happening okay. God knows that with all my words and both my languages there are still times when I am unhelpful, unsubtle, too carried away by my own feelings of heroism or sadness or too overwhelmed to know what to do or say.

There are also people there who know they are stuck with English but, when something happens outside of their comprehension, they don't panic. Instead, they look for the need and make themselves busy by filling it: buying snacks for the office, coloring with kids, or even just sitting with someone, smiling reassuringly, drinking coffee quietly together. Katie must have walked the length of downtown Tijuana twice over trying to find a pair of leggings for a woman who was about to cross over and was dreading the frigid temperatures of the hieleras. More than once, I see her have full conversations with children and adults alike, without a word understood between them, speaking instead through a pack of stickers and expansive hand gestures and willing smiles.

But, there are so many people here—*so* many—who, when confronted with the first sign of something unknown, flutter up to me in a panic, call in the reserves, pull away almost as if horrified. It's not xenophobia, exactly, but it isn't not that either. Somehow, I have become the person who might reassure them, who might act as a bridge between the good work these people imagined themselves to be doing and what is actually getting done.

I have a guess as to why I am the one they latch on to, why my labor feels like the thing that can be expended without consideration, both to them and to me. They are more comfortable asking me, a brown woman, to do this work for them than admitting that they themselves might be powerless, incapable of providing the help that they so desperately want to perform.

Even here, in a place where we are presumably present to be of help to others, I am expected to hierarchize my service: to white people's goodness first, to people who actually need help second.

And even though their anxieties take advantage of me, I still understand the impulse. Being in Tijuana, I feel the most concentrated sense of utter powerlessness and overwhelm in the face of an actual literal system of oppression that I have ever encountered. It is impossible to ignore the damage the United States did and does around the world—we can see the proof of it here, in the people whose lives have been so severely disrupted that they had to flee their home countries. We are not experiencing need in the abstract here in the way that we may at home, through news reports of

U.S.-backed instability or by barely seeing the same unhoused person in the exact same place every day on our morning commutes, so every day they blend into the neighborhood. We are being forced to look it straight in the eyes. I am here to help, and that means actually noticing that my help is both sorely needed and not nearly enough. If I was able to feel even the slightest sense of control over one thing that normally wasn't within my purview—say, having a translator available to say any little silly thing I wanted to—I can't say I wouldn't have tried to avail myself of it.

Tijuana was difficult in large part because of the scale, the newness, the way that if you let it, you might, like Kayla, find that it had taken over your whole life. I had experience getting involved on the level of my neighborhood, of my community, thanks to the clinic in New York, so I thought I would be prepared for what Tijuana had to show me. I had called countless congresspeople—my actual representatives, those for my old addresses, at my parents' place in Texas—had voted in the midterms, was closely following the work to get drivers licenses for undocumented people living in Massachusetts and still, and still, and still Tijuana makes me feel unbearably small, unbearably out of control, unbearably unable to help. It was only my training from my time at the asylum clinic that saved me. We were trained to ask consent, to never pass judgment in any way, to ask how we could help and what their goals were and figure out how to meet them. That training, applied to something on a far vaster scale than some paperwork in an office, proved helpful. It let me witness what people needed me to witness, let me at least talk to people as people even when their circumstances were beyond what I could imagine.

Writer and theologian Simone Weil wrote that loving your neighbor, attending to them, simply means recognizing that a suffering person "exists, not only as a unit in a collection, or a specimen from the social category labeled 'unfortunate' but as a man, exactly like us." This is, like a lot of theology, something that is far, far easier said than done, in part because of the protective urges of our natures, convincing us we could never be so unfortunate, in part because generally, here in the United States many of us have lived lives such that we may never actually be so unfortunate, or know anyone who has been so unfortunate. But people are people, and treating them as such—instead of like narratives or problems or opportunities for self-aggrandizement or feeling good about yourself—is the first step.

I'm not sure I finished realizing all this, finished learning all of this at El Chaparral, but now, with the benefit of time and a lot more practice, this strikes me as the thing between the volunteers I saw helping and those I saw fluttering their hands or making a fuss.

The need at El Chaparral is deep and wide and urgent, and we step into the breach with tamales and Hot Wheels and holographic superhero stickers and our stupid little words because that is all we are comfortably able to give, all we have power over in that moment. I still don't entirely know what it looks like to help selflessly, in a way that effects meaningful change in the lives of those who need it. And while I do know what it felt like to see someone else failing at the task, I can't confirm that I, myself, was succeeding at it.

During that week in Tijuana and thereafter, I wonder if I unintentionally made people perform gratitude for meaningless things—the toys we handed out to children, the games of distraction, the tamales and the coffee—just so I, too, could feel myself doing something good. I can imagine the bridge I needed between the good I thought I was doing, and those polite, quiet smiles pointed my way.

16

I AM NOT CALLED ON to translate prayer in the plaza because I am in my second year of divinity school, because I can tell the difference between intercessory prayer and supplicatory prayer and contemplative prayer, because I know the Lord's Prayer or the Jesus Prayer. I am called on to translate prayer because I can take that plea, made in English, by a member of the clergy wearing a collar and everything, and replicate it into Spanish right there, on the spot, in front of the people it is meant for.

I wonder about the efficacy of that prayer, about the moment in which it becomes understood by God and zapped into action. Is the moment it turns into true prayer when the pastor begins, "Dear Heavenly Father," or when I say "Padre Nuestro," when the person whose hands we are holding knows the prayer has begun? Or another moment, much farther afield, in whatever divine language God receives all prayer?

One of the pastors calls me over to the line one afternoon and asks me to translate a prayer for a family. A mom, a dad, and a daughter in her early teens, who somehow looks like me at that age—square teeth in a big grin, messy ponytail, and despite it all, a choker, and chipped black nail polish. I circle up with them, between the pastor and the girl, one of my hands in each of theirs.

I was about her age when I articulated to myself that not only did I not believe in God, but that I was done even trying to believe in God. But, I also remember being prayed over around that time and how lovely and comforting it felt whether or not I could say I believed. I want so badly for her to be okay, want so badly for her to come out the other side of this, to write terrible poems in a journal and go to high school and make her own decisions about whether or not to believe in God.

And so, even as I am sliding language like beads on a rosary, just in case mine is the version that counts, I do more than just translate the prayer. I actually pray it. I send it up to a God I care deeply about but don't always want to believe in, and hope it makes it there. And, just in case, I send it to the people whose hands I am holding too, send it to the girl and through her, to her mother and her father. I try to create that strange and funny little spark that happens when someone squeezes your hand as they say "Amen."

ALTHOUGH IT REFERS to a different saint, "San Diego" is also the Spanish name for Saint James the Apostle, whose remains are rumored to lie at the Cathedral of Santiago de Compostela in Galicia, Spain. The pilgrimage to that cathedral, known as "El Camino," has remained in continuous usage from the early Middle Ages to the present day. Pilgrims along the route travel for penance, for grace, for quiet and peace, for exercise, for the challenge of it, on the off chance that every step brings them closer to God. What they are more literally approaching is the Cathedral of Santiago de Compostela, and a Pilgrim's Mass that's celebrated twice a day, every day, where those with aching feet receive a blessing and recognition for their travels.

After leaving the mass, many of the pilgrims keep going, another two days' walk all the way to Finisterre, Latin for "the ends of the earth." There, the land drops into the sea, and the pilgrim's path fans out into an ocean of possibilities, although the one most taken is to turn around and go home.

At the western end of the American continent where the border wall plunges into the Pacific Ocean, the wall between San Diego and Tijuana extends a good 50 feet out into the ocean. If you tried to walk out into the water to its end, you'd be in over your head. This design is purposeful, though that is not to say that people don't try to swim around it, to head far enough north by cover of night that Border Patrol won't catch them as soon as they stagger onto the beach.

This portion of the wall has been there since the 1990s, but if you drive east along it, farther into Tijuana proper, you'll start seeing portions of the wall that are newly (re)built but are already beginning to rust in the sea air. This place where the border wall falls into the sea feels like the height of human folly—a literal line in the sand that's been defended to the death, the starting point of an empire.

It's also a place where God comes down: There's a church service here every Sunday, largely attended by volunteers and a few locals. On the Sunday that I'm in town, I go with a group of other volunteers. We climb up the beach to Friendship Park, past where deported veterans have painted their names on the wall next to murals and bible verses, past food vendors and blaring boom boxes and dogs on walks.

In a lot of ways, it's an ordinary ecumenical church service, like the kind I went to as a kid but don't go to anymore. There are prayers, announcements, and a young guy with a guitar leading visitors in a song. In other ways, it isn't just another service. We're outside, where the wind whips everyone's hair and carries the sound of our voices out over the Pacific. And looming over us is the wall, some 20 feet tall. Through its slats and razor wire, we can see another sermon, this one in English. On our side, we sing Spanish versions of the hymns I have known since I was a kid, songs that bring with them a powerful nostalgia as I stare at a cross painted on the wall and a tableclothed card table set with bread and wine in a chalice.

While regular church services sometimes feel to me like uneasy compromises between the human and the divine, the beauty of the Eucharist feels uncomplicated—it is about sanctifying the regular, life-sustaining ritual of a meal, calling attention to a God who is present not only in this bread and in this wine, but also everywhere in a world bright and buzzing with grace. But looking at that bread and wine, laid out against the border wall, something about it feels out of place, as if it is in some way calling for the sanctification of this scar in the landscape.

That Sunday, walking up to the altar, I feel like I am pinned to the center of everything. Between Mexico and the United States, between land and sea, between hard days and harder ones. Taking bread and wine in the shadow of the wall doesn't resolve anything for me, doesn't make anything clearer or make me feel any less alone. The grief and anger I brought with me into the service only gets heavier. The Eucharist has the potential to be a symbol of suffering turned into salvation, of the way in which our very bodies are holy, and the ways that communities bind everyone up within their protection. But that afternoon, the reminder that God is present in our physical reality seems cruel rather than hopeful.

When it comes time for the closing prayer, the pastor offers me the microphone, someone having told him I was a student at a theological school. I put my hands out in front of me, shake my head no. I have barely gotten back into prayer in my own life, after years and years of a frosty silence between me and God. I had grown up in the church—charismatic evangelical—and after an eternity of quiet from God while all around me people had ecstatic encounters, I decided to ignore God back. Divinity school, which I had gone to halfway out of the same kind of desire that leads to picking at a scab, had also surrounded me with people who prayed ritually, who prayed conversationally, who prayed meditatively, who prayed constantly. By the time I arrive in Tijuana, I am cautiously dipping a toe back into the waters of prayer, but only in the quietest, most vulnerable parts of my mind, alone and silent. I can't pray in front of others, not out loud, not like this, and not today, when the thing most likely to erupt from me if I address myself to God is a rage-filled scream or a babble of my own doubts and abandonment.

The pastor shrugs and keeps the microphone, tells us to put our hands on the border wall, to bow our heads.

"Father God," he intones. "We ask you to meet us here, at the border. You are Lord of All, God of everything. You are Lord over all the people here; You are Lord over the governments and the Nations of Men. We forgive the governments for their actions, for everything that has occurred here, just as You forgive us, sinners before this wall."

My fingers tighten on the steel in front of me, my eyes snap open, the pastor's words blanketing out into a microphone hum whipped away by the ocean wind. I will forgive *no one* for this, not the governments, not the people, not even God. This is unforgivable. I owe nothing to a God that might let this happen—the evil of the border is on a biblical scale. Earlier in the church service, a visiting rabbi had spoken about the Israelites fleeing Egypt. The Israelites had gotten manna in the desert to feed them, had gotten an entire sea opening up before their feet, had gotten plagues on their behalf. Migrants in Tijuana got me and a couple hundred other well-intentioned gringos, got José Andrés' World Central Kitchen, and got fucking Border Patrol officers and the desert.

Annie Dillard writes that "there is no less holiness at this time—as you are reading this—than there was the day the Red Sea parted." But as the waves keep lapping up against the shore and the wall, people keep getting loaded into vans and taken into detention centers for wanting to be safe. They keep being fed into a system designed to humiliate and dehumanize them. We are not at the shores of the Red Sea, and this wall is stronger than Jericho's. We don't have trumpets, we don't have an army, and most of the time, it feels like we don't even have God on our side. It feels like all that's left here is the slow work of time and the waves, mechanical and unstoppable.

THEN, MY SECOND to last morning in Tijuana, Sara shows up at the shelter, early as always, grinning from ear to ear. Family in Florida have gotten a phone call from her partner and right now—she checks the clock on her phone—at this very moment(!), he and her daughter are flying through the air on an airplane. Thanks to a last-minute ticket purchase by an aunt, they are on their way to Miami to stay with his extended family.

"Bueno," she says, with a sudden, businesslike nod. "Es hora que yo cruce."

17

GROWING UP IN TEXAS, MY border was the same one as Anzaldúa's, still the Rio Grande where the third culture she describes grows out of the friction between two countries, but also utterly different. I lived more than 300 miles away from the nearest border crossing at Piedras Negras, just within the bounds of ICE's 100-mile jurisdiction zone, but every year, sometimes twice a year, we would cross over that border in our family car, stuffed full of suitcases and gifts and encargos, to my grandmother's house in San Luis Potosí.

The border crossing itself is never not absolute chaos. Lines stretching out the doors, people that have driven through the night from Michigan or Iowa barely holding it together as they navigate the strange bureaucracy of car permits; families unfolding themselves from the backseats of minivans for breaks in the tiled bathroom that smells like Fabuloso; pickup trucks towing other cars blinking their hazards halfway across the country; mattresses, bikes, and washing machines strapped to roofs; pickup trucks riding low with the full bounty of all that American Walmarts might provide. Capitalizing on the long lines, vendors set up with elotes and gorditas and peanut candy and potato chips bathed in off-brand Valentina and crucifixes and little Guadalupe figurines, shaking bags of candy in front of car windows. If you're lucky, if you have all or most of your papers in order, you might spend three, four, seven hours there, waiting and wading through bureaucratic swampland in the desert. Every time we get ready to cross, it's a flurry of making sure our passports are not expired, that my mom has her green card ready, that we have all the information we need about the ownership of the car we're traveling in. All of us, except for my mom, have dual citizenship, and the main way we're held up is in making sure we're not illegally importing our car to Mexico. The invisible protection of my passport means I don't know what it's like to cross the border any other way.

The border is, has always been, the place where I feel the least Mexican. It is here, surrounded by all the people who are roughly in the same situation as I am—immigrant parents, first generation children, with a mishmash of different immigration statuses under one roof, and everyone trying to find a way to live between two worlds, caught at that very point where both worlds meet. And yet, nothing here feels like home, and it isn't just because of the bureaucracy. The language these families speak isn't the same Spanish of my family, their Spanglish isn't the same as mine and my siblings', the way they're moving through the world doesn't always look like the way I move through the world.

In reading someone else's translation, especially alongside an original, one of the first things you want to do is critique it, pick it apart for the changes you'd make. It's certainly my first impulse, and in spending time with other translators, others of us obsessed with the gap between languages,

I can tell I'm not alone in this: "Well, I would have done it this way and not the other, this phrase here I would argue means something else, a particular assonance was lost here that I'd work harder to preserve." At the border, I feel like a translation under the microscope, wonder if I've done it right, feel flat and strange or like my seams are showing, wonder if I've used the right words to frame myself. I wonder if I'm identifiable as Mexican to the other people crossing, wonder to what degree the place we're going to feels like home to any of us. I'm also, always and of course, critiquing everyone else's choices in their translations.

This critique becomes complicated because the other thing I'm pointing to, I think, is class difference. At a time when only 15 percent of Mexicans went to college, both my parents graduated—my mom, in the first generation of her family, my dad the third or fourth. My family has wealth in the generational-accumulation-of-capital, land-owning type of way, in the type of way that means that each generation could take risks that the previous one had not been able to afford, in the type of way that means that my parents *could* immigrate, not that they *had* to, in the type of way that means that I changed my major from economics and political science to creative writing before I was even done with a year of college.

Given my family history, the side of the border I was born on is a matter of chance, and I don't think my life would have changed significantly in either case. My parents left Mexico not because there wasn't enough food or enough work, but because there wasn't enough space for my dad's ambition, a ceiling to how much he could do without becoming complicit in the tangled webs of political power and corruption in Mexico. If things didn't work out in the States, he and my mother could go back, have a comfortable life, live in a big city near his parents, probably have a girl come in a few times a week to help with the dishes and the mopping. Inasmuch as it wasn't a matter of life-or-death whether they succeeded in their new lives, they also had a better chance of success when bolstered by their savings, and family money to fall back on in the case of dire emergency.

Talking about class, here, in the context of this border, and of myself within it, thinking of my family's wealth as it coils between two countries and keeps me safe in both, makes even my nail beds itch. But I need to. There are experiences I share with the families here, I'm sure of it—of having people at checkout counters practice their mangled Spanish on us, of being called a wetback in school, of being told to go back to where we came from, of our abilities being doubted before we even opened our mouths, a certain way we're regarded when we're in ratty jeans and T-shirts. We also share the assumptions people make about us, the ones we fight against tooth and claw until it becomes too hard to keep fighting, so we let them settle on our skin instead. If everyone is saying it, it must be true. These are the places where my experience reaches towards theirs, but there are so, so many other places where only my solidarity can.

There are many ways in which my parents' wealth makes us a family of ideal immigrants, exceptions to the rule. There are people who see my family and hold us as a standard for what anyone else graced with permission to enter the country should achieve.

That word, "achievement"—here in the U.S., it means assimilation. It means knowing how to act middle class, means putting things like college and a salary and a job as the ultimate markers of success. It means perfect, unaccented English and perfect, unaccented Spanish, but only when appropriate, like in an AP language classroom. It means looking a certain way, speaking a certain way. We're immigrants who don't "seem" like immigrants, achieving enough to be a feel-good story about a land of opportunity but not necessarily enough to be threatening. When other families don't have the resources or the institutional knowledge or the desire to assimilate in these ways, to buy into white American systems of achievement and value, they're shunted aside as less than, as not worthy, as wastes of a visa. While there was still some grumbling, especially around college admissions—we're the product of affirmative action, taking the place of some more deserving white person—in general my siblings and I, my parents and I are held up as some kind of gold standard, the minimum level any-one should achieve out of sheer gratitude for being let into the hallowed halls of the United States of America. Anyone else is lazy, isn't trying hard enough, isn't grateful enough.

These are the ways in which my existence has been weaponized against that of many other immigrants, many of them Latinx. I don't want to speak for that part of the experience—about what it's like to grow up poor, about facing the double barriers of race and class, about not being able to or not wanting to align yourself with someone else's idea of success. I don't want to speak to that part of the experience because I can't, because it isn't my place to and I don't want to take up the oxygen in the room with it, but I do want to speak for the ways and places where skin color comes into the room before money does, for all the times in which we do speak the same lan-guages, for all the places where our translations are read in the same ways.

When we're done filing all the paperwork, when the German shep-herds have walked past, straining on tight leashes and after we've all shared a too sweet Sidral Mundet from a vending machine, we all climb back into my parents' SUV and drive across a bridge called Free Trade or Gateway to the Americas, which arcs over a surprisingly narrow, slow-moving river, thick with silt and significance.

18

THERE'S THIS IDEA, HALF A myth, half a reality, that the Rio Grande can't be uncrossed, that once you've submerged yourself for a migratory baptism, it can't be undone.

To wit: one of the pejoratives for Mexican immigrants coming into this country is "wetback." In Mexico, they might be called "mojados," and the reason for these two names is the same: because at some point in their journey, they crossed the Rio Grande. I haven't heard "wetback" in a while, although it is hard to say if it's because the word has gone out of favor, or just because I've left high school and Texas. The term "wetback"—once used by the Eisenhower administration as the name of a mass deportation operation—narrows the wide web of migration experiences into a singular action, connotes a singular (economic) reason for crossing.

The people arriving at the United States southern border today, although no longer only Mexican, are also river crossers, the muddied waters of the Grande, of the Usumacinta cling to them. We have this myth that immigration changes a person, that crossing a border means you can't uncross it, even if you were to walk yourself back. When I've asked them, my own parents say they couldn't do it, couldn't imagine living in Mexico again. "We're just not like that anymore," my mom will say, "like that," alluding to some idea of Mexicanness I've never understood for myself. Ni de aquí ni de allá.

On the other hand, there's also a group of people who long for nothing more than to return home. I've interviewed so many people who say that, if given the chance, if it was safe, if there was enough food and work to go around, if their whole families could come, they would go back home in a heartbeat. This is often especially true of seasonal workers, who come to make enough money for their family to build a house or get through the next few growing seasons and then realize the crossing is so risky, the need so great that they end up staying for longer than they wanted.

When those who have migrated are returned to their countries of birth, either by choice or by force, the Americanness clings, somehow—there are stories of deported DREAMers taking call center jobs only to end up shooting the shit with U.S. customers, reminiscing, asking them if Crunchwrap Supremes® still exist over there, del otro lado. In the States, of course, the fact of the river crossing means that un mojado, by default, se tiene que quedar en las orillas de todo.

AND SOMETIMES, THE crossing erases you.

We are sitting around in the shelter after the afternoon van had left when Katie brings me her phone, apologetically. She reminds me that she had given her contact information to a man named Rodrigo on our very first day, agreed to be his sponsor as he boarded the vans. Together, we had watched as he hastily wrote her phone number down on the corner of a folder holding his birth certificate, identity card, and paperwork. Now, five days later, she's gotten a text from an unknown number.

"I need your help translating! I can't tell what's going on, but I think it's something to do with Rodrigo, with the sponsorship?"

I take the phone and translate as I read.

"Hello, this phone number was found with some papers in my brother's suitcase when we picked him up from the processing center. The papers are for a Rodrigo. Can you get these back to him?"

"Wait," Katie says, confused. "Why does this guy's brother have Rodrigo's papers? Where's Rodrigo?"

With the rush towards the vans, Katie hadn't had time to get Rodrigo's contact information and we couldn't know whether he had saved her number somewhere else, if he had also made it out of the processing center. We knew his first name, his country of origin, and when and where he had crossed the border, and the state he was heading to—nothing more.

Knowing we have no way to reach Rodrigo and worried how he might have ended up without his identifying documents, we reply: "Who is your brother? Where was he detained?"

"Why do you want to know? Who are you?" You could almost hear the crackle of discomfort on the other end.

The week Katie and I are in Tijuana falls within the month that the United States government shutdown, which had started at around the end of December, reaches an untenable fever pitch. ICE's detention locator isn't being regularly updated, and it's unclear whether this is due to apathy or malice or being overwhelmed. The end result is that when someone climbs into a van to cross the border, they disappear. There is no digital trace of them, at least for a few weeks. They will have little to no access to phones or directories, no way of communicating with the world outside of the insulated horror of the detention system, regardless of whether they are being detained at the San Ysidro border processing center or sent to small county jails in Kenosha, Wisconsin or Pike County, Pennsylvania or LaSalle Parish, Louisiana. If we are lucky, we may hear from someone stuck at a Greyhound station in San Diego after being released, without money or their belongs but with a fever. These phone calls come only because a volunteer like Katie gave them a cell phone number to call.

This is what it looks like to follow the rules: to be made literally ill by the system depriving you of your freedom, to be kept locked up with no way for anyone to find you, to be disappeared. You may be moved from center to center in an effort to fulfill mysterious bed occupation quotas, spat out in the middle of nowhere with only a bus token and your cellphone, long since drained of its charge. And this is what the process looks like in the best scenario, an application for asylum handled the "right" way. This is the welcome we give to someone fleeing a credible harm.

IT'S NEARLY IMPOSSIBLE to translate something perfectly back into the original. It's a fun experiment you can do with plain machine translation—feed your favorite line of poetry into Google Translate over and over again and watch the meaning disintegrate and distort before your eyes.

This is the gap between languages where translation exists, where translation theory holds up solutions to a problem that is more like an opportunity. These spaces are where a culture is reflected in its language, where the contours of an individual mind show through the letters. It's what makes translation an art and not something that's doable with an infinite recursion of Google Translate; it's the key that holds the proof that translation is profoundly human.

When you carry something—a language, a story, a text, a person—you can't set it down again without it bearing the traces of your having held it in your hands.

· · ·

THE MAN ON the other end of the phone won't tell us his brother's name or what detention center his brother had been in, just that he isn't the Rodrigo we're looking for. When we give him the address of a legal organization in San Diego, he agrees to mail them Rodrigo's documents. We hope that Rodrigo might remember the name of our organization, might call around and look for his documentation if he was somehow able to make it through without it. There is no other way we can think of to reconnect someone lost within this system with documents lost from him.

We ask the volunteer in charge of data processing for our organization to sweep the detention locator once, twice, three times a day, hoping to find a digital trace of Rodrigo that we might be able to follow. The computer spits out the same message, over and over again.

Search Results: 0.

19

EVERY NIGHT, AS THE SUN sets, we gather in our hostel-office that has been essentially taken over by volunteers staying in Tijuana long-term. We go around the room with reminders and updates for what had happened that day, the last number called or the menu items prepared by folks at the World Central Kitchen, the highs and lows. We are assigned roles for the next day, say goodbye to volunteers that are heading back home, then carpool back to San Diego.

Evening meetings are sometimes comfortable and lovely—it's reassuring to know that other people hate those vans with the grates over the windows as much as I do—and sometimes an irritant—struggling to keep my eyes open through a thirty-person recounting of that day's minutiae when all I want to do is collapse into my hotel bed.

Tonight, it is one of the longer running volunteer's last day, and she asks if, instead of the customary parting words, she might sing instead. I like the idea of a song in this grubby hostel, relish the thought of a little sweetness to end the day. She is maybe a few years older than me, with a buzz cut and the kind of smile that takes up her whole face. We had chatted a few times, were friendly, but she had always been assigned to a different location, so I only ever really see her at these evening meetings. As she stands in front of all of us, though, she is solemn, eyes closed.

> *"When the world is sick*
> *can't no one be well*
> *but I dreamt we was all beautiful and strong."*

Her voice starts out thin and nervous but, by the time she returns to the same refrain again, it has grown rounder, more solid, blooming into the room. On the third repetition, another volunteer picks up the song, weaving her voice in.

I don't know why she's chosen the song, where she first heard it. It's the chorus to a song by Thee Silver Mt. Zion Memorial Orchestra that is now a popular refrain for hippieish singing groups on YouTube. It feels like a camp song, like a church song, like a benediction and a prayer for what we are noticing, what we want the world to be.

When I was little, my favorite thing about going to church was worship—a roomful of people, hands outstretched, coming together to lift one song heavenward. After I stopped going to church, there wasn't really anywhere else like a worship service, nowhere that might punch those specific buttons for me. Until tonight, in a shitty hostel in Tijuana. The singers raise their hands to us, inviting us to join in, and so we do: Some of us lean forward on the couches or sit up from where we are sprawled on the floor, some of us sway, some of us sing with our eyes closed and others open, our

voices swell and lift—not in praise of a God that feels far away on this
January night, but for our capacity to imagine a future in which everyone
is whole, and healthy, and has everything they need.

> *"When the world is sick*
> *can't no one be well*
> *but I dreamt we was all beautiful and strong."*

AND THEN, SUDDENLY, it was my own time to leave. I had been crossing
the border every day to get to and from Tijuana, but there would be something different about walking that maze of corridors for the last time.

The San Ysidro border crossing, a ten-minute drive east of El Chaparral and the port through which I've crossed every day this week, is named
after Saint Isidro the Laborer, a Spanish saint that, in life, was a field-
worker. His story is usually used to extol the virtues of a simple life of hard
work, of keeping your head down and working hard, even through deplor-
able conditions. Miracles attributed to him include the supernaturally fast
ploughing of a field thanks to angelic help and being able to redouble the
amount of food in his meager allowance to feed his fellow workers. He is
the patron saint of La Ceiba, Honduras, which is the home city of many
asylum seekers. The city's biggest annual tourist attraction is their carnival
in his honor.

San Ysidro is also where the vans with the grates over their window are
headed. The asylum seekers in the vans will be unloaded in San Ysidro,
processed, assigned numbers and marked as EWI, Entry Without Inspection. What happens next is a complete mystery, not just to those of us on
the outside, but to people moving through the system itself. Someone might
be released that same day to the Greyhound station on the other side, sent
to a Customs and Border Protection hielera, then deported straight away.
I've talked to people who were put on planes late at night, their arms and

legs shackled. They were transported into an aleatory detention center in the middle of the country because the center had trouble making their minimum occupancy quotas that night.

The entirety of the half-mile walk it takes to actually cross the border is studded with both visible and invisible surveillance cameras, menacingly labeled locked doors, rooms behind barely frosted glass where you can see people waiting, slumped into the poses of those held for hours without updates. This stretch is the strangest part of my daily commute; I avert my eyes and hurry through, worrying that if I stare too hard, take too much notice, I'll end up on the other side of those windows.

While there's a brass line embedded in the sidewalk at some point in the ten-minute walk across to mark the line between one country and the next, the whole area feels like one continuous line, one long march separate from both the outlet malls and highways on the one side, the food stands and mercaditos for tourists on the other. This space is instead entirely reserved for the idea of Government or Nation or Military.

Every morning, as I walk down the ramp into El Chaparral, I wonder about the person who designed this pathway and the signs all along that seem to imply you're lucky that you're not already standing in an unmoving line. I wonder about the people for whom this walk takes hours, days, years, instead of the five minutes it takes me to flash my American passport and be waved through. I wonder how much your average American, crossing into Tijuana at San Ysidro for cheap margaritas or Viagra or dental work, is aware of these back rooms. Do they feel the ominous hand of government, pressing down on the low ceilings, making all of it feel like the clean and law-abiding and gently menacing prelude to a prison? On one of my morning walks to El Chaparral, I pass a tour group of golfers—middle-aged white men ambling aimlessly around their bus in the parking lot, drinking coffee, sighing at how long it was taking. Another evening, on the footbridge on the way back across into California, I pass a bachelorette party, all satin sashes and glitter and rhinestones. I wonder what it's like to walk through these gates with entirely different eyes.

I suppose if you're golfing or coming to Tijuana to party, the government isn't much interested in your activities, and you're able to ignore the closeness of the surveillance. The same isn't true for the volunteers. No one in the group is sure how closely we are being watched, if at all. The work we're doing—this kind of accompaniment, providing intangible bits of aid—isn't illegal. We know it isn't. But we have all heard stories about members of our group being "held for further questioning" when crossing back into the U.S., of migrants who were seen as having received too much help being retaliated against by border guards. So, we try to keep a low profile knowing that, at any moment, some authority may decide the work we're doing isn't permissible anymore.

About a month after I get home, in February 2019, news breaks that the United States government has been keeping a watch list of journalists and aid workers and pastors who cross the border "too often," or who are believed to be closely connected with the caravan. There are reports of Border Patrol seizing a photojournalist's camera and destroying memory cards, rifling through a reporter's computer files and confiscating notes, aid workers being dragged into back rooms and shown pictures of strangers and asked over and over if they know who organized the caravan.

On my second to last day, a U.S. Customs and Border Protection agent stops me after a week of being waved through without question. "Says here you've been crossing every day. You volunteering or something?"

"What? Nah. Just visiting friends. I'm down here for a little sun, the beaches, you know, but my mom was like," I pitch my voice up into a nag. "'Oh no, Tijuana is so unsafe! Stay in San Diego!' so now I have to do this every day." I roll my eyes.

He looks back at the screen, at me. I try my best to school my face into a mix of boredom and impatience until, finally, he waves me through.

Katie is waiting for me up ahead, out of earshot but clearly trying to play the part of my impatient friend, knowing to play along rather than risk outing ourselves. Even though I've only known her for a few days, I can recognize the worry creasing at the corners of her eyes.

We send our bags through the scanner then walk out together, totally silent until we reach the stoplight 100 yards away from the doors of the border station.

"What happened?" Katie asks, her voice still hushed and tight with concern.

"They asked if I was volunteering. I told them that no, joked around, you know, the whole thing."

"What time are you leaving tomorrow? I'll walk across with you."

Neither one of us believes that Katie crossing with me will actually do anything, but it means having a first line of alert if I do get detained or shuffled into a back room. I appreciate the offer, understanding in my bones what accompaniment actually feels like. It's as simple and as complicated as the knowledge that if something bad happens to you, someone else will know about it, will see you, will do whatever they can to save you.

SARA LEAVES TIJUANA the same day I do.

By the time she crosses the border, I am already in a cab on my way to the San Diego airport, a route that is all freeways and palm trees and glittering ugly convention centers. I don't get to see her wait in line or climb into the van or watch her disappear down the street.

Tijuana itself is just a waypoint on people's longer journeys, nowhere more than El Chaparral. I talk to a lot of people the week I'm in Tijuana, but it's rare that I meet anyone more than once, have more than one conversation with someone. There were only a few people I saw, day after day, and Sara was one of them. I don't speculate on what it would be like to watch a van, with her so brave and careful and bright in it, disappear down the street and fall off the edge of the planet, because I know it would have been harder than watching any of the other vans I saw disappear in that same way. But it would also be more joyful knowing she was on her way to her partner and her baby girl.

The day before we leave, Sara adds me on Facebook. That night at the hotel, I scroll through pictures of her with her baby, pictures of her with her partner, selfies with elaborately done makeup, jokes and memes about no-good boyfriends and tacos and wanting to shop.

In the days that come, I refresh that page over and over again.

20

"DO YOU DREAM IN SPANISH, or in English?"

It's kind of a truism that you're not *really* bilingual until you dream in the other language, until you can fully translate yourself over both waking and sleeping. I rarely dream, and I've never dreamt in Spanish. There are huge portions of me that remain untranslated, perhaps largely because they remain illegible to me.

For about two weeks after I get home from Tijuana—twice as long as I was there—though, I dream of El Chaparral. They aren't nightmares, exactly, but everything in them is rushed, tense, vivid. I wake up with the feeling of having forgotten to do something, with the feeling of having let someone down. My feet ache and pinprick, just as they did after hours of standing in the plaza. While these dreams center around language—the dream-task I've been assigned has to do with the transmission of an urgent message—the language is as mysterious and slippery as anything else in the dream. When I awake, I not only don't remember the message I need to relay, but I can't remember the language it is in.

ENCOUNTERING A RIVER in your dreams can mean any number of things.

If the river is broad, and placid, and wide like the Rio Grande, it means that you're in a state of contentment or complacency, the water sweeping you along.

If the river is turbulent or raging like the Rio Bravo, it means your life is out of control, that there are challenges ahead and you are in turmoil.

A river of any kind, which picks up earth and stones and carries them out towards the sea, can symbolize the things you are doing now that will create your future.

It may seem self-evident, but we are, even today, creating the country we and our children will inhabit in the future. The policies passed today will have an impact on this generation and the next—families will not soon forget their separation, nor detainees their mistreatment, nor children the way their parents held their hands while crossing into the U.S., the anxiety of those months in Tijuana waiting and waiting to cross. Children will remember their deported parents, families around the world will remember their children who did not come home. This is the silt in our river, the soil we will plant our next harvest into.

Everything in a comfortable American life is set up for complacency, for letting the river flow lazily past you. To get involved, to step in yourself means muddying the waters, creating a commotion where there was none.

An empty riverbed, like the Rio Grande during the dry months, means numbness, an absence of feeling.

Rivers are life-giving—where the water flows, life follows. Crossing rivers can get you into heaven, into the Promised Land, into a new world shining with possibilities, but the crossing is part of the journey. Allowing apathy or blankness or exhaustion to keep us on the banks means that these new and brighter opportunities are foreclosed to us.

Building a bridge means that not only do you make it across the river, so can anyone coming behind you on the road. As Americans, we were born, both figuratively and literally, on the right side of the river, the side everyone tries to cross to. We sit here, on our prosperous shores, surrounded by the materials to build bridges, to build homes, to build cathedrals, to build irrigation canals and make plenty for everyone. It's time to start building.

21

THE FIRST MORNING I AM back home, a Wednesday, I call a friend and ask her to come to church with me. I have already cried—quietly at the airport bar, at my gate, with my head leaning against the airplane window—in a kind of grief that feels selfish and inadequate to what I've just seen.

Whenever I go to church, it is always after a long absence, and usually in extremis. My whole life I've been waiting for that moment, like St. Augustine's conversion, when the exact right words are enough to overcome my years of skepticism, when that day's psalm is enough to meet my specific needs and deliver me into a comforting, uncomplicated faith. I've never found what I'm looking for, but the monk's chanting as solid as the stone around us calms me at least.

The Society of Saint John the Evangelist is a brotherhood of Anglican Episcopalian monks who live on the banks of the Charles River. They open their heavy wooden doors for their morning prayers, noonday prayers, and compline in a bare, gray-stone chapel with a soaring ceiling that always smells faintly of incense. The seats are in a long, thin, U-shape, so there is usually someone facing you. The brothers sit facing the cross.

Their prayer is minimal; the call and response chanting of a psalm, the voices rising and responding to the cantor's tune that modulates in pitch but never in register. Most of them are in their sixties, and when they sing you get the sense of not only the history of this brotherhood—the last twenty, thirty, or more years they've spent learning to harmonize and settle into each other's voices—but of all the monks, with their sandaled feet and long habits, marching back through the ages to make this music.

The psalm today is wrong, but I don't know that the psalm that I need exists. I need something halfway between the "how long, O Lord?" of Psalm 13 and the "still waters" of the 23rd, of being angry at God, but still wanting God to be the one to lift the sorrow up from my shoulders, the psalmist all the while coy about God's existence.

Then comes the remembrances of the community in prayer. A monk raises up his mother, recently deceased. Another lists off a series of the beloved ill. Another asks for prayers for those on the road, those making journeys. I love the feeling of this kind of prayer, love feeling the tendrils of attention pushing out from the chapel to grave sites and hospital beds and airports, to people discerning calls, or waiting for phone calls, or calling out for help.

But when the silence opens up for us to pray our own prayers, those tendrils of attention vanish. Any progress I had made in figuring out how to pray, what prayer is, has disappeared. I don't know how to tell even God about the things I've seen happen and how angry I am.

THIS ENTIRE TIME, without even knowing it, I have been doing a second kind of translation.

Experts talk of second-hand trauma, common among social workers and EMTs and anyone else whose job involves stepping into the worst days in people's lives, as a shadow of knowledge that wraps around you when you have come to know, through observation, the depths of cruelty that exists in the world. Second-hand trauma is complex, working in many of the same ways that first-hand trauma does: Your brain gets rewired in the same ways, your physiological responses are the same.

However, second-hand trauma also carries the privilege and shame of safety, awareness that you were removed from the suffering itself, that your reactions are outsized for someone who had merely heard about the pain, that you were protected even if your body doesn't recognize that. Why should I find myself sobbing in my San Diego hotel room after a day mostly spent playing with children? Once I'm back home, what makes me raise my voice at the soft-spoken lady at work who asks me if Tijuana was "very depressing"? Nothing had, after all, really happened to me.

I am wrapped up in grief for a world I thought existed but doesn't, for a country I still somehow feel has to be good but isn't at all. I am horrified by my own safety and comfort; I am in danger of flying apart at any moment.

One morning, I cry in a coffee shop, holding hands with a friend. I am set off by a question he asks about the LGBTQ+ caravan, whether I'd seen them. Excited to be able to say "yes" to even one question about my time in Tijuana, I tell him how I had gotten to watch some of the last of that group cross. And then, all of a sudden, I remember them: kids, close to my own age that looked like my friends, that had formed into a family on the road. They had made it to the wall, all jutting chins and rainbow flags and tear-stained goodbyes and shaky cigarettes, knowing they would be separated in order to head into their new unknown lives. Because they were not actually a family, there was no promise that they would be kept together. I remember a trans girl carefully folding her wig into her backpack and wiping her lipstick off with the back of her hand as her number got closer. I remember the couple that were yelled at by the man with the mustache for pausing to share a long kiss before they got in the van. It's not that I had forgotten them, but that I hadn't yet had the time to pull their stories out one by one, to celebrate and mourn them, to wonder where these people ended up once they left my view. Now, I do.

I feel guilty for feeling this grief. If I wasn't so privileged, so blind, so thoughtless, would it have taken seeing this need in person to recognize the scale? I am angry about the stories I've told myself about who migrates and why, like all migrants were victims in need of help instead of individuals who have carefully considered their alternatives, who understood the gravity of their own choices.

For weeks, I am an inferno dressed up in borrowed sorrows. I feel like lashing out, like I have either no words or far too many to tell someone exactly how it was. I resent everyone who asks me about it and anyone that doesn't. No words feel adequate—I simultaneously don't want to burden people and want everyone to feel the same kind of anger and grief I'm carrying.

Friends, classmates, ask, "So how was it?"

I can sometimes manage "hard," or "you know," but most of the time, my answer comes in the form of a shrug, hands open wide. All of it feels wrong and I am angry at myself for not knowing how to tell it better.

My partner, who sent me pictures of our dog every night while I was gone, asks me about it my first night home, and then doesn't ask me about it again, seeming to sense that I need space to find my own way into talking about what I had seen. On some days, his silence feels incurious and uncaring (it isn't); other times, it gives me room to allow something more to rise up, to be able to tell him a story or test out an idea. And other times still, even when the silence feels open and welcoming and ready, I hate myself for not having words to fill it.

Here is where second-hand trauma does differ from first though: I'll give it time. Just a little, a matter of weeks or months, and the howling rage will stop, the winds will die down. It will get quiet enough for me to work, to put words to the things that I saw and felt, to find the way to bring other people into what I'm feeling.

This trauma translation—my weaker, ghost-version of the original trauma I witnessed—I'm hoping it works like a real translation. In the same way translating a text brings it to a new audience, I want my work to bring a reality that was previously invisible and illegible to light. I'm hoping that it builds a bridge to greater understanding, or rather, a bridge across the gaps when you realize that, like me, you understand so very little of anything.

I hope it is clear that what I'm giving you is not, cannot, be the real thing. I couldn't even hold the real thing myself, have felt it slip through my fingers as I tried. It's far from Walter Benjamin's ideal invisible translator, but I am doing the only thing I can: making myself visible, taking your hand and walking you through the inferno, pointing out the places where I've left things out or omitted details, critiquing my own translating as we go.

KNOWING THIS, THOUGH, doesn't make it any easier to sit with myself. I'm still angry, still grief-stricken, full of a kind of restless energy that doesn't have an easy outlet in my day-to-day life of going to classes and making dinner and walking my dog.

I ask a friend how to cope. As a chaplain-in-training, she's familiar with accompaniment work, with the kind of aftermath I'm in the middle of.

"We're given all these things," she says, "and then we have nowhere to put them, so all we can do is archive it, put it away somewhere safe."

Building an archive is inherently an act of service, a gift for others to explore. Historians often speak of the joy of the archives, diving deep into the murky river of the past in order to discover some perfect, unexpected thing. The letters, the papers, the ephemera of the dead are stored together, as if just being in proximity to one another might provide some answer, some silhouetted clue that could bring the dead back to life.

A close friend of mine, Mounia, died a few years ago. She loved books deeply, loved a good leather binding and a yellowed page. I have this mental image of her, probably incorrect but somehow spiritually true of her lugging steamer trunks full of books around the world. Many of us who loved her got an email from her mother a few months later, letting us know that she was selling these steamer trunks of books to pay for a memorial video, and did we want to contribute a short clip of ourselves talking about her. I kept imagining those books, well-loved and tucked under an arm I knew so well, being handed over to strangers, indiscriminate hands that wouldn't quite know how to hold them with the care they deserved. It felt like a separate kind of loss, stacked on top of the first one. Something about her books all being in the same place, all having been chosen, handled, annotated and dog-eared by her was the mark of her mind on the world in a way a loose book jammed into someone else's shelves could never be. Archives prove a life, somehow.

I THINK ABOUT the missing and incomplete information in the ICE Detainee Locator, about Rodrigo's paperwork found in another man's suitcase, about the National Archives allowing ICE to destroy records from 2017 on detainee deaths and sexual assaults. I think about the detainee grievances relating to discrimination by guards, shoddy medical care, civil rights violations, uses of force. This is one kind of archive that needs to be kept. In the years to come, it will matter the way we treated the people who came to us looking for safety, it will matter who was wronged and how because I believe in a future where we make reparation for these harms. However, the witnesses also need tending—there are stories, moments, scenes that will never be captured in government paperwork. That is the work I want to do.

• • • •

AND THEN, ON a random refresh of Sara's Facebook, I see it: the three of them, on a beach, wind whipping through Sara's hair, the sun setting next to them.

I remember a slow afternoon at the shelter, after her partner had left, Sara and I and a few other women sat around. As we drank milky instant coffee, she told us about how her baby was named.

Her daughter was born a few months early with serious cardiac complications, a little slip of a thing. As they waited in the hospital room to find out if their baby would survive, Sara's partner began to pray in his parents' language, different from her own. As he spoke, Sara noticed a single word recurring, over and over. When she asked him what it meant, he said it meant "blessing."

A little girl named "Blessing" crossed the border, and a few days later, her mother crossed too. Their little family settled somewhere sunny and warm. And while they're still waiting for so much—their court date, the permanence a positive decision will bring—they are together now, safe.

This may be an easy way to end, but it is a true one. In the years since, I've seen a thousand pictures of Sara and her baby girl, have watched her learn to walk and give enthusiastic, near incomprehensible toddler monologues into the camera of her mother's phone. I have gotten to witness Sara's story continue, unfold past the moment we met. It's a sample size so small as to be meaningless, only made significant by the fact that it's the one I've been granted access to follow. I don't know what happened to anyone else that I met, but I can imagine happy endings for them too: tearful reunions, legal help, work authorizations, money sent back home to a hungry family. But because of the way this country treats people who come to its borders asking for help, I know it's likely that my imagined endings are just that: fiction.

I don't know how to become the kind of archive I want to be, don't know how to keep the details together so that no one or nothing gets lost. I'm struggling with my own "I," and where it belongs, how it's been both irrevocably altered by bearing witness and still somehow untouched and safe from suffering. In this way, translation of trauma is like a hurricane making landfall, like a river overflowing its banks. Eventually, the storm passes, the water settles back into its banks, and there's again a placid river winding its way through the landscape. The land remembers the flood, though—trees are uprooted, animals displaced, earth washed away.

And so, here I am, and here are dozens of other translators and inter-preters: not actually marked by the stories we have torn through in the same way they have torn through us, but feeling marked somehow. And what do we do with this markedness?

It is hard to have a real answer, to see how the things I have heard and am sharing will be useful to you or to someone else, how someone else's pain, refracted through my life, might change the course of a different life altogether. But the answer I have settled on is to archive, to submit what I have seen as a body of proof. I do it in part because I don't have a choice: The stories I have seen and heard are a part of me now. I cannot set them down, and there's no way to carry them easily without at least trying to change their endings.

The task of the archivist translator of anonymous texts is this: to be able to surface from within herself a story that will move people into ac-tion, that might change a mind or at least turn it to contemplation, to elide the boundaries so I'm not the only one carrying it.

PART II

Sobremesa

New York City, January 2017

22

DINNER IS MOSTLY OVER, BUT we still have our plates, salad-dressing-slicked and chicken-grease-dripped, in front of us, silverware piled on top. My sister is picking parmesan shreds out of the tablecloth, and I've got a hand in the salad bowl, mopping up dressing with a stray arugula leaf and delicately licking the ends of my fingers. Our cat is eyeing the remains of the meal from the extra chair that's always out more or less for her, while my dad scratches her ears. My sibling is peeling a label off their beer. My mom has cleared her plate and is scrolling through her Instagram, pausing to show us a watercolorist's page.

We stopped eating in earnest maybe an hour or so ago, but we're all still here around the kitchen table. I've gotten up to get myself another beer, my mom her iPad, my dad a finger or two of whiskey. My sister's telling a long-winded story I'm half paying attention to, mostly in Spanish but every once in a while she breaks into English when she gets to something frustrating, or makes a point. Whenever she does, my dad raises his eyebrows at her.

"En Español, muchacha!"

She rolls her eyes but translates herself. "Sí, 'pá, yo sé."

While we've been sitting at the table, the sky outside has gotten dark, cicadas have started singing into the muggy east Texas air. My family's sobremesas sometimes last until bedtime, all of us sitting around the table refilling drinks and arguing and chatting about nothing in particular. The living room, with its loveseats and couches all of us can sprawl on is just one room over, but especially since my siblings and I have moved out, when we're home, we're always right here, sitting around the same faux-weathered fading into actually weathered table where we did our homework all through high school. The varnish is rubbing off at each of our usually occupied spaces, crumbs gather in the interstices except in front of my dad's spot, because he'll sometimes idly wedge them out with a butter knife while we're all sitting here.

Sobremesa is the word we use to refer to both the conversations held over the table and the time spent sitting together after the meal. Sobremesa literally means above or on the table, the conversation a warm haze building up from the table's surface to encompass everyone sitting around it. Sobremesa is the thing that happens somewhere between the cozy but ultimately rule-bound meal and the scattering, chaotic forces of the outside world. It embodies a different way to circle around the nourishing nucleus of food and the traditions and care of making a meal, without having to worry about table manners or cloth napkins or whether anyone is watching you eat. Sobremesa knows there's work to do ahead: dishes to clean, a table to wipe down, something to get back to beyond the kitchen, even, but is content to linger, spend a little longer with good company in the space carved out in between.

Because of the specific circumstances of who we are, how we were brought up, and the ways we move in the world, my family's sobremesa conversation moves fluidly between English and Spanish. Sometimes the conversation, if it veers too far into English, will get course-corrected by my parents, but they're just as likely to drift back and forth—my dad when he's emphasizing a point, my mom when she's struggling to find a word, or talking about her paints or her plants, hobbies picked up in the U.S.

"En Español!" was the constant reminder of my childhood, the battle cry of my parents, intent on raising three children to be bilingual. They mostly succeeded, even if the three of us speak a little formally, a little schoolmarmishly—I for one can't curse or do math in Spanish, and I don't know why but when my siblings say "um," I can tell it's in English. Our entire childhood, it was a struggle to get the Spanish to stick—the three of us would revert whenever and however we could into English. And then, when I married someone who spoke only a little Spanish (he's working on it!) our dinner conversations were pulled out of Spanish, and we had to remind ourselves and each other to speak in English, sometimes pulling up mid-sentence with an abashed apology thrown Jason's way, and then switching back if he went off to go read a book or watch the hockey game. In sobremesa, the language—like the seats at the table and the food on the plates—ebbs and flows, changing to make space for everyone as chairs are pulled up or people wander off.

Sobremesa takes everything that is best about a meal—the nourishment, the intimacy—and translates its spell into a common language, accessible to everyone.

WHAT CAN I tell you about growing up in two languages? What can I tell you about the way that Spanish folded me into my family, the house I grew up in? What can I tell you about how a language spoken by 38 million people at home felt like it belonged only in mine? Even now, my bilingualism feels like a cheat code, a secret experience, something that belongs to me and my siblings alone, incommunicable.

Most of my life is conducted in English. That is the language I use to think, read, write, argue, calculate tips, chat, swear, name myself. Most days, my Spanish is like a phantom limb: never used, a fun fact rather than an active part of my life. Still, sometimes it itches.

Whenever I hear Spanish on the street, especially strong, Mexican Spanish, a feeling of tenderness, of family, springs up inside me—this, more than anything else, signifies my kinship. Even though so much of my life happens in another language, this well of feeling that Spanish uncovers means that my life, lived only in English, would be incomplete.

We never lived anywhere with big communities of Mexican families, or if there were, we weren't really part of them. My Spanish was not the Spanish of backyard barbecues or entire weekends spent together with a herd of other children my age, or the Spanish of telling secrets under the covers at late-night sleepovers. It was the Spanish of deep inside jokes, of my parents' 1980s slang, all cleaned up for us, the Spanish of Guadalupe Pineda and Cri-Cri.

Summer was the time we lived in Spanish. Every summer when I was in elementary school, we did Spanish homeschool. Other than our afternoons at a local pond playing Marco Polo and practicing our backstroke, we spent all our days in Spanish, swam in it, dove deep daily. For those few months each year, the language got closer, clearer, felt more like our home than a borrowed one. The rest of the year, Spanish was like pajamas—only for home and the rest of the time scarcely even thought about.

Translation was a way, the only way, in which Spanish became social. It allowed me to reach beyond the boundaries of my family and my own mind. In kindergarten and first grade, my best friend was Camila, a girl whose family had recently arrived from Colombia. I would translate for her in the classroom, but at lunch and on the playground, we would talk to each other in Spanish. Later, my cousin Paola, who spoke English like you might if you had mainly learned it in a classroom, came to stay with us for a year and I did the same thing—stepping in, easing the way, acting as a go-between. This was probably presumptuous and unnecessary—both did speak English—but I liked the way translating for them made me feel useful, gave me the same kind of virtuous rush as holding the door open for someone or giving up my seat on the subway.

When I moved out of my parents' house and came to New York City for college, Spanish became a way of engaging with the city—I'd help tourists with directions on the train, chat with the cafeteria workers and the guys in the mail room. I'm short, and brown, and have a round face and dark, straight hair and so people would sometimes come up to me: "¿Habla Español?" It was always a rush to be recognized like that—despite my uncertainty, despite my fear of not fitting in or of my Spanish being suitable to only the people I loved, people would look at me and *know*.

And then that knowing curdled.

23

IN JANUARY OF 2017, I was living in New York City. My morning commute every weekday led me through Union Square Station, which had become papered over in sticky notes of support and fear. "Fuck Trump," they said, or "We All Stand Together," or "#Resist." They were supposed to make me feel good, feel like the city, in some undefinable way, had my back, but they were mostly just sticky notes, slips of paper whose adhesive failed in the weird damp of the January subway and would flutter to the ground as multicolored, well-meaning trash, eventually trodden into grayish pulp on the slushy subway floor. After a week or so, as the sticky notes spread through the station in tendrils, I began to have to push past people, locals and tourists alike, who had stopped, midpassage, to photograph them, to remind themselves that we were living in an exceptional city, in an exceptional time.

And even though I rolled my eyes at it, I wasn't immune to that feeling. Every train ride felt like I was waiting for an inevitable attack from an ICE agent or a cop or a hijab-puller or a MAGA-hat-wearing goon, or just generally subjected me to a mass of people I could eye speculatively, wondering which way they had voted, and why. Occasionally someone made eye contact back, gestured at a safety pin on their lapel, made a little nod of solidarity that felt just as hollow and weird as my panic.

Every part of being in the city at that time—of being in public at that time, I suspect—reminded you of the danger you were in, both ironically and not. There were too many people you didn't know and couldn't trust, a sense of hidden ugliness coming unveiled, and the most visible attempts at combating it were weak and corny. I had known that there was ugliness, that there was injustice and struggle before this election but, as it didn't affect me, it was easy to convince myself that there were checks on it, that something like decency might prevail because my own life was decent. Every divinity student worth their salt will tell you that "apocalypse" comes from the Greek word for "unveiling." We joked the world was ending, but the only thing that had actually changed was that we could see the process a little more clearly, and we could see that no one was coming to save us.

And still, I Googled whether the three-years-past expired Texas driver's license I hadn't renewed since I moved to the city would be enough to prove my citizenship, and told my roommates, just in case, where to find my passport, all the while knowing these preparations were ridiculous.

So, when a friend asked if I wanted to do translation work at a weekly *pro se* asylum application clinic, I said yes, unsure what that actually meant, either logistically or emotionally, but desperately wanting to keep my hands and my brain busy with something new. "There's soup!" she said, but I don't think I needed the extra motivation. We met at a Starbucks near the clinic, the little group of translators, or at least bilingües, that my friend had recruited, most of us in our twenties, Latinx, bundled up against the cold.

I got there early enough to buy and nurse a drink, something sweet and warm to hold while I waited for the rest of the group to trickle in. I knew my friend from my undergrad at Columbia, and looking around the coffee shop, I saw a few people I suspected were here for the same reason, faces I recognized from around campus. Whatever our homes and families had been growing up, we had all received some expensive educations, all had enough free time to be here, at a Starbucks at 5:30 p.m. on a Tuesday, hoping to make ourselves useful in some way. This, at any other time, would have been enough: to know that there were other people like me, who had been given so much but were just as angry as I was, just as hungry for more than aimless anger.

After talking for a little bit about what to expect—asylum applications and bureaucracy, asylum seekers, usually from the Northern Triangle of Guatemala, Honduras, and El Salvador, almost always traumatized—we trudge a few blocks through wintry slush to a church basement off Washington Square Park. When we arrive, it's already a sardine-packed jumble of volunteers and photocopies and manila file folders. The other volunteers, arrayed on fraying couches and leaning on cabinets or bustling from one end of the basement to another are largely white—either young people, with glasses and artfully cut hair and whimsically layered clothes, or old-school New York socialists who had spent their lives running to where the need felt the greatest, or lawyers, working pro bono but still in their suits from their corporate-ish office jobs. We go around the room and introduce ourselves even though the group, some thirty or forty people, is already too big to make this a feasible proposition. One of the organizers, Kitty, a compact woman in her seventies with a wide smile and close-cropped strawberry blonde hair, explains the processes for the evening, and asks that if we are new, we try to spend a week or two observing.

"If you're a translator though, you may end up stepping in anyways. We are a little short, so if you see the need, please do join a group."

Sara, another one of the leaders, brings in a group of people who are here tonight to get help, each of them holding a folder with either their half-completed applications, or blank versions of all the forms we sign—contact information, waivers stating that we won't give legal advice, and the I-589 (Application for Asylum and for Withholding of Removal). True enough, as the volunteers find the people they've worked with previously or are partnered with first-time attendees, it becomes obvious that there are groups that don't have anyone to interpret, and so eventually I raise my hand and find myself teamed up with two well-meaning retirees sitting across the table from someone who needs help to fill out a document I haven't ever seen before.

This is Mayra. She greets me with a grin and a nod, I tell her it's my first time at the clinic, and that it's my first time in a while interpreting like this, so I'm sorry if I mess up, and I'm probably going to be very slow. The other two volunteers reassure us that they've been here for longer, and more or less know what they're doing. I ask her if she can go slow—to say a sentence or two and then let me catch up to her, but that it's okay if she forgets. I let her know she can stop at any time, that she can take a break if she needs—a strategy my friend had suggested at the Starbucks. She's a head shorter than me, and as we start the interview, she's shrinking back in her chair, playing with the sleeve of her sweater, looking up at the ceiling as she tries to remember a detail. We are sitting at the end of a long table almost in a hallway in this church basement—people bustle past on their way to the bathroom or the copier, we can hear the dull murmur of other groups going through their questionnaires.

Talking to Mayra, we start outlining her life as it was before—a small house in San Pedro Sula with her mother, two daughters, a brother who came in and out of the house as his job took him in and out of the city, a job of her own as a hairdresser that she practiced from her living room, an occasional involvement with the local church mostly on holidays and saints' days. This is the first time I have seen how much an application for asylum goes into detail on the mundanity of a life. I learn the names of all Mayra's siblings and where they live, the political party her brother belonged to, her addresses and occupations going back five years.

And then, Mayra and I find out together just how difficult filling out the I-589 can be. It's my first time filling out the form, so I ask her the questions, exactly as they are written.

"Have you, your family, close friends, or colleagues ever experienced harm or mistreatment or threats in the past by anyone?"

"If 'Yes,' explain in detail what happened, when the harm or mistreatment or threats occurred; who caused the harm or mistreatment or threats; and why you believe the harm or mistreatment, or threats occurred."

"Do you fear harm or mistreatment if you return to your home country?"

"If 'Yes,' explain in detail what harm or mistreatment you fear; who you believe would harm or mistreat you; and why you believe you would or could be harmed or mistreated."

"Are you afraid of being subjected to torture in your home country or any other country to which you may be returned?"

"If 'Yes,' explain why you are afraid and describe the nature of torture you fear, by whom, and why it would be inflicted."

As each question lands, Mayra shrinks farther back in her chair, her eyes more often seeking out the corners of the room, her sleeve in danger of being picked apart entirely. I offer tissues even though she is dry-eyed, water even though her voice does not crack, a break, though when I ask she looks at me with a grim set to her jaw and shakes her head no. And so, we keep going.

She's been through this before, answered these questions or ones just like them when they were posed to her, a few weeks ago, by a Border Patrol officer or an asylum official during her Credible Fear Interview—if she hadn't had that, if she hadn't passed it, she wouldn't be sitting in front of me now. But that doesn't make this any easier.

As I talk to her, I am also talking to the other two people around the table with us, explaining to them, in my own voice and a different language, what Mayra is telling me. They are writing it down so that the ways in which I am hurting Mayra by asking her to remember does not go to waste.

A few minutes before 9 p.m., Kitty wanders around to all the groups, giving them a time check and reminding them that there's soup and snacks available in the lobby. When Kitty comes by our table, I translate her message for Mayra, and let her know that we should wind down. She asks how many more questions we have left, and I say just the one, and I ask it, and she asks me the difference between this question about torture and the question about being afraid of being hurt. I don't know the answer, nor do any of the other team members, although they suggest just repeating the same answer as the previous question about harm, but we decide maybe it's better to hold off until we can ask one of the lawyers floating around to advise on the form. I ask Mayra if it's okay if we leave it for next week, while I find out, and she says okay. I watch as the wire-strung tension holding her shoulders rigid and her jaw tight relaxes fractionally.

"¿Quieres ir por comida?" I ask her, and she nods, so we get up, and I serve us both small plastic bowls of Italian wedding soup with tiny meatballs bobbing in broth, serve out bowls for the other two volunteers, and we eat together, in silence, until one by one, we put on our coats and head out into the city night.

24

METAPHORS FOR THE TRANSLATOR ABOUND: She is a windowpane, a bridge builder, a diplomat, a spy, a traitor. Like any traitor, I hold one allegiance close to my heart, and let everything else slide by the wayside. If you were to ask someone fundamentally different from me, they'd tell you that my translating for asylum seekers constitutes a kind of treason, a refusal to align myself with what's best for the country. They're ultimately not wrong—my allegiance isn't to a country that defines itself through exclusion.

However, I'm also not in league with you, reader—there's a way in which I'm playing coy. I suspect your heart is in the right place, but you don't yet—and won't ever—know anyone's name or their real stories. I'll give you pastiche, narratives in asymptote to reality, but never the real thing.

The allegiances I keep are instead to myself and to the people I've met, to the hours together in church basements and at the border, to their right, however wan it feels, to keep their stories between them and the U.S. government, and me.

There's also, always and of course, more. Just because someone told me a story about the worst days of their life, just because I took some hours, one day a week, to sit with them and listen to that story that was forced out of them by a need for survival doesn't mean I actually know them at all. Every time I encounter someone moving through the immigration system, I encounter them at points of trauma and pain, where even their self-concept is fragmented and strange. In order to believe the world is capable of being more than its worst moments, you have to believe any one person is capable of that.

However, since the United States Application for Asylum and for Withholding of Removal is solely focused on that worst moment, since waiting at the border or in court or for a reply to a form to come back is the moment when the worst options can bloom into the imagination as ever-more-solid possibilities, all I get is the worst moment.

And that's fine. I'm no more entitled to the totality of an asylum seeker's life than I am to that of any other complete stranger, but it is my responsibility to remember that I do not know the totality of that life, and to make space for the rest of that life to occur in safety and comfort. I make my work a door into verdant pastures, a bridge into a quiet future.

LET'S TALK ABOUT the origin of languages. It's not a true story, but it is a useful one.

Some time had passed after the great flood—the one that Noah famously survived in his ark—and the people of Earth, who all spoke the same language, decided that they would build a tower "that reaches to the heavens" so that they would not be "scattered over the face of the Earth."

After calamity, they wanted to build a monument to their own permanence, create a point where they might reach God, but the rising floodwaters God sent could not reach them.

As they built and reached towards heaven, God realized that the tower was too tall, came too close to where God lived. "Come, let us go down and confuse their language so they will not understand each other," God said. And God did.

Some versions of the story, especially in children's bibles, show the languages coming down like a lightning strike to the top of the tower, shattering it. However, the text itself makes no mention of this, only saying that the people stopped building. We are left to imagine the tower, reaching towards heaven, and then, over time, slowly crumbling into dust.

I do wonder how much language was actually needed to continue building a tower—if it was tall enough to make God nervous, then surely the brickmakers knew how to continue shaping and baking bricks out of earth; and the masons knew how to lay down thin, careful layers of mortar at the very top of the tower; and those who carried the bricks up the ever-growing staircase knew the best way to set their shoulders against the load. So when the languages came down not with a thunderclap, but in a persistent rain, it must have been something else that was halted, something else that made people stop working and move apart from one another.

I have a theory that the Tower of Babel is both the birthplace of languages and the birthplace of differences. The real thing that halted production wasn't being unable to communicate about mortar consistency or kiln temperatures, but rather the distrust that rushed in to fill the space between understanding. When God sent down the languages, the thing that was accomplished was the splintering of a community.

In translating Genesis 11:1-9—or any other work, really—translators are slowly beginning the task of pulling that community back together, of stacking bricks one on top of another.

Or, in the case of a border, dismantling a wall brick by brick to ensure people can find their way to one another. The border walls are the consequence for what happened at Babel, a manifestation of a community, splintered. No one I have met that has encountered a border is safer or more whole or happier for it. Before we can start rebuilding the tower, we have to start by tearing down what keeps us apart.

25

"I WANT TO BE CLEAR to folks in this region who are thinking about making that dangerous trek to the United States–Mexico border: Do not come. Do not come." Even after the overt cruelty of the Trump administration, in 2021 the Biden administration's "humanitarian" answer to the immigration problem has been to counsel people to stay home, to stay in places like Guatemala, where Vice President Kamala Harris delivered these remarks, and Honduras and Nicaragua and El Salvador and Venezuela and Mexico. If you know nothing else about the world, it's maybe not such an absurd proposition: Don't come here, we don't have room for you, and the journey is dangerous. The Statue of Liberty and the Great American Melting Pot and Cher Horowitz aside, being a person alive in the United States of America today is often enough evidence that it's not a country that's doing particularly well, or that's particularly welcoming.

And yet, people keep coming, keep making dangerous journeys, risking separation and death and deportation, and so it falls to us to ask why? What is it like where immigrants are *from* for them to think that this country is a better alternative? The answer is countries that are deeply, grindingly poor, countries with corrupt politicians despite decades of attempted self-governance, countries with flourishing crime syndicates and depleted resources. And how did they get that way?

The United States.

Through a century and a half of continual diplomatic and military intervention, exploitative U.S.-based multinationals run riot, as do deeply unjust trade deals. We've rendered many (most?) of the countries south of our borders dangerous to all but the wealthiest, a pattern continuing as we contribute far beyond proportion to global warming. There's no better way to see the long history of U.S.-led devastation of Latin American states than through a contemplation of our food systems, the ways we feed American excess.

Today, the United States' gardens and food fields are worked in large part by Indigenous and Latinx workers, a tradition that began with the Spanish Missions in the 1800s, where missionary monks would conscript Indigenous communities to work the land in exchange for "civilization" and Christianization. This pattern was continued and made explicit by the Bracero Program that brought mostly Mexican guest workers north to work the fields during the labor shortages of World War II, only to be deported if they attempted to negotiate for better conditions or flee exploitative bosses, and is still visible in the demographics of those that harvest the vegetables and butcher the meat that ends up on our tables.

The surplus of cheap Latinx and Indigenous labor is not a coincidence— and it all begins with a banana.

"OK, ¿ESTÁ LISTA PARA EMPEZAR? Esta entrevista a veces puede ser un poco difícil, así que, si necesita tomarse el tiempo, tomar agua, lo que sea, avísame y podemos pausar, o seguir la semana siguiente. Es importante que me diga todo lo que puede recordar, pero yo sé que puede ser muy difícil recordar cosas. ¿Lista?"

"Sí."

"Okay, I'm going to ask her if there was an event or something that happened that made her decide to come to the U.S. Ready? Okay. ¿Hubo algún evento o algo que la hizo decidir venir a los Estados Unidos?"

"Bueno, sí."

"¿Me puede decir lo que pasó?"

"Yo salí con mis amigas a bailar una noche, y de repente oímos balazos, y gente gritando, y habían matado a alguien ahí en el medio del club."

"*She says she was out dancing with her friends, and they heard gunshots, and they had killed someone in the middle of the dance floor.*"

"*Y fue mi primo.*"

"*¿Él que mataron?*"

"*Sí. Le dieron dos balazos, aquí y aquí, y yo grité, y me vieron los que estaban ahí.*"

"*She's saying that the person that was killed was her cousin, they shot him twice in the chest, and I screamed and they saw me. ¿Sabía quienes eran los que le mataron a su primo?*"

"*No sabía sus nombres, pero eran mareros de por ahí del barrio.*"

"*¿Cómo sabía que eran mareros?*"

"*Pues, no sé, na'más sabes. Tenían tatuajes, estaban vestidos así, mataron a mi primo, no sé.*"

"*She said they were gangsters, and I asked her how she knew, and she said she just knew, but not how—they were dressed like it and had tattoos, they killed her cousin. ¿Qué paso después?*"

"*Nos dijeron, 'si les dicen a alguien lo que vieron, las vamos a matar'. Y nosotras dijimos que sí, que sí, y nos dejaron ir, pero el día siguiente, estaban ahí los mismos, frente a mi casa, y me estaban viendo entrar y salir, y otra vez el día siguiente, y otra vez después.*"

"*¿Le decían algo?*"

"*A veces. A veces me amenazaban, o decían que me iban a matar, una noche, creo la segunda o tercera que estaban ahí, empezaron a golpear la puerta, y uno de ellos rompió una ventana, aventó una piedra, y solo fue porque una vecina empezó a gritar que se fueron. Fue entonces que decidí que tenía que irme. Me fui a quedar con mi mamá, en otro barrio, y con mi hija, y estuvo bien unas semanas, pero entonces aparecieron ahí, frente a la casa de mi mamá, y esa noche me junté con otros que venían, y me vine para aquí.*"

"*Ok, ¿un momento? Uh, the gangsters said that if they talked to anyone, they'd kill them, and they all said yes, yes, okay, and they let them go, but the next day, they were all waiting in front of her house, and again and again,*" *sometimes like, threatening her, telling her they'd kill her. And one night they tried to break in, broke a window, were yelling, but only left when a neighbor started screaming, so she decided to leave. Um, she and her daughter went to stay with her mom, but then they showed up there too, so she decided that night to join up with some other people who were coming here and left."*

"Can you ask her about her daughter?"

"Sure thing. Y, su hija, ¿dónde está?"

"Pensé que iba a ser muy peligroso traérmela, así que la dejé ahí, con mi mamá, y—y—"

"Ay no, mi amor, lo siento, lo siento. ¿Quiere pañuelo?"

"No, no, está bien, está bien, gracias, solo es que—"

AND THUS, IN the first month of the Trump administration, I began to work as a volunteer interpreter for undocumented immigrants. I met them in the basement of a church a ten-minute walk from the office where I was working as a marketing assistant, sitting in a cubicle tweeting and compiling spreadsheets all day. They came after long days of childcare or construction jobs or the occasional under-the-table gig as a hairdresser. They were mostly asylum seekers, mostly from Honduras, had mostly arrived in New York City within the last year, cold and disoriented.

I, too, arrived at the church cold and disoriented most weeks. I came to the work because I was exhausted, heartsick, looking to do something to stem the tide of despair flowing knee-deep around and through me. And so, on Tuesday nights, I would find myself among a crowd of volunteers in that church basement, or in one of the student lounges at the NYU School of Law, volunteers on one side, and asylum applicants, who we were instructed to call our friends, on the other.

I always hated calling them this—it felt patronizing and forcedly intimate. However, it did serve the dual purpose of giving the people we interviewed a relational identity to us beyond their legal status—not just an asylum seeker or an undocumented person but a friend. It also gave us plausible deniability if we were ever questioned: "No, no, I was just spending time with some friends!"

It was unclear at any given time if we expected to be questioned, but we prepared for it nonetheless. Surveillance hygiene, we called it, keeping clinic files and notes off Google or cloud storage, preferring pen and paper locked up in a file cabinet in the basement when we could—it wasn't perfect, but the feds would need a warrant to access the information—leaving vague messages on friends' phones if we needed to reach them, only loosely alluding to the location of the clinic. These measures often felt like we were trying to create a small island of relative safety, as if washing our hands often enough could keep the sickness of the country itself from spreading.

Every week, we started off in these bifurcated crowds, volunteers on one side, asylum seekers on the other, and as they called out the names on a thick stack of manila folders, we would come together, returning friends first. The crowd on my side of the room was often homogenous—largely white, largely middle- and upper-class, although diverse in ages. The crowd on the friends' side was a little more diverse, although we had a reputation as largely a Spanish-speaking clinic, so we didn't often get people from outside of the Americas. You could kind of tell as news of the clinic spread through the neighborhoods and micro-communities of New York—for a few weeks, everyone showing up would be from San Pedro Sula or Tegucigalpa or Guerrero or La Ceiba, sometimes even down to the neighborhood in the city. For a month or two, many of the people showing up were Garifuna, members of a community of Black Indigenous people living largely in coastal Honduras and St. Vincent who had been, over the years, displaced by the resort and farming industries.

Our task, all of us, every week, was to interview the applicants, and to answer the questions, roughly following the contours of form I-589, the Application for Asylum and for Withholding of Removal. It always struck me as strange that we called it that, withholding of removal, as if removal was the default option, and it was only through the exposure of this trauma that it might be held off for a time, as if the lack of deportation was a massive favor the federal government was doing for our friends.

But there I was every week, to ask the government for this favor on behalf of someone new. I sat across the table from a new or somewhat familiar face, asking the same questions, and getting distinctive stories in return—stories that were different, but rhymed, that had assonance with each other, that were born of the same desperate conditions, some combination of violence and poverty and exploitation by the country we were all sitting in.

The form was complicated. It required not only excavation of past trauma, but the kind of extra-detailed minutiae of a tax form. Because of this, we met with the same friends weekly, three or four weeks at a time. While the first and last weeks were usually dedicated to logistics—names and addresses and later finding the passport-sized picture that needed to be stapled on the second-to-last page and photocopying, stapling, and collating the entire application in triplicate—the middle weeks were dedicated to going over the details of what we called "their story." This meant asking about exactly where he was when his neighbor or brother or best friend had been murdered, about exactly how often or for how long he had followed her home from school, spewing threats, about whether there was a racial undertone to the insults he had used while beating her, about whether his family had gone to the hospital or the police or the church or the train into Mexico and then further north.

The people across the table from us often had the dazed look of someone who has just gotten off an airplane, even if they had been in the States for weeks or months. I heard stories of people walking up the continent, of riding atop speeding trains through the night, of people left behind at home or along the road. I became familiarized with the geography of detention, of border check-ins and waystations. Many of the people I had talked to had crossed the border on foot. Sometimes in Tijuana, yes, but more commonly in other places, even the ones I knew from my own crossings: Eagle Pass, Piedras Negras, Karnes, Eloy, Otay Mesa, the names of border towns and the detention or processing centers on their outskirts interchangeable. Trauma and violence marked every step of the journey, from the midnight flight from something pounding at the door to traveling companions falling off rushing trains or being kidnapped somewhere in the middle of Mexico, to horrifying conditions in an ICE or CBP detention center.

There was a sense among us volunteers that the worse the story was, the better chances our friend had of being granted asylum, and so, like ghouls, we would hope for racial epithets, for beatings so bad they necessitated the ever-elusive physical evidence of hospital records, for the death certificate of a relative within reach, cause of death: shooting, stabbing, anything. We had the sense that a return to their home country would mean death for any of the people we were talking to, but also had to hope that they had felt its touch before—and better yet, had the evidence to prove it.

Then, right around 9 p.m., the manila folders would close, chairs would get pushed back from tables, and we would eat snacks together, take breaks, pass tissues, play with rosy-cheeked, bundled-up babies, ask about weekend plans or how their new apartment was working out, give tips on surviving New York winters.

And at the end of each Tuesday night, I'd walk down into the subway and wait for the B train to come thundering to a stop. I would sit there as it crossed over the darkened river and made its way into Brooklyn, not looking at my phone or a book or anything, trying to let what I had heard that night stream out behind me as I went.

GROWING UP, A lot of the most serious conversations I had with my mom happened in the front seat of her car. It's easier to talk that way, without having to look at each other, leaving the things we say strewn behind us on the highway as we go. Even now, when I no longer live at home, I only ever call her when I'm on the move between point A and point B, or in the interstices of my day, as I'm preparing dinner or doing laundry. Walking around New York, there are certain streets, certain benches that are marked because I walked up and down those blocks, sat on those benches for hours while on the phone with her.

Her way of talking is extremely her own: She will pick up a thread of conversation abandoned some twenty minutes ago, or trail off, mid-thought, trying to remember a place name or the year something happened. This isn't a symptom of anything, it's just the way she talks. As I've gotten older, my own speech patterns are moving in this direction also. My dad and my husband now will stop us in the same ways, especially when we've started up on a new subject, mid-thought. They'll say hold on, back up, start over: "Why are you talking about this? Why is this coming up?"

I never have to ask. My mom's digressions and equivocations have always made sense to me. When she picks up a subject, I can trace its roots back to an earlier conversation, or something we drove past, or even just the branching paths of her thoughts. Of course talking about a trip to the Antique Rose Emporium means that a minute from now we'll be talking about the difficulties in finding cadmium red watercolor tubes at the local Michael's or her asking me if I'm sure I don't want to go pick up some kolaches before I leave town—she often uses the photos she takes at botanical gardens as references for her watercolors, and our kolache spot is in the same town as the Antique Rose Emporium. I'm the one she turns to when she forgets a name or wants reassurance that what she brings up makes some kind of sense. I fill in the gaps in her conversation when she pauses, offer up names and words and connective tissue for everyone else. When it's just us, my mom and I talk mostly in Spanish. English is reserved for some kind of public conversation—when there's someone else, someone outside the family involved. But even when there's just us and my dad and siblings, I still sometimes feel like the way we talk involves a translation—from her way to our way of being in conversation to a different, more widely recognized one. It's this translation that means I'm prone to interrupting other people, that means I have to remind myself that people generally don't need my help to finish thoughts or find the right words, that I only know my mom in that kind of way.

And yet, a language gap persists. It's strange to think of there being a language gap between us, but there is. When I do the work of being myself, of inscribing and circumscribing myself into language, the language I do it in is English. And so, in my conversations with my mother, what comes out is a translated version of me, a version that I can feel being constrained by a limited vocabulary, an unease, however slight, in a language that isn't always my home.

It is fitting then, that to talk to her at all about myself, there is also travel: from the language of my adult self, backwards through a narrowing vocabulary, into the language of my childhood. I don't know how much of it gets lost in translation, how many gaps I'm leaving that neither of us can see, much less fill in.

27

KATE BRIGGS, IN HER BOOK on the task of the translator, *This Little Art*, compares translation to Robinson Crusoe making a table for himself on his deserted island. He doesn't need a table: A rock or a lap or a tree trunk will do; you can eat food off anything, really. Still, he's reaching for the model, for the idea of it, because having the item "table" in the context of "deserted island" would say something about the kind of person he is, the kind of life he can make for himself so far from home. He sets out to build the table out of the materials and tools he has at his disposal—making this like no table he has ever known. But he is an Englishman, he has sat at hundreds, possibly thousands of tables to eat, to write, to have conversations. He has embodied knowledge of what a table feels like when you sit down in front of its smooth surface. Much like a table itself, this metaphor is useful in more ways than one.

As Briggs says, "If translation is like a table, then it has known and is open to different kinds of making." A table, of course, makes its own community by being a gathering place of basic necessity. It is the surface that undergirds the meal, and everything else that flowers from it. In making a translation, like in making a table, you (re)create a blank surface that draws people around it, allows for places to be set, for meals to be made and served, for sobremesa to extend its warm glow late into the evening. A translation not only makes the table but puts extra leaves in, lays out a few extra places for whoever drops in. Donde comen dos, comen tres.

IN THE UPSTAIRS rooms of an inn tucked away in some side street in ancient Jerusalem, Jesus sat down for a final meal with his twelve disciples. It was like any family meal: someone reclining on Jesus' breast; lamb, and wine, and bread; accusations of poor behavior; tensions; eleventh-hour revelations. We have a fairly comprehensive, if somewhat blurred account of the Last Supper because each of the Four Evangelists mentions it.

John tells us about how Jesus attended to his apostles' bodies, not just through feeding them a meal, but by kneeling before them and washing their feet. Matthew tells us about how Judas is taken aback at the news of his betrayal, Mark about all the disciples' dismay. Luke recounts a petty squabble among the apostles about which of them is the greatest. When Jesus interrupts, I imagine them all sitting shame-faced, knowing that for this occasion they had wanted to be better than themselves, but had not been able to be anything other than what they were.

What three of the apostles agree on, and the fourth makes slant mention of, is that at some point in the meal, Jesus lifted up bread and gave thanks and broke it, telling the apostles, "This is my body, which is given for you; do this in remembrance of me." He then took a cup of wine, and repeated himself: "This cup is the new covenant in my blood, which is shed for you."

The next day, this would be true in a more literal fashion. That day, we have the actual blood of Jesus, spilling down from the wounds on his body, the actual body of Jesus, rendered lifeless, but on this Passover, we have wine and bread and twelve men on the precipice of grief.

The Eucharist—which is what we now call the ritual in which we consume bread and wine in remembrance of Jesus—is a ceremony that imbues the ordinary with meaning. I've read bemused tweets from congregants at churches in which teen boy altar servers are responsible for obtaining the Eucharistic bread, which naturally leads to celebrating the body of Christ as it manifests in a cut-up bit of hot dog bun; there's a meme popular among divinity school students that suggests that, depending on your feelings about purity in ingredients vs. structure, foodstuffs as diverse as Lunchables and Mountain Dew might be consecrated for communion. The point is this: God can be found in the ordinary.

I have a complicated relationship to God and Christianity, but I've always loved the Eucharist, have taken it in the desire to be found by the holiness that inhabits hot dog buns and inexpertly performed rituals. In the end, like delicious slices of pizza eaten standing up at the end of a really good night out or even a disastrous Thanksgiving dinner, it is less about the food and more about the occasion that calls you to it, the person eating next to you.

WHEN THE UNITED FRUIT COMPANY (UFCO) arrived on a new parcel of land, they would begin by transforming it to look like every other piece of land they owned. They would rip out all the preexisting vegetation and smooth out the landscape like shaking out a tablecloth: leveling out hills, removing rocky outcroppings, filling marshlands and creeks and replacing them with orderly rows of irrigation. When the land was ready, they would plant row after row of banana trees, all the same kind. Banana plants are all clones of each other—you may have noticed that the fruit of a banana tree doesn't actually have seeds, and the big multilayered flowers that slowly turn into banana chandeliers are largely for show. As a result, most bananas reproduce by creating genetically identical suckers that propagate off the main root system.

At first, the vast majority of the bananas planted were the Gros Michel, or "Big Mike" banana—the banana frozen in time as artificial "banana flavoring." However, the plants were unaccustomed to growing side-by-side in orderly rows, and so when disease came for the Gros Michel, the trees' proximity meant it tore through plantations, decimating supplies, and the United Fruit Company switched to the Cavendish banana.

The Cavendish banana was favored not because it was particularly beautiful or flavorful, but because it was largely resistant to disease and had a high yield. No one actually knows where the Cavendish first grew, it's called that because Lord Cavendish found it on an expedition and had it growing in a greenhouse on his estate when the United Fruit Company came calling. It's speculated that it's originally from Southeast Asia—Thailand or India, perhaps—but it became an unwitting colonist of the Americas as it was spread across the United Fruit Company's vast holdings.

After a number of growing seasons, when the nutrients in the soil were depleted and banana yields dropped, or when fungal diseases at last managed to infect the trees, they simply picked up and left, leaving the land razed and empty. The United Fruit Company also made it a point to keep over half the land they owned unplanted and unproductive, buying up vast tracts largely to keep competitors—and the local peasant farmworkers—from accessing it. The company, now better known by their U.S. successor, Chiquita Brand, owned plantations in Cuba, Ecuador, Guatemala, Honduras, Colombia, Puerto Rico, and Nicaragua. By the 1930s, they owned 3.5 million acres of land across all Central America and the Caribbean, including 42 percent of the land in Guatemala.

The company began amidst Gilded Age excesses—channeling the adventurers and exploiters at loose ends in a post-Civil War U.S. into a tropical land of opportunity. When bananas first arrived in the United States, they were seen as markers of wealth and prosperity, signs of the United States' dominance of faraway climes. Unsurprisingly, labor conditions on early plantations were horrifying for locals, while American expats lived in company towns of shimmering pools and shiny cars.

In *One Hundred Years of Solitude*, Gabriel García Márquez has one of his many José Arcadios hide while members of the Colombian army slaughter three thousand striking banana workers, only to have every last trace of the massacre wiped from the collective memory of Macondo. In reality, the Colombian army killed anywhere from forty-seven to two thousand striking banana workers during the 1928 strike at the Santa Marta plantation in Colombia. The workers were striking for compensation for workplace accidents, a six-day workweek, hygienic dormitories, and payment in actual money as opposed to company scrip. Meanwhile, telegrams went back and forth between U.S. and Colombian officials and the executives of the United Fruit Company, assuring each other that American interests would be protected, but just in case, it might be a good idea to have a United States warship anchored off the coast to step in if necessary. Part of the confusion over the death toll of this strike lies in the unknown last resting place of the people murdered.

By the 1950s, bananas were ubiquitous, sliced over the cornflakes of a prosperous postwar breakfast, and congealed into terrifyingly kitschy publicity recipes. They no longer *suggested* the United States' domination of lands across the globe, they were proof of it. It was around this time also that the countries of Central America began to more visibly chafe under the dictatorial yoke of the United Fruit Company. Guatemala, having recently elected a democratic socialist president, began redistributing some of the massive landholding of UFCO to their peasant class. This obviously was unacceptable to the United Fruit Company, and so they called in the United States Government, which was already itching to exercise "anti-communist" measures in Central America. At the time, the Secretary of State, John Foster Dulles, and the head of the CIA, Allen Dulles, were brothers who had been on UFCO's payroll for thirty-eight years. In 1954, the brothers organized a successful coup to depose the president, replacing him with a U.S.-backed military man. The coup kicked off the Guatemalan Civil War, which ended officially in 1996 and from which the country is very much still recovering. It's estimated that 200,000 civilians died during the war, not to mention the campaigns of terror, rape, and disappearances carried out by the Guatemalan government with U.S. support.

Guatemala was far from the only country affected in this way. The United Fruit Company caused political revolts and massacres in Cuba, Guatemala, Honduras, and Colombia, all under the aegis of the CIA and the United States government. This is the kind of political instability that causes people to migrate, the kind that has far-reaching consequences years and decades down the line. It's been nearly one hundred years since the massacre at Santa Marta, and in that time, Colombia has hardly achieved political stability thanks to constant U.S. interventions that range from deposing leaders to bombing peasant enclaves in the jungle with napalm. What each of these interventions demonstrates, both to the United States and to the residents of the countries in question, is that if the land has been taken once, when it's been reshaped in the interest of a foreign power or a multinational corporation, there is little stopping it from being taken again and again. You may as well put on your pack and see if you can claim a bit of the colonizing power, a bit of their stability for yourself and your family.

"Y ¿POR QUÉ VINISTE A los Estados Unidos? ¿Cuándo decidiste que tenías que venir?"

"Bueno. Yo me decidí venir porque estaba pasando muchos, muchos problemas allí en El Salvador, y una amiga mía me dijo que estaba mucho mejor aquí, que no me iban a maltratar."

"He decided to come here because he was having many, many problems in El Salvador, and a friend of his told him that it was better here, that he wouldn't be mistreated. ¿Quién lo estaba maltratando?"

"Ay pues todos. Después que mi familia se dio cuenta que era gay, mi mamá me sacó de la casa, me dijo que no podía vivir con ellos ya. Me costó mucho trabajo, pero encontré donde vivir, y aun así. Un día me vio un policía con mi novio, Raúl, y nos siguió y nos estaba amenazando, y nos dijo que le diéramos *dinero para que nos dejara en paz, para que no nos reportara. Le dimos el dinero, y aun así nos golpeó, todo el rato diciendo cosas así muy homofóbicas, muy feas."*

"I asked who was mistreating him, and he said everyone. After his family found out he was gay, his mom kicked him out of the house, said he couldn't live with them anymore. It was hard, but he found a new place to live. One day a police officer saw him with his partner, Raúl, and followed him, he was threatening them and telling them to give him money to leave them alone, to not report them. Even after they paid him, he beat them both up, saying really ugly, really homophobic things."

"Después de eso, nosotros dos decidimos, ya, basta, nos venimos y a ver que pasa. Queríamos estar juntos, y Ana, mi amiga, me dijo que aquí había toda manera de gays en el abierto, y que sería más fácil."

"After that, we both decided, enough, we will come and see what happens. We wanted to be together, and Ana, my friend, said that here there were all kinds of gay people out in the open, and it would be easier. Y ¿cómo le ha ido?"

"Muy bien, muy bien, la verdad. Los dos estamos aquí ya, hemos estado viviendo con Ana aquí en un departamentico por ahí en, en Queens. Estamos buscando nuestro propio lugar, pero por ahora, es completamente diferente salir a la calle. Podemos estar caminando, así nada más en la calle, agarrados de la mano, y es una bendición, es algo que no tenía yo en mi país."

"He says it's been good since he got here, him and his boyfriend are living with his friend Ana in Queens. They're looking for a place of their own. But for now, he says it feels like a blessing to be able to walk down the street, holding hands, something he didn't have in his own country."

THE NIGHT MY parents describe as being the first in their relationship, they went out in a big group with friends and classmates. My mom's boyfriend hadn't wanted her to go out because he was studying, but she wasn't, so there she was at the disco, sweating drink in hand. My parents knew each other from class, and had talked a little bit, but didn't really know each other like that. They end up dancing, and in the middle of the dance floor, my mom is fanning her face, trying to get a little breeze going, and so my dad takes over. My mom, obviously charmed, says the first part of an Octavio Paz poem to him. My dad finishes the quote. Boom, she's done for. They stay up until 5 a.m. talking, my mom breaks up with her boyfriend the following day.

At our wedding, Jason and I wanted his brother, our officiant, to read Clare Cavanagh's gorgeous translation of one of Wisława Szymborska's poems. Jason had read me the poem on one of our first dates. It ends like this:

"And it so happened that I'm here with you.
And I really see nothing
Usual in that."

It's the kind of move that only works well in those early, heady dates, when you are, as Jason put it, *deeply* un-chill about how smitten you are, but as he was reading it, I knew, irrevocably, that I was done for.

The poem wasn't actually read at our wedding, mostly because Matt decided to joyfully and spontaneously improvise the whole ceremony, forgetting poem, ring exchange, just about everything but the kissing. Still, the inside of our bands read "nothing usual"—because there really isn't anything usual about finding love, intimacy, a shared language with someone who was once a stranger.

Jason doesn't speak Spanish. Or, he does, but the kind of Spanish that comes from a few high school- and college-level courses and a facility with language—he's got a surprisingly wide vocabulary, can stammeringly put sentences together and tease out meaning in an overheard conversation even though he hasn't sat in a Spanish class in some ten years. Most of the time, this is something I barely need to think about. We talk to each other in English, we always have, and I can't really imagine conducting our entire lives in Spanish.

The only time I really feel it is when my family is all together, extended or even just nuclear. All of them speak English, the majority of them extremely well, but we just . . . *don't*. Not when you're with family. Jason is family, has been from about thirty seconds after he finished reading me that poem, and it feels strange to me to have him be left on the outskirts of this language we use to wrap each other up and call each other home.

My immediate family is careful about it, conscientiously switching to English if he's in the room, immediately apologizing when they forget or slide into Spanish. Ima, my grandmother, is also pretty good—when Jason comes into the room, she'll wave her hands and call out "English, English!" in her deep Texas twang, but my uncles don't really care unless one of them wants to talk sports. I try to sit next to him and translate bits and pieces, but my whole family are fast talkers and I (mercifully) don't always get my uncles' jokes, so Jason is mostly just left nursing his beer or watching the conversation ping-pong across the room and catching whatever drifts he can.

He'll tell me afterwards that he caught about a third of it, will ask questions about a particular moment or confirm he got some shade of meaning right, but mostly he's just easygoing—nodding along if an aunt tries to talk to him in very slow Spanish, flagging down waiters, participating to the extent that he can.

He talks all the time about learning more, better Spanish, how it feels important for him to be folded into the family in that way. Usually, for a couple of weeks after seeing my family, I see him bent over a Spanish-English dictionary, sure that he's just a couple of vocabulary lessons away from feeling confident. Him learning Spanish is something I want so badly I don't trust myself to ask or offer anything beyond finding a TV show we can watch together, suggesting an app or two that lets him listen to spoken Spanish.

The one thing we're agreed on is that in the future, when we have kids, they'll be raised in the same way I was—in two languages. This means that eventually, he and some small child that looks a little like both of us will learn, side-by-side, the language that to me most sounds like tenderness.

And even though it's not so unusual, there is nothing usual in that.

30

IF TRANSLATION IS A TABLE, Kate Briggs says, then it must also be the meal on it and the people sitting around it, making up the imaginary dinner party where the writer, you (the translator), and your eventual reader hold down three corners of the table and the rest of the seats are filled by a whole ghostly community of writers and characters you're so desperately trying to hold séance with. All of the writers of the other books on the shelf as your writer worked, the friend he called up late at night to work through a thorny question, the waitress who brought him his morning coffees, and the one who brings you yours, the teacher who introduced you to your writer's work, all of them.

I think a lot about who is in the room, who is at the table when I'm translating an asylum application. There's me, and the other people on my team, and the person we're interviewing, the friend seeking asylum. There's also ICE agents, and immigration judges, and often there are also gang members, and abusive boyfriends and husbands. There are the children there in the room with us, bouncing on a knee or playing quietly in a corner, and the children left behind in a home country—some sullen teens leaning in a corner or babies on ghostly grandmothers' laps. The dead frequently take their seats as well, hoping someone will be able to pass along their stories. My mom is in the room, and so is the asylum seeker's.

And then, depending on how big I decide to make the table, there are also CIA agents just back from fomenting a coup or politicians, stockholders and board members. They don't usually realize they're in the room, much less sitting down to a meal with all of us, but here they are anyways, diffidently fiddling with the silverware.

I also think about what's at the center of the table, what, exactly it is we are feasting on. Some days, I worry that, like the vampiric ICE agents and government workers, I'm here to make a grisly feast out of the worst moments of someone's life. I worry that rather than helping or resisting, I'm serving up the choicest cuts, the most picturesque of traumas. On a good day, I can see more clearly that the meal at the center of the table is not the kind of meal I would normally serve to so many guests—it's a meal of survival. It's not a feast, just enough to keep body and soul together. That it is a hard-won meal doesn't mean it isn't prepared with care and attention, but it would be a mistake to assume this meal is comforting or serves any purpose beyond bare nourishment.

Sometimes, back in that church basement, a volunteer will have made soup or an enormous salad or a cheese plate, and after getting as far as we're able on any given day, we'll sit together and eat it. It is nearly impossible to make small talk with someone after spending an hour or two unpacking their most visceral traumas, so these are small meals often eaten in relative silence. It's a friendly silence, though, full of smiles and murmurs about how good the food is.

31

IN 1957, PHOTOGRAPHER SID AVERY was sent on assignment by the *Saturday Evening Post* to the fields just outside of the glittering edges of Los Angeles. While Avery's usual beat was the studio starlets and leading men of Golden-Age Hollywood, his job this time was to photograph the braceros, Mexican guest workers brought north by the promise of plentiful jobs and enough money to send home to wives and children. In the photographs taken at the time, they're often smiling, or conveying the kind of serious, wary looks of men at work, handsome in a clean-cut, mid-century kind of way.

While Avery's photos show men, yes, bent over in fields, yes, climbing narrow ladders to the tops of date palms, yes, holding crates full of produce; they also show the men playing cards in an orderly barracks, cooking a meal over a camp stove, celebrating a white-lace-frosted little girl's first communion, show them styled and posed like a kind of brown Jimmy Stewart working-class hero of a Hollywood film. The photographs make life as a bracero look like some kind of aspirational Western dream, the kind of life where a man, by the sweat of his brow, might better his lot in life and provide for his family. This was, in fact, how the program was sold, both to Americans and the Mexican campesinos who were most often already farming someone else's land for a poverty wage when the program was introduced. You don't have to pay attention for long to know that this isn't necessarily how the program worked.

The 2020s are likely among the final years when it will be possible to hear firsthand testimony from braceros on what the program was like for them. The program, which brought over able-bodied men from areas of Mexico with a "surplus of labor" as guest workers to tend the fields emptied of U.S. workers by World War II and landowners' intransigence in the face of labor organization, ended in 1964. Many of the young men who had bent over rows of grapes and asparagus and strawberries are now old men, faces still bronzed by long days in the sun.

In 2010, documentary filmmakers set out to capture some of these testimonies, and turned it into a movie, *Harvest of Loneliness*. The film is mostly made up of the voices of former braceros, their widows, their wives, their children and grandchildren who have settled today on both sides of the border. This is the story of the Bracero Program, as they tell it.

A journey northward on crowded trains, leaving behind wives and children and mothers and families to processing stations south of the border. There, they waited, much like the migrants of today, for their numbers to be called up, all the while quickly running out of the food and money brought from home. They recount watching people eat watermelon rinds, banana peels, scraps to quiet a protesting belly. Then, a train northward again, another processing center, invasive medical examinations, including

a stranger examining their hands for calluses to ensure they were really laborers, poking and prodding to ensure their eventual employers were "getting their money's worth." Stripped down to underwear and sprayed with
a cloud of DDT dust, a pesticide eventually banned by the U.S. government for its carcinogenic effects on humans. From there, corrals where landowners and farmers would review them, picking and choosing men who
looked docile, who looked poor, who looked unlikely to revolt.

And by and large, it worked. Not because the men were docile, but
because they were poor. Braceros were brought in regularly to break farmworker strikes and were threatened with deportation if they themselves organized. Deportation could mean being unable to return to the United
States, could mean a hungry family and no way to provide for them. And
the farm owners took advantage: Housing was Quonset huts with no ven-
tilation in the Arizona desert, meals were sour rice and undercooked beans,
the "clean habitations" and regular meals promised in bracero contracts were
often nowhere to be seen. Farm owners often charged the braceros inordi-
nately for their meals and ran "company stores" with outrageous prices.
The government also took a portion: Ten percent of all bracero earnings
were squirreled away by the U.S. and Mexican governments in so-called
"savings accounts" that were, in many cases, never paid out. Men recall
seeing end-of-week paychecks of cents after seven days of twelve-hour shifts
bent over beet fields, recall owing the bosses more than they had earned so
nothing could be sent home.

Meanwhile, an entire generation of Mexican women and children lived
on their own—it's estimated that something around four million braceros
came to the United States during the length of the program, as many as
500,000 in a single growing season in 1957. The remittances, the money
sent home was sometimes good, sometimes bad, but always extracted at a
high price of loneliness. I don't know whose first communion Sid Avery
photographed, but the vast majority of the men would not have been able

to see their children's milestone moments because their children were not allowed to accompany them into the United States.

This is the real horror of the bracero program—the thousand little cuts of dehumanization they endured in order to have their labor extracted from them at maximum profit for the United States was, as a matter of policy, heaped onto their separation from many of the things and people and places that might make them feel human, feel valued for more than their work. This becomes particularly obvious at the end of the film, where one after another, these tough men, these campesinos in their sixties raised on a steady diet of machismo, of aguantate ya, talk about the emotional toll of the program. They cry remembering their mothers worrying over the household budget, blink back tears and avert their eyes while their wives tell the filmmakers about the loneliness they went through with their families separated, find their voices failing as they try to talk about their own suffering.

The Bracero Program ended in the mid-1960s, in part because of massive labor violations and in part because new developments in mechanization meant that fewer farmworkers were needed. Even so, today the United States' agricultural system still largely relies on migrant farm laborers, perhaps in the U.S. on the slim protections of an H-2A visa or, given the relatively restricted numbers and restrictive nature of that visa, undocumented. U.S. policy has only furthered the reliance on cheap labor on the U.S. side and remittances on the Mexican side—the passage of the North American Free Trade Agreement flooded Mexico with cheap American corn and made it nearly impossible for small-scale farmers to survive. Instead, families send their sons and daughters, mothers and fathers to the United States to work the fields. Since U.S. child labor laws carve out an exception for farm work, oftentimes children will join in to meet daily picking minimums and ease the load.

Just about every piece of produce you pick up at the grocery store will have, in every way that matters, been grown, tended to, and harvested by a largely undocumented, largely Latinx and Indigenous workforce, oftentimes paid well below the minimum wage for U.S. workers, despite being exposed to harsh chemicals and physically exhausting conditions. In this way, we are intimately bound to these people many of us have never met and, in most cases, will rarely even see as they bend over fields or with their heads and hands amidst the branches of fruit trees.

32

THERE'S A COUNTERPOINT TO THE Babel story, much later on in the
Bible. The New Testament, in fact, after Jesus has come and gone. It happens early on in the Acts of the Apostles, which is sort of the sequel to the
Matthew-Mark-Luke-John gospels, and goes into the events after the death
of Jesus, with the apostles traveling and evangelizing and infighting.

The story comes early in the book. It's the feast of the Pentecost and all
the apostles, and maybe a few other early Christians are gathered together
in the upper rooms of a house. Jesus had been crucified a little while back,
and there's a sense, even in the Bible's sketchy, unemotional narration, of
both mourning and planning for great works ahead. This meal is somehow
the *real* last supper. Not Jesus' of course, but of the apostles as a family, the
last time they'll be together in the same space as a matched set. They've just

shared a meal, and are sitting around together, perhaps starting to discuss the business that brought them into the same space—plans to split up the known world in order to evangelize it, each one of them rising from this table to head out in a new direction. Maybe they're aware that once this meal is over, they won't really meet anyone else who had *known* Jesus, who had been there when he joked and when he said the inscrutable, puzzling things he so loved to volley at them, no one else who had seen the crowds, both adoring and hostile, no one else who had touched the hand of God made man.

I imagine the room as comfortable in the way my grandmother's living room is comfortable on the last day of Christmas vacation, and buzzing in the way that a room full of activists buzzes when they're embarking on a new campaign.

And then, from heaven comes "a sound as of the rushing of a mighty wind," and tongues of fire appear over each of the disciples' heads. Then, "devout men, from every nation under heaven" hear strangers speaking in their own language. A Galilean hears a Cretan speaking his mother tongue. A Roman speaks to a Judean in the language the Judean's grandmother used to lay him down to sleep, and the Roman hears the Judean respond in Latin. I wonder if it is actually a matter of Aramaic and Latin and Greek, or if what is actually being spoken, being understood, is the "divine language" that translators of the Bible are always gesturing towards. Because this moment, the moment of the apostles' sobremesa gone cosmic, of their drunkenness on language, is the moment the Holy Spirit enters the world.

33

"*¿LISTA?*"

"*Sí.*"

"*Ok, la próxima pregunta en la forma es que si alguien alguna vez la ha lastimado o amenazado a usted, o a alguien en su familia.*"

"*Sí, a mí, el papá de mi hija.*"

"*She says yes, the father of her daughter. ¿Me puede contar lo que pasó?*"

"*Sí, bueno, empezamos a salir y todo estaba bien, me trataba bien, ya sabes, pero después que tuve a mi hija empezó a salir más y más tarde, y se enojaba más y más conmigo.*"

"*When they started going out, he treated her well, but when she had her daughter, he'd stay out later, and get angrier and angrier with her.*"

"*Y luego me empezó a golpear. Una vez tuve que ir al hospital, porque me quemó con un rizador, mira, aquí, y otra vez me dejó con toda la cara, el labio partido, todo."*

"And he started hitting her. Once, he burned her with a curling iron, on her leg there, and another time he left her face all messed up, split her lip, everything. *¿Está bien para seguir?*"

"Sí, sí."

"¿Cuándo fue que decidió irse?"

"Pues, antes, nada más me pegaba cuando estábamos a solas, y solo a mí, y después, poco a poco empezó a ser delante de la niña, y el día que me fui, fue porque la golpeó a ella también."

"He used to only hit her, and just when they were alone, but little by little he would do it in front of the girl, but the day she left, it was because he hit her daughter also. *¿Vino directo a los Estados Unidos después?*"

"No, no, me fui a quedar con mi tía en otra ciudad, mi hija y yo."

"¿Y porque se salió de ahí?"

"Me encontró. Mi pareja era marero, y pensé que había estado viendo más y más de ellos cerca de la casa de mi tía, y como al mes, él mismo se me apareció ahí, afuera de la casa, y trató de agarrarnos, a la niña y a mí, y estaba amenazando, y gritando, todo con una pistola y todo, ya sabes."

"She went to her aunt's house first, where she was for about a month before he found her. He was a gang member, and she saw more and more of them around her aunt's house, and then he showed up, yelling threats and with a gun."

"Esa noche, mi tía me pide que nos vayamos, y pues sí, lo hice. Me junté con un grupo que se venía, y así nos pasamos."

"That night, her aunt asked her to leave, and she did. She met up with a group that was traveling together, and that's how she ended up here."

AS THAT WINTER of 2017 turned to spring, the clinic grew, the number of friends and volunteers expanding week by week as things outside the clinic walls got worse and worse. As I got better at interviewing, became more of a fixture at the church just off Washington Square Park, the leaders started assigning me to cases that indicated on their intake that they might be eligible to apply for asylum because of domestic violence.

Asylum requires that the harm someone has suffered be related to their belonging to a "particular social group"—some kind of identity they cannot or should not be required to change, like political party or religion or sexuality or, in these cases, gender—and enacted either by a government force, or an entity the government is "unwilling or unable to stop." Domestic violence is, of course, not limited to women, or even to women in a particular country, but in places like Latin America, with legal systems already buckling under the weight of unprosecuted crimes and a generations-long colonial legacy of machismo that makes things like beating your wife not only acceptable but expected, domestic violence is entrenched into everyday life in a way that feels difficult to get around, makes gender in general and femininity specifically something that must be carefully managed. I sat across the table from girls as young as twelve and mothers holding the babies of men who had left scars on their skin, women who had left their children behind in the care of their own mothers, who understood all too well why they had to run.

The way that we processed domestic violence cases at the clinic was a little bit different from other asylum cases—we were allowed rooms with doors instead of being crammed, elbows brushing, with other groups at long tables, usually classrooms with one full wall, covered floor-to-ceiling in law books and with video cameras for mock trials that we threw sweatshirts over, or pastors' offices with overcrowded calendars and inspirational posters. The whole team was usually made up of young women.

In a time that felt far from this pastor's office or that law classroom, but had actually been only a few months before, I facilitated a gender and sexuality discussion group for women like those on my application processing team—in our twenties and early thirties, progressive, largely queer. The culmination of the several-week program was a night we called "Violation of Boundaries," where we sat on pillows on the floor, with lit candles and community guidelines, and made space for people to share their experiences of sexual assault and harassment. People told stories they had never shared before, cried, got angry, sat in meditative silence, or wrote something down for themselves. You could choose whether to share, could just choose to feel less alone in silence instead. After everyone who wanted to had shared, we thanked them for their story, and spent some time before closing out the session talking about self-care and sharing affirmations with one another.

And then, several months later, here we were, with the luxury of a closed door and bright overhead lighting, not making space for a story, but insisting on it, asking, demanding for it to be told, and told in a certain way that fit the frame the government had provided for us. Here we were, with lips pressed into somber lines, looking down at the floor, with a thirteen-year-old girl who held her mother's hand the whole time I talked to her, trying to find the least damaging way to ask her whether the twenty-something-year-old gang member that had taken an interest in her had ever gone farther than following her home from school, spewing death threats. As I asked, for the sake of a government form to be read by a faceless bureaucrat in charge of deciding whether or not she would be allowed to stay with her mother, if a man nearly twice her age had tried to kiss her, had touched her, or whether he had merely frightened her badly enough that she left the country. I needed an answer from her because otherwise she *would* be separated from her mother.

WHEN I STARTED working more closely with immigration attorneys, rather than just volunteers, I found out that they call the I-589 on its own a "skeleton application." Just the bare bones of it. When a lawyer helps someone apply for asylum—something that is true for eighty to ninety percent of all asylum applicants, given that most people will not attempt the complex process without legal representation—the skeleton is enfleshed. Affidavits, expert witness testimonies, reports from forensic pathologists on clients' living bodies, fat files of reporting on "country conditions." An asylum application completed by an immigration attorney usually runs somewhere between three hundred and five hundred pages—solid bricks of paperwork that are stacked up as a defensive wall when someone goes into court. The translations I need to do for asylum applicants filling out their I-589 forms are also skeletal; they make up the twelve flimsy pages of the application alone.

I DON'T EVER think of this translation as enrobing myself in someone else's ideas, of taking on their speech patterns or their ways of thinking. There's no trying to capture the nuance of a turn of phrase, no attempt to do anything but the near-mechanical passage from one language to another. Instead, as I work, I find myself wanting to shelter myself from the contents of their mind, shying away from thinking about their subjectivity. I try not to think about the ways that the things I hear as stories live as memories in someone else's head, there after they leave the clinic and after they go to sleep at night. I also know that I can't ever really understand the story I'm tasked with transmitting.

In addition, the text I end up producing is, by necessity, skeletal, a bone shard in the desert. One hundred and fifty words, clipped and factual, describing the things that have left a mark on a single body, but never what it is like to live inside that body—dry-mouth, palm-sweating terror, or the effervescent joy of a first kiss or of a newborn making a small fist around a finger or the heaviness in the lower back after a day spent standing.

When you talk about a translator as a bridge, you generally mean that it's the translator's job to make meanings meet in the middle—you're not transliterating the source language into the target, you're not rewriting the original text with cultural references and ideas that are common in the target language's culture. Asylum translation is more like the translation of saintly relics.

When a saint is canonized, they are brought out of their resting place—usually somewhere they lived and grew up and did their holy works and instead brought to a place that is the center of power. When Constantinople became the center of the Christian world, a flock of holy bones was translated there from the surrounding areas. This legitimated the divinity of the tibia of St. Leocadia, the splinter of the Holy Cross, the skull of St. Cordula, but it also gave sanctity and legitimacy to the church itself, marking it as holy for being able to gather holiness to itself. When a saint's bones enter a church, they are gilded and boxed up, removed from their context of a grave, of a living person somewhere, and presented alongside calcified hagiographies as proof of the church's power. You don't know St. Leocadia or St. Cordula, all you know are their bones, their holiness, their presence in some cathedral's basement reliquary, proof that the church is worth dying for. The translation of bones serves only the church and not the stories of those interred.

The U.S. government is not the Catholic Church, but it does require asylum seekers to be saints. It gathers their stories to itself, forces them to be translated—in language and in fact, since they only accept paper files—into their own language and space. The power here only moves in one direction, and everything done by asylum seekers, every translation done by them and their allies, serves only the reader: the United States government. The text, the presentation of it, the imprisonment of it within the forms' boxes, away from the messiness of real life and into the beats of a known and understood narrative—a quiet and virtuous life, shattered by a single act of explicitly politically motivated violence, an escape by night, a plea for safety. These are meant not at all as an expression of the person telling the story and entirely to satisfy the entity processing it.

If I do my job right, if in those 150 words I succeed as a translator, what my friend gets is a grudging acceptance of their humanity, a big official rubber stamp that says that their suffering matters, but not much else does about the ways in which they have stayed alive or lived at all. Just the suffering.

You can argue about how much, or whether, any one person needs the acknowledgement of an inherently violent state apparatus on their worth as a human. It's not really necessary, I don't think, but part of the violence the state inflicts is the lack of that acknowledgement. A lawyer I worked with at the clinic called it "bureaucratic violence," the carrying across of people out of their own words, their own language, the mutilation of the stories they tell. A violence I participated in, even if it was as gentle as I could make it.

No matter how softly I asked the questions, how much time I gave anyone to answer or how much cushion I gave to their telling of it, the form still demanded filling. I was still forcing stories onto boxes on a form that would make them visible to the U.S. government, would be playing into a rigged system set up by people who had difficulty recognizing, in all likelihood, both of our humanities. And here I was, with no risk to myself, kindly, gently, with infinite patience, asking them to tell me stories they might never repeat again, all so I could mine them for parts and shove them under the bright, unblinking light of government surveillance.

34

WHEN I FIRST MOVED IN with Jason, right when I started grad school in 2017, it felt like a good opportunity to reach for the kind of domesticity that had so far eluded me in my rotating-cast-of-roommates-in-a-Brooklyn-apartment life. I thought the best place to start was to get really, really good at making a roast chicken, and found a butcher near us that sold broiler hens for five dollars apiece. I watched YouTube videos on spatch-cocking for a more even roast, carefully arranged potato slices in concentric circles underneath the bird to catch drippings, watched my oven like, well, a broody hen. I eventually learned to debone thighs and breasts on my own to ensure that we always had good stock bones in the freezer, learned how to brine a bird and dry out the surface to get crackling, perfect skin while it roasted. I did this work slowly and leisurely, a way to show my partner I cared, a way to bring myself back to my body after long days in grad school. A few years later, like for many other people, this kind of slow cooking became one of my pandemic coping mechanisms—a way to dissociate from the anxiety at hand and care for a body that felt suddenly precarious.

Meanwhile, just a few miles down the road from the house I grew up in, from the table where I first learned how to sobremesa with people I loved, people in my community were putting their lives on the actual line, all for the sake of supplying chicken to American families.

Sanderson Farms, the third-largest poultry processer in the United States, has a plant in Bryan, Texas, a town over from where I went to high school. On March 20, 2020, just four days before the company would report its first COVID-19 case, the president of the company sent a memo to his employees, including those working at the plant in Bryan. "If people like you and me stop coming to work every day, people will go hungry . . . . We call upon you to look at this crisis as an opportunity to serve."

Sanderson Farms is one of the largest employers of undocumented people in the Brazos Valley—it pays a few dollars an hour more than fast food jobs or farm labor—and it is also regularly the subject of labor activism, with workers, both documented and not, protesting for better working conditions. In 2014, labor complaints were filed with the National Labor Relations Board by workers at the Bryan plant over changes in the terms and conditions of employment. In 2018, workers picketed the plant wearing diapers, protesting the fact that line workers were often forced to urinate on themselves when line supervisors did not allow them adequate toilet breaks. In 2019, they picketed the company for regularly misclassifying workers' injuries as "non-job related" to skimp out on workers' comp. These complaints are not unique to the Bryan location, or even to Sanderson Farms as a whole. Poultry workers end up with higher levels of repetitive motion injuries than those in other industries, and meatpacking as a whole has had a bad rap as a dirty, overwhelming business since at least Upton Sinclair's *The Jungle.*

And the problems only got worse during COVID-19. Like many other meat processing employees, those at Sanderson Farms were given no paid sick leave, were given financial incentives to come to work with little to no monitoring of symptoms, no health and safety instructions in Spanish— the language spoken by many of the workers at the plant—no PPE until after at least May of 2020, working closely side-by-side to butcher the chickens that would end up cooked into elaborate pandemic meals by bored work-from-home white-collar workers, that would end up fried into fast food by yet another set of vulnerable workers classed as "front line" employees to ensure the wealthy still had the pretense of normal luxuries during a time when nothing should have been allowed to keep going as usual.

Chicken, for all that it's not the sizzling red meat of a special occasion steak or the weekend grill master's burger, is nevertheless a symbol of prosperity. From Hoover's Depression-era promise of "a chicken for every pot" as a return to economic health, to the Norman Rockwell vision of what is essentially an oversized, overabundant chicken lowered onto a holiday table, to my own associations between a beautifully roasted chicken and somehow having made it as an adult, it's the kind of everyday prosperity that we believe to be a baseline to our national prosperity. It's comfort food, an everyday luxury that signals that everything is alright, or will be. We make chicken noodle soup when we're sick, engagement chicken when we're in love, quick weeknight chicken recipes when we're working moms.

And all the while, like so much else that we rely on, that we love, that we take for granted as part of our daily bread, there are people, invisible to most of us, working to ensure that our access to comfort remains unencumbered.

What made working in a poultry plant particularly dangerous during COVID-19 wasn't just the painful repetitive motions of butchery, or the horrifying labor conditions and the expectation that some of the poorest, most disenfranchised workers see the pandemic as "an opportunity to serve," it was the chemistry of a poultry processing plant.

Peracetic acid is used in small quantities throughout meat processing plants as a sanitizer and disinfectant for the chicken. In humans, when aspirated, it tends to cause a dry cough, nearly identical to the one produced by the COVID-19 virus. With so many disincentives to staying home, with such minimal safeguards to ensure that people reporting to work each morning were healthy, with a dry cough as the constant side effect of the job for as long as they had worked there, with the people working the lines packed nearly as close as the chicken thighs they plastic-wrapped onto Styrofoam trays, it was no wonder that COVID-19 spread through meat processing plants.

This problem was not limited to Sanderson Farms, or to Bryan, Texas, or even to poultry processing, but was widespread throughout any meat processing plant in the United States. A few plants closed indefinitely in the early days of COVID-19, when it became clear that their business model was incompatible with stopping the spread of disease because hundreds of employees at a time called out sick with the virus. In December 2020, before COVID-19 vaccines were widely available, seven managers at a Tyson pork processing plant in Waterloo, Iowa, were fired after they were found betting on how many of their employees would contract COVID-19. At that time, six of the plant's employees, many of whom were immigrants and refugees, had died, and 90 percent of the cases in Black Hawk County could be traced to the processing plant. And through it all, thanks to a Presidential Executive Order, the vast majority of meat processing plants stayed open. Companies were able to use the excuse of "national emergency" to usher in an incredibly profitable year, and workers continued to get sick with COVID-19.

EVEN NOW, IN all the communities across the country just like Bryan, ten minutes down the road from the house I grew up, there are people missing.

Mothers, sisters, fathers, uncles, neighbors, sons, and daughters are not meeting, bleary-eyed, around the breakfast table before a shift or arriving in the backyard with a sweaty six-pack in hand for a parrillada. This is the price we paid, all of us, gone unacknowledged and unnoted, for the continued presence of chicken that was just a few dollars a pound on our pandemic tables. This is the kind of blindness capitalism forces us into—equivalencies and choices we would never make if they were presented to us in the form of a thought experiment, of a nightmare post-apocalyptic world: Would you trade your neighbor's life for a chicken in your pot? The answer, if asked, is likely "no," but the reality is more complicated. Chicken is cheap, it's plentiful, and the people who slaughter, pluck, and butcher it and pack it are often already at the edges of society—they speak different languages, have immigration statuses that keep them trapped at jobs few others will take and make them fearful of organizing. The chicken on your table has already cost that much, whatever else you paid for it.

35

EVERY FEW WEEKS, DEPENDING ON which volunteers were waiting around in the lobby without cases, and who the new arrivals were, teams of interpreters and notetakers would be shuffled around, and you would wind up sitting across the table from a completely new set of people.

I loved meeting the other volunteers. As a twenty-four-year-old in a city where I knew almost no one except the people I had gone to college with, being able to spend time with people who were older than me and weren't my supervisors at work was a rare chance. Between cases, on snack breaks, waiting by the copier, we were able to talk a little about our own lives, why we were there in that church basement. Many of the older volunteers were people in their sixties and seventies who had spent a lifetime in activist circles in New York City. They told stories about movement lawyering, about being longtime New Yorkers, living in neighborhoods that I could only dream about. I wanted to be like them when I grew up, or at least have lives something like them, comfortable yet involved in their communities, deeply rooted in the realities of a romanticized city.

There was Marta and Sam, a married couple who lived on the Upper West Side. I was never on a team with them—Marta was Cuban, spoke Spanish, and they stuck together during sessions, so they wouldn't need another translator on their team—but Marta was one of those people that was endlessly warm and easy to talk to, while Sam was just a quiet beanpole of a man who would sometimes cut in on his wife's pleasant chatter with a droll observation or a quietly funny aside to me. Helen was a no-nonsense former Brooklyn schoolteacher, and sometimes ran our meetings with friends like a classroom—brisk questions, an air of crowd management even in your one-on-one conversations with her. Sally was sweet and affable and would take notes by hand in beautiful handwriting I had only seen in inscriptions in old books. Jean was always making jokes and then waggling her eyebrows at the friend the entire time I translated the joke (sometimes ineffectively), waiting for them to be in on it.

Then there were the founders and the leaders: Ravi was a legend around the clinic—one of its founders, he had begun his activism nearly a decade beforehand when he had been ordered deported himself. Juan Carlos was a former Catholic priest who had become fierce in his activism after meeting the Berrigan brothers, activist Jesuits who had known Dorothy Day and been members of the Catholic Worker movement since its early days. He was from the same part of Mexico as my dad. Kitty, who had started the union I had been part of at my ill-fated first job, and now ran the meeting logistics; Sara, who greeted every single person at the clinic as if she had known them for years. Gia was an actual, honest-to-God immigration attorney who led our trainings resplendently tattooed and wrote poetry in her off-hours.

Other people were around my age—brilliant law students like Noah, who vibrated with fury at what the system was and expected him to acquiesce to, nonprofit workers and teachers who couldn't leave it behind at the end of the day. These were the people I would run around with all evening, making copies and tracking down staplers and then meet in dark NYU basement bars after clinic sometimes, to plan better futures.

The lack of translators and the dynamic of the volunteers meant that I was almost always in a group with two or three other white people, and the hispanohablantes, the "heritage speakers," if you will, were scattered among the groups, our relationships not usually extending beyond solidarity nods.

And yet, despite all the kinship I felt, the closeness I had with so many of the volunteers, it didn't take me long, working in this way, to realize that working with some people was almost unbearable for reasons I couldn't exactly identify. Talking with another volunteer, years later, she described the scene as being full of people who got off on the sense of emergency surrounding the applications we did, the high drama of Helping Others. She was right about that, but the dynamic extended to just how that help was offered.

I think the main thing it boiled down to is, like an emergency room doctor, some of the volunteers assumed they were in charge. More than that, that they knew better than anyone else around the table what would best serve the friend and their interests. They interrupted, they sometimes spoke over me or tried to cut in and ask a question themselves in pidgin Spanish, they patted hands and gave advice, even though we were told not to, especially on a friend's legal case. If I tried to have a side conversation with our friend to explain a procedural point or answer a question about finding the bathroom or where to get passport photos done, they'd cut in, asking me "What's she saying? What's going on?" Like every conversation that happened around that table needed to be presented to them for surveillance and inspection. Every time they wanted me to translate, they'd start "Tell her that . . ." instead of just talking to the person that was right there in front of them. They offered absolutely impractical and unearned advice in declarative sentences: "You should find a lawyer." "You should be honest with us." They'd turn to me after someone told us their story and say things like "I don't know if they have a good case," either damning the person through my translation, or, unlike conversations I had, assuming their words wouldn't make it to our friends' ears.

It's important to emphasize here that they had just as much training as I did—at first, likely an hour or two in that same church basement with Gia and Sara, clinic mainstays. Part of that training had included constant reminders that we, ourselves, were not attorneys, that this hour was not legal training, that we were in no position to advise or instruct. The non-legal part of our training, the parts that instructed us to call the people we met with weekly "friends," and taught us the very basics of trauma-informed interviewing, emphasized that we were there solely as amanuenses. We were told that honesty was important to fill out the I-589 form, and to get our friends to be honest, we needed to build trust. And for that, we needed to be open, we needed to be nonjudgmental, we needed to be ready to meet them where they were and let people come to us. We should not judge, we should not advise, we should not push or flex an authority we did not have.

I spent one clinic shadowing one of the immigration attorneys, John, who was only there every few weeks. His job was to double-check completed applications, and to actually be the one that might provide advice to strengthen our arguments. That day, I watched as one woman, a volunteer I had never worked with, discussed a case, literally over the head of an increasingly anxious friend, who sat on the couch between her and the lawyer, wringing her hands and asking the same question over and over again. Finally, the woman snapped at the friend that she was talking and to wait before her question would be answered. I had tried to quietly translate the conversation happening, but when the friend directed her questions to me, I, unsure and unable to answer, stayed quiet out of awkwardness.

Another time, towards the end of a session with a friend, we spent two hours unpacking her traumatic past with an ex-partner that had led her to leave her home and her country. She had recounted horrific events as if describing her morning routine, had minimized and joked about her partner's behavior, but she had gotten through it all, every horrible fact that might secure her safety. Her court date was set for just a few months out, looming over our conversation both because we needed to ensure the application was finished rather quickly and because we knew that in just a few short weeks she would have to recite this same litany of facts in front of the judge that would determine her fate.

As we were wrapping up, re-filing papers and closing laptops and zipping up coats, Helen leaned across the table to the friend.

"You really need to practice your story," she said. "You should be more compelling."

I froze, and the friend looked over at me. "¿Qué dijo?"

"Que buena suerte," I told her.

And yet, I understood the impulse to give advice. Many of the people across the table from us were dazed by the city, by the cold, by the unrelenting nature of the immigration system. Many of them asked directly for advice, were exhausted at the prospect of making even more life-changing choices and decisions. It felt like throwing yet another obstacle in their way when I insisted that I couldn't do anything but offer more options in a wave of unremitting options. Worse, because after filling out the same form a dozen times, it was hard not to feel like I knew everything about the form, about the person in front of me as they were unspooling their story, about what they wanted to get from the immigration system, from the United States as a whole. It was our role to make a little clearing in the snarls and dense underbrush of bureaucracy for someone to stand and walk around for a moment, to assess the terrain and make their own way forward. We didn't know the lay of the land any better for having bushwhacked, we just knew these six square feet of terrain in a different way than the person we had made it for—and it frustrated me that, despite our shared first impulses, I still understood that better than people who had been alive for much longer than I had. They meant well, but they weren't *doing* very well at all.

I felt like I couldn't push back, not in the ways I needed to, my own deference and comfort overriding the need to provide a comfortable and safe space for the asylum seekers coming in every week. Sure, as a translator, I was able to ignore or mistranslate the worst comments, like the advice to "be more compelling." This at least blunted the edges of a too sharp comment, but didn't exactly get at the root of the problem, which was people who should have known better feeling comfortable enough to say these things in the first place. Because it was a matter of tone, a matter of an entire approach that was clearly invisible to the volunteer, but not to me, who had spent a lifetime dealing with all the little nuances of white people speaking to non-white people—all the little assumptions and interruptions and head tilts and ways of talking that I had been so good at ignoring, had suddenly become unbearable. All the little "so smart for a Mexican girl" and the "oh, but your English is so good," that I had never known how to tell someone was not actually a compliment. I didn't know how to push back in a way that would actually help, that would open the volunteers' eyes to whatever was getting in the way of them seeing the friends as full people. Somewhere in the gap between English and Spanish, between San Pedro Sula and Washington Square Park, there had been a mistranslation, and so they spoke to them like children. And I, the translator-advocate, was stuck somewhere in between, trying to translate into existence a respect that wasn't there.

Roberto Tijerina had predicted exactly this in his curriculum for the Highlander Center entitled, "Interpreting for Social Justice." In a lesson centered on ethics, he separates out the roles of interpreter and advocate, assigning to each a different set of goals and values. An interpreter is neutral, translates everything in the "public sphere" of the room, and promotes the autonomy of all agents in the conversation. An advocate, on the other hand, takes a specific side, speaks on behalf of someone, and can take a more active role in decision-making. Preserving this distinction is particularly important, Tijerina notes, because "interpreting, when done well, empowers folks to advocate for themselves and not rely on the interpreter for advocacy."

I didn't find Tijerina's curriculum until long after my days regularly interpreting in small-group settings like those of the *pro se* clinic, but even reading them now, I feel a flush of shame rise through me. Like the people I railed against, I thought I knew better. I tried to protect people that hadn't asked for my protection, had turned myself into an advocate in a way that insulated people from the real circumstances they had found themselves in. There were ways in which my job as an interpreter with the clinic *did* require me to be an advocate—explaining the form, providing more information and context than what was given in those sparse dozen pages, asking questions and participating in the interview as both interpreter and facilitator. By assuming people wouldn't ask for breaks when they needed them, wouldn't ask for clarification when they needed it, wouldn't have their own snappy retorts to the gentle paternalism I had been shielding them from, I was engaging in my own form of paternalism, my own assumptions about what someone could or could not handle, what they might or might not want to know about the people sitting around a table with them.

36

A LITERARY TRANSLATION PROJECT INVOLVES making yourself porous to the text, allowing it into you, and allowing yourself into it. To be so deeply involved, so enmeshed, you don't have much of a choice. All reading involves this kind of cross-pollination, but translation also asks and answers a different question. I'd like to think it is, to some extent, self-sacrificing. When you are translating, you are giving over room in your brain, days of your one single life to the careful, minute study of someone else's work, in order that others might have the privilege of encountering it. You're not only recognizing that your voice isn't the most important one, but you're sinking precious hours into that belief. That's one way of thinking about it, but I don't think that's quite right either, because there's a return. In making yourself porous, you also make yourself expansive, are allowed to reach beyond yourself. Theorists often talk about translation as an act of expanding the target language by allowing for the importation of foreign turns of speech and clever constructions, but it has often seemed to me that the real expansion occurs largely in the mind of the translator.

CICERO AND THE ancient Romans saw translation as a form of colonial victory, of reaching into the language of the conquered and importing it for the greater glory of the Roman Empire, much like elephants or silks might be displayed in an emperor's palace.

When I translate for the I-589, I feel like I'm translating like a Roman, but rather than an elephant, I'm adorning the palace with prisoners of war. This is, of course, because I am. The United States has been deeply involved in Central and South America for years—behind every revolution, every uprising and coup of the 20th century, there were CIA agents or congressmen making colonial decisions to "stop the spread of communism" or, more commonly, to protect U.S. investments and corporations.

The people I translate for are survivors among generations of desaparecidos, the few farmers with land not yet seized or ruined by multinational corporations, the people who were not left to die in the desert or dumped into mass graves in the sea or corralled into camps to die of neglect. The translation I take part in is the most meager form of reparations and has more to do with the CIA agents and congressmen than the utopian promise that more contemporary literary translators make for us.

Like the United States, which welcomed European immigrants as low-level workers with a plea for the world's "tired and hungry," which bills itself as a great melting pot, with fine words about the equality of "all men," translation likes to describe itself as a diplomat, bridging cultures, or a bridge itself, spanning the Rio Grande, the kind of thing that can transcend borders. But ignoring the ways that power can thrum through and across the bridge—the way a diplomat always, always has his own nation's best interests at heart—you run the risk of making yourself complicit in this power.

When I translate for an asylum seeker, I like to think I'm working against the powers that be, but the truth is that I'm filling out the form, I'm making people findable, searchable, cross-indexable for a government machine that has proven time and time again that the only way in which it cares about these lives is as resources to be extracted to exhaustion.

I don't know how else to help, don't know if I'm brave or smart or strong enough to find another way to wipe away the fear of separation, the fear of return, to remake the world into the place it needs to be to make sure everyone is safe. I haven't even figured out how to talk to people in a way that grants them agency, that treats them like real people instead of the fragile aftermath of their own experiences. I don't know if bravery or smarts or strength on an individual or collective level are even capable of fixing this problem. For now, the form is all we have. And perhaps that means that I put too much stock in words, in the empty promises of these government forms, in the mealymouthed assurances meted out from behind podiums.

And yet.

The stories I've been told, the lives opened up to me, both by the force of the form and later, sometimes, with the shy triumph of something won at great cost, the photographs of grinning children held up on shaky camera phones by proud parents have changed my life. Stories are not enough, but they are a place to start.

AGUA PASA POR MI CASA
Cate de mi corazón

It's a common riddle for children that loses its meaning in translation, but what is important is that the answer is "el aguacate"—avocado. I'll translate it for you anyways. *Water goes by my house/cate of my heart.* There's no great translation for "cate"—in Spain-Spanish it can mean a strike or a thump, but I always associate it with the "cate" of "mecate," a word derived from Nahuatl meaning a rope or a cord. The riddle takes the cord of Nahuatl to tie the fruit to your home, your heart. There's a little Mexican nationalism around the avocado, the idea that it belongs more to Mexico than anywhere else it grows. They are mentioned in the *Florentine Codex*, and the oldest avocado pit was found in an archeological dig of human settlement of a cave in Puebla from 9,000 to 10,000 years ago.

Every time noise is made about tariffs in trade with Mexico increasing or the borders closing, news outlets begin fretting about the avocado. Many of the avocados that you can find in grocery stores in the U.S. are grown in farms and orchards along the western coast of Mexico. Avocado trees are full of dark green, wide, leathery leaves. The fruits hang heavy from long stems, fattening and turning from a lizard green to a nearly black plum color in the sun and humidity.

As Super Bowl season approaches, the avocados are picked and packed, usually on-site. A sizable avocado orchard will have a company town that grows up around it, and it will be a valuable source of employment through-out the year. Hass avocados, the most common cultivar, is known for pro-ducing fruit across the growing season. However, in many cases, in order for the cases of avocados to even leave the orchards, landowners must pay fees to the drug cartels that control the area. Nonpayment is known to re-sult in violence and death.

After the cartels are paid off, though, it is all business as usual, with all its invisible intricacies. International produce shippers kick in, NAFTA takes its own cut as things cross the border (trains and trucks, refrigerated ware-houses) all so that on the first Saturday in February, you can reach into the produce bins at your local grocery store and touch an avocado the exact texture of the inside of your elbow. Perfectly ripe.

38

"*ESTA SEMANA, TOMAMOS TODA LA información que usted nos dio, y llenamos la forma para usted. Queremos leerle lo que preparamos, para que sepa lo que va a entregar, lo que va a saber el juez, todo, así que, si oye algo mal, algo que no le agrada, díganos, y se lo arreglamos, ¿ok?*"

"*Sí, está bien.*"

"*Okay, he's ready for you whenever you want to start reading out the questions and answers.*"

"*Have you, your family, close friends, or colleagues ever experienced harm or mistreatment or threats from anyone? Yes.*"

"*La primera pregunta es si usted o sus familiares han sufrido daño, maltrato, o amenazas de cualquier persona, y pusimos que sí. Después, la forma nos pide más detalles, así que le vamos a leer lo que pusimos.*"

"*In Honduras, my wife and I had a business selling bread out of my house.*"

"*En Honduras, mi esposa y yo teníamos un negocio vendiendo pan desde mi casa.*"

"*In April 2016, two men came into the business, and told me that I needed to pay them, or bad things would happen. These men were gang members.*"

"*En abril 2016, dos hombres entraron al negocio, y me dijeron que tenía que pagarles, o cosas malas pasarían. Ellos eran mareros.*"

"*I told them I didn't have the money then, so they pointed their guns at me and said they'd be back the next day.*"

"*Yo les dije que no tenía el dinero entonces, así que me apuntaron sus pistolas, y dijeron que regresarían el día siguiente.*"

"*I had to borrow money from friends and family, but I was able to gather the amount they wanted by the next day. We gave it to them, and they left.*"

"*Tuve que pedir dinero prestado de familia, pero pude reunir lo que querían para el día siguiente. Se los dimos, y se fueron.*"

"*But the next week, I got a text message telling me I needed to start gathering money again, or they'd kill my wife.*"

"*La semana siguiente, me llegó un texto diciendo que tenía que empezar a conseguir dinero otra vez o matarían a mi esposa.*"

"*That week, we escaped to another city in Honduras, but I got another text with just the name of the city.*"

"*Esa semana, escapamos a otra ciudad en Honduras, pero me llego otro texto diciendo solo el nombre de la ciudad.*"

"*After that, we decided to come to the U.S. to be safe.*"

"*Después de eso, decidimos venir a los Estados Unidos para estar seguros. Esa fue la primera pregunta. ¿Todo eso está bien?*"

"*Sí, sí.*"

"*Okay, the next question is 'Do you fear harm or mistreatment if you return to your home country?' and we put down 'Yes.'*"

"*La siguiente pregunta es si temes que te lastimen o te maltraten si regresa a su país, y pusimos que sí.*"

"Sí, así es."

"Y aquí también nos piden la explicación. ¿Listo? Podemos pausar si necesita."

"No, no, está bien, está bien."

"After arriving in the United States, I continued to get threatening text messages, telling me that the senders knew that I was in the U.S., and that they would find a way to get money from me here."

"Después de llegar a los Estados Unidos, seguí recibiendo textos amenazantes, diciéndome que sabían que estaba en los Estados Unidos, y que encontrarían como sacarme dinero aquí."

"I have been in the United States for nine months now, and I still get about one text message a week."

"He estado en los Estados Unidos por nueve meses, y sigo recibiendo más o menos un texto a la semana."

"I know that if I went back to Honduras, they would find me very quickly, and kill me if I did not continue to pay them. I do not have the money to do so, as I no longer have my business, and immigrating was very expensive."

"Yo sé que si regreso a Honduras, ellos me encontrarían rápidamente, y me matarían si no les pago. Yo no tengo el dinero para hacer esto, ya que ya no tengo mi negocio, e inmigrar costó mucho dinero."

"Sí, sí, está bien. Necesito salir por un poco de agua, ¿está bien?"

39

THE I-589 IS A FORM of fragments. It is not interested in the totality of a person; it cannot capture anything but a partial rendering. It is also incredibly important, especially to a *pro se* applicant, like the ones I was meeting every week.

Pro se, in Latin, means "on behalf of oneself." In practice, with the friends I met every week, it means that after they left from our weekly clinic, they were entirely on their own as they navigated the immigration system. There were no lawyers by their side in the courtroom, no translator but the one provided by the court, a woman who often looked bored or tired or disconnected from the job she was there to do.

Cases in immigration court are actually classified as civil, and not criminal cases, despite the fact they often have life-or-death consequences, and that they're so often punitive. As a result, immigrants, who are often utterly unprepared to face the realities of immigration court—including adversarial attorneys, proceedings in an intentionally complex and obfuscating version of a language not usually their own—do not have the benefit of court-appointed representation. Demand for pro bono and nonprofit immigration lawyers far exceeds supply, and scammers and notarios abound. Help filling out the application for asylum is more than most people get.

The organization I volunteered with also did court and ICE check-in accompaniment, providing volunteers to stand by people as they entered the belly of the beast: the federal building at 26 Federal Plaza. These check-ins and appointments happened during business hours, and so accompaniment was most often carried out by retirees, many of whom did not speak Spanish. This distilled accompaniment to its most basic function: a warm hand to hold, the knowledge that someone was looking out for you. I, on the other hand, was usually stuck behind a computer composing tweets about recently published books or formatting HTML on a blog post. Because of this, I lost track of people after we got up and walked away from the table between us. My view of the immigration system was similarly fragmented. All I saw was the same thing as an immigration judge—a steady stream of people, all of them at the same step in the process, stuck between home and safety.

Every part of the immigration system echoes its largest function: to fracture. The I-589 fractures the story of a life; ICE check-ins, court and detention systems fracture families and communities; the rhetoric of immigration numbers and countries of origin and displacement fracture the ability of people to come together across their different nations of origin to decry a fundamentally unjust system.

ONCE WE WERE done interviewing our friends, it was our little group of volunteers' task to do another kind of translation: to transform the testimonies culled from hours of interviewing into little blocks of text to fit into the boxes of form I-589, no more than 150 words each. There was overflow room on each form, of course, but the lawyers that were there for us to consult told us that for this application, it was best to stay within the boxes, as judges and opposing counsel couldn't always be trusted to turn the page and read the information on the back of the form.

The I-589 demands an "I" to have suffered and demands a specific kind of suffering—political, but of the body, of specific and explicit violence. We translated and read back unimaginable sentences in the first person, all the more unimaginable for having happened to the person sitting in front of us:

"In April 2017, my brother was killed in front of me by members of MS-13."

"A few months later, he pressed a curling iron into my leg."

"I left my daughter with my mother and left the country. She is still there."

We were instructed to conduct our interviews as groups, in part so that nothing was missed, and in part to prevent us from having to hold another person's trauma all on our own. That still left the person sitting at the table in front of us, palms sweating and looking at the ground, listening to their stories in our mouths.

WHEN I STARTED working at the clinic, I was warm and polite to everyone I got in touch with, and we got along just fine. I'm not always great with strangers, and especially when doing the asylum application, I assumed that a slightly businesslike demeanor would avoid too much embarrassment on either end by keeping things cool and removed. It wasn't until a few months in, after I was able to watch Sara, the clinic coordinator, that I realized I was fucking up.

Sara was only a few years older than me—big, round glasses, the kind of smile that changed her whole face around, a Madrileña. I wanted to hang out with her, be her friend, wanted her to like me, and so I spent a lot of my unassigned time at the clinic sort of hovering around her. I watched her go up to a woman, a friend, who was trying to figure out where the copier was while also shuffling through her massive file folder for the specific paper she wanted copies of. "¿Qué buscas, cariño?" she asked. She stayed close to the woman as she listened before waving me over.

"Ok, no hay problema! Aquí, Alejandra se va a cuidar de ti, mi amor," she told the woman, squeezing her arm. To me: "Necesita ayuda con la copiadora, ¿si le echas la mano?"

"Ay, gracias, gracias," she said, turning to me in the reflective afterglow of a warmth I didn't know I had been missing.

Sara's speech was peppered with gentle little terms of affection—cariño, mi amor, querida—that I knew but rarely used. This was not the way my parents talked, or my grandmother. It was, instead, a way of talking that I associated with older women, some distant aunts, people who grabbed hold of my hand at weddings and said it had been so long since they last saw me, would you believe I was only thiiiis big? It was the way you were able to transmit affection to strangers and near-strangers, to perform warmth in the way a diner waitress will call you "hon" as she slides a plate of eggs in front of your disastrously hungover self.

In my family, the Spanish alone, this secret language we spoke, was enough to transmit affection because it reminded us of the ways we were more like each other than anyone else in the world. Or, it was weirder—my family nickname is Alita de Pollo, my mom calls my little sibling mi Príncipe Azul after an old song. You just can't go around calling strangers that. Outside of my family, Spanish was a fact and not an exception, and so it took a while for me to figure out that I had to *tell* people, to spell out that I was here to care for them, that they were more than just chips moving through a bureaucratic machinery. By calling someone "querida," I was able to acknowledge to them that they were a person, that I could see in them the ways that they were dear, that they were loved—maybe not quite by me, but by *someone*—and that this love would have some bearing on how I talked to them.

So, I made it a point to watch Sara, watch the ways her hands, her body, her voice warmed up when she was talking to a friend at the clinic. I tried, tentatively, to append "queridas" and "cariños" onto the ends of my sentences, tried to offer a hand on the shoulder or a quick squeeze of the arm. I . . . was not good at it. It was obvious, at least to me, that this was a kind of affection unfamiliar to me, that I was trying a persona on for size, and it fit weirdly. I don't know how much individual friends realized it, but I could tell that they weren't warming up the way they did for Sara, weren't returning the little gestures of affection. This wasn't a Spanish I knew how to speak, so I turned to one I could figure out.

Instead of overt displays of affection, I tried for the kind of contagious self-assuredness I got from conversations with my dad, trying to go into every conversation with the hope that in it would be the key for my friend figuring out how the application worked, and how they wanted to tell their story, both on this form and as they moved through the immigration system. This, alongside the exhaustive explanations I was learning to give on the I-589 form and the questions within it, I'd like to think made me maybe not a friend or a figure of immediate affection, but rather someone efficient and calm when that feels like the right thing to have. And as I set up the framework of these sessions like discussions with my dad, I tried to listen like my mom does—making small sounds, giving people the space to come to their own conclusions, asking small questions every now and then.

The way I was able to give care—within the bounds of my own awkwardness, within my own limited ways of using Spanish—turned out to be the exact same kind of care my parents extended to me every time I spoke to them. Giving this kind of attention felt like welcoming new people into the language of my family each week, and hoping they felt the affection at the heart of it.

40

THE PHILOSOPHER WALTER BENJAMIN ASSIGNS to the translator the task of reviving a text: "The life of the original attains in [a translation] its ever-renewed latest and most abundant flowering." This is a literal resurrection when it comes to asylum applications. The application is a last-ditch attempt to stay in a safe-haven country, to shut the door, at least somewhat, against the wolves outside.

I think sometimes about the warehouse where all the asylum applications must exist, in triplicate, rubber stamped, with a passport photo stapled to the second-to-last page of the I-589 form staring ahead into the following sheet. Overhead fluorescent lights blinking on to reveal an infinite array of banker's boxes on metal shelving.

Around 60 percent of all asylum applications are rejected—the burden of proof for asylum is high to begin with (hence those four-hundred-page applications) and having to prove something will happen that hasn't happened yet is never an easy task. We also don't have a good system for finding out what happens when someone's asylum claim is rejected—once they're deported across our borders, it is as if, to the U.S. government, they disappear off the edges of the earth. Every now and then, thanks to vocal family members or activists and supporters, we get news of someone being murdered or imprisoned or disappeared in their first days back in the country they fled. Their names and photographs are more or less part of an anonymous mass to the vast majority of us, up until the moment they spark across newscaster screens and up and down Facebook and Twitter pages or are enshrined in flowers for an Instagram-friendly post for just a moment before they flare out, again becoming part of the anonymous mass of the deported dead. Activist groups say there is no real way to know what the scale of these deaths are.

It's impossible to know, then, how many of these translated asylum applications have survived their original authors, for how many of the dead these bankers' boxes represent not the seed for an "ever-renewed and most abundant flowering," but rather a last gasp of life, the record of someone fighting to survive with the fragmented tools they were given.

A LOT OF TRANSLATION THEORY is ultimately biblical translation theory. This is why, even when you're not necessarily talking about the word of God, the original is held as a bright, inviolable light that the translator must struggle to approach, much less replicate. To find the source of this brightness, theorists keep pointing not just behind the original text but behind language itself.

There's a sense in which looking at *any* original in the light of divine origination makes total sense. The creation of any text is a miracle of individuation, of reference and self-reference, of idiosyncratic experiences—just as miraculous as the idea of an individual consciousness. When you're translating literary texts, there's a kind of slow awareness of this as you find your sentences unfurling along paths that are not your usual, a different understanding of the creator of the text. When you translate, you become aware that this author, your author, uses the word "cuerpo," the word "casa," the word "tierra" like no one else ever has or will again. You also realize that you can only ever know a part of it, can only ever skim the surface of their meaning. The dizzying individuality of any single writer or mind, multiplied by all the possible writers or minds, or even your own, as you read or translate, unfolds a world that feels too intricate to be anything but the traces of God's fingerprint.

My investment in this idea, however, stops short when I think of my other source texts, which are not usually the product of slow mornings sitting at one's desk, or even the stress of looming deadlines, but rather, the product of extreme violence and fear, created not to serve a creative desire but to fill a bureaucrat's form. This leads me right back to the doorway of one of the oldest and most persistent theological questions in the book— literally. The Book of Job asks why bad things happen to good people, or why bad things happen at all. It starts with Job, who is a fortunate and wealthy man with a large family. When Satan says that he would turn away from God if he were to lose his good fortune, God says, "Hmmm, interesting," and sets about plunging Job into a personal apocalypse of famine, disease, and grief. Job, throughout, remains steadfast. The book ends with Job's fortunes generally restored while God spits out enigmas in his direction before disappearing into a storm.

It is since Job's suffering, but more critically since Christ's, that Christianity has recast suffering in a redemptive, sacrificatory light. Paul, in his second letter to the Corinthians, recounts his suffering, enumerating beatings, shipwrecks, and sleepless nights as echoes and mediations of Christ's sufferings, making him a mirror of God-made-man. St. Teresa of Ávila speaks of the blessings of suffering, which allow her to learn patience and endurance, Christlike qualities. When using translation theory that has its roots in biblical translation, I'm using a theory that centers the divine—and in Christianity, the divine is often both shrouded and elevated by suffering.

I don't like the implication that there's something holy about suffering that's present in so much of Christian philosophy. I hate the idea that there's a pure and shining light at the back of any of the trauma I've borne witness to, that it was a necessary step on the path to anyone's holiness. None of it feels like what I want God to be. I don't want to honor the original, don't want to revere it like I might the words from God's mouth, because it seems patently obvious to me that any God I might believe in could not have been involved. On the other hand, I also don't want to mutilate the stories I'm given, like I do every time I fill out an asylum application. It feels sacrilegious to cut up someone's life in the interest of the government, because there's something of value in their story, something that deserves careful treatment, deserves to be honored and respected and not pried out with pliers and smashed up. This something isn't about the divinity or the foreordination of any story, or the sacredness of the idea of stories in general, or about the beauty of suffering, but because the people telling them are viscerally, embodiedly human, as I'm reminded with every tissue or glass of water. These stories are important because the person sitting in front of me and I share the fragility of our flesh, are entrusted to one another because of the thinness of our skins, the delicate workings of our insides.

At the very same time, our bodies are not enough. The asylum application is a skeleton that, like the worst horror movie cliché, longs for a body. The immigration system is hungry for bodies: bodies to suffer, bodies to fill up beds in for-profit detention centers, bodies to work in the fields and factories and behind the scenes of everything, all the while rejecting their humanity. The I-589 pretends to care about biography, asks for a narrative in a specific person's voice, but in reality, is only concerned with violence on the body, glancing off anything deeper than the skin.

A bad translation does this same work—it lives on the surface of a text, is concerned with the physical shape, the surface meaning, whatever reflection momentarily blinds you. A good translation dives deep into the beating heart of a text. You can only translate what you see, and if all that is visible to you is a body, if all that is presented is the surface, then there is something about the human that is still invisible to you, to the government, to the immigration judge in his chambers and the Border Patrolman in his truck.

I THINK THE real function of that soup at the end of each clinic was to bring us back into ourselves and our bodies, to honor the hard work we had done in filling out the forms by nourishing us. It allowed us to make a little time for care in the midst of a struggle for survival, gave us space to find common ground outside the confines of the boxes of the I-589 form.

We were bodies, yes, but not in the way the form demanded. Our physical selves became not just sites of pain or danger or violence but of care and comfort. Eating together allowed me and the volunteers and the friend—all wound tightly together in a specific configuration of translator-asylum seeker-notetaker-questioner while we filled out the form—to relax into something more like ourselves. It allowed us to gently clear the table of all we had discussed and returned us to this singular moment of hunger, and its meeting.

PART III

El Azote

Boston Immigration Court, March 2019
Immigration Detention Center, Southeastern U.S., December 2019

42

THERE ARE TWO BILINGUAL-BUT-STILL-DUMB JOKES my dad likes to tell. They're apocryphally the invention of my great-grandfather, a man known in my family as "Mr. Wilson." He was born in Mercedes, Texas, and according to my dad, the only person he's ever met that could fluently curse in two languages. "A true bilingual," my dad says. Mr. Wilson died before I was born, but his larger-than-life presence looms in family stories, he looks out from photos on my grandmother's wall, blue-eyed, blond, tan, and squinting, with a handsome, straight-nosed profile.

The first of Mr. Wilson's jokes is the story of the mariposita: "Once upon a time, there was a little mariposita, and she was aleteando around the garden, when, de repente! she azoted. "Oh no," she cried, "I forgot to open my little alitas!"

The other is this: "Between, between, drink a chair, for the water zero is coming!" which is funny because it's a sort of perfect, entirely terrible word-for-word translation of another phrase in Spanish "Entre, entre, tome una silla, porque viene el aguacero!"

I worry that in explaining them, or even writing them down, I've robbed them of some essential humor: I remember laughing hysterically as a child at "De repente! she azoted," but it's also maybe the kind of joke that's largely dependent on you being six and your usually serious dad putting on a weird voice and speaking in Spanglish and clapping his hands together in front of your face, so you jump back a little, the idea of a little butterfly slamming into a wall, bemoaning her wings.

Still, I risk the over-explanation of these very particular my-dad jokes because I think both of them, in their own way, get at something about my experiences living in two languages. There comes a moment, regardless of how fluent, how natural, how expert you are in whatever language when de repente! You will azote against one of its walls. Your wings will fail you and you will find yourself wordless, or with the wrong word, and will grasp for something that's on the other side and come up short.

LET'S TALK MARIPOSITAS. Every year, for three generations of short lives, monarch butterflies fly northward, tracing out branching routes that spread across the United States, and as far as the southernmost border of Canada. The third generation, often born in late summer or early fall, emerges from its chrysalis, shakes out crumpled wings, and flies the entire route back south to the overwinter site its great-great-grandparents left from, so many months ago. Many of these overwinter sites are concentrated in the Reserva de la Biósfera Santuario Mariposa Monarca, a sprawling pine forest to the west of Mexico City.

In the heart of the Reserva, branches are weighed down by lightness, orange and fluttering, populating the forest with a kind of pine tree that might become airborne, disappearing into the sky if you turn your back on it. The pines themselves haven't disappeared, or not much, but the orange, fluttering trees so particular to the fall arrival of the monarch migration are vanishing, year by year. Climate change, logging, the decimation of the kinds of tangled wildernesses and unmown meadows where milkweed, the monarchs' food and nursery, grows, all of these have had a hand in decreasing the numbers of monarchs that make it back from their long migrations.

It seems fitting in a variety of ways, then, that the monarch has been adopted by artists and activists as a symbol for open borders, for fluid migrations, for the ways in which migration is natural and walls are not. You can find clumsily painted monarchs on the walls of shelters, nonprofits, and children's detention centers, find them vast and swirling, spray painted onto city walls along both sides of the border, Sharpie outlines of monarchs on posters held up by protesters, thin and elegantly rendered in logos and digital campaigns. And just as monarch butterflies are finding their progress impeded by the changing shape of the world, finding it harder and harder both to navigate north and to return back to the trees of their forefathers, so too are people finding it harder to move across borders.

The southern border of Mexico has been hardened with accreting layers of steel and guns and troops and helicopters in response to American pressure. The southern border of the United States is at this point nearly impenetrable to anything other than capital, cheap goods and labor flowing north, and remittances back to waiting families in the south, unable to earn a living in the shadow of the United States. With every round of increasingly restrictive policies, with every additional limitation on immigration or rise in filing fees, the number of people who successfully make it across the border gets smaller. Not only that, but the number of people who might make it back home is decreasing as well. These are the people who are able to get their green cards or citizenships. With the ability to stay they also gain the ability to leave again without imperiling everything they have worked so hard for. At my day job, I often interview people who have won status after many years in the United States. The first thing many of them do is buy plane tickets home to finally return to visit parents and grandparents unseen for decades; in one quick plane flight, they make a journey to return to a home that took years to leave, watching the hard-won miles rewind beneath the plane's shadow on the earth. Family histories like mine, that span the border as often as they do generations, are vanishingly rare.

LET ME BE very clear though: As lovely, as delicate, as picturesque as the symbol may be, migrants are not butterflies. They're people—complex, and individual, with memories and thoughts and opinions on politics and the state of the world and the ways that they have been treated. I talk about butterflies here because, given their shared migration paths, it seems that through this metaphor, people find it easier to care about immigrants, because people seem to find it easier to care about these simple, uncomplicated insects and their disrupted migration paths than those of people. Comparing immigrants to insects, no matter how lovely, is a way of dehumanizing them, of rendering them slightly grotesque and 100 percent unthreatening.

In the words of undocumented writer Karla Cornejo Villavicencio: "I fucking hate thinking of migrants as butterflies. Butterflies can't fuck a bitch up."

43

I'M SITTING IN A COURTROOM in Boston, in a shallow wooden pew, next to two other volunteer court observers. In the pew across the aisle from us, there's a few people, two men and a woman, shackled at the wrists and ankles. A man in a Suffolk County Corrections jacket made it clear as soon as we walked in that we should not be trying to sit next to them by blocking off the end of the pew with his body and nodding us further down the aisle. A few other attorneys and maybe a family of someone in the room make up the rest of our small congregation. When the judge comes in, harried in a black robe, we all rise like church, and sit back down.

Behind the judge, who sits on a raised dais at the front of the room, there is a seal for the United States Department of Justice: an eagle on a shield, clutching an olive branch and a quiver of arrows in its claws, and these words: Qui pro domina justitia sequitur.

The judge, all the while looking at his computer, incantates his daily opening: He tells those of us assembled the date and the time, and that we're in the Boston immigration court, then calls us into session. He reads off a name and four digits from the end of an A-number, and one of the shackled men stands up, shuffling down the aisle, the chains around his waist clanking. Because of the angles of the room, the angles of his body, it's hard to see his face, but it seems like he's in his mid-thirties. He's a tall man and has to hunch over to keep the chains from pulling at his ankles and wrists. The bailiff swings open the gate to admit him to the court, and in a move that might almost be chivalrous were it not obvious that the man cannot physically perform this small service for himself, pulls out a chair for him at the table across the aisle from the government attorney, a tiny, sharp woman with a cart crammed full of neatly filed papers and manila accordion folders. As the man sits, she pulls one out, flicks it open with a practiced movement, smooths out the papers in front of her.

"What language do you speak and understand best?" the judge asks.

"English is okay," the man replies, softly.

"Okay, sounds good." The judge tells the room again that this is an initial deportation hearing in his courtroom, he tells us the date and the time again, and repeats the name of the man. He rushes through this, reading off his monitor. "Please raise your right hand."

The man hunches down even farther in his chair, elbows on knees, to give the chain enough slack to allow him to raise his right hand, bringing his left hand along with it.

"Do you affirm that the testimony you will provide in these proceedings will be the truth, the whole truth and nothing but the truth?"

"Yes." He speaks softly.

"The purpose of this hearing will be to determine whether or not you should be allowed to remain in the United States. The Department of

Homeland Security alleges that you do not have a legal reason to remain in the United States. Do you understand?"

The man says yes.

"At this time, we will discuss the government's allegations and charges as outlined in the Notice to Appear. The government charges that you are subject to removal because you are an alien. First, that you are not a citizen or national of the United States. Second, that you are a citizen or national of Haiti. Third, that you entered the country unlawfully on June 3, 1994. Fourth, that on February 18, 2019, there was found in your possession a schedule one drug: one and a half grams of marijuana."

(Possession of small amounts of marijuana in Massachusetts has been legal since 2008. The state had recently legalized recreational marijuana sales and brought in over 4 million dollars in tax revenue in the first two months alone. However, immigration court is federal court, and marijuana is still illegal under federal laws.)

The judge tells the man that because of these allegations, the government has charged him with removal. "Now I will ask you some questions to see what forms of relief from removal, if any, may be available to you."

The judge asks a few questions about possible roads to citizenship—a U.S. citizen parent or spouse, a previously filed visa languishing somewhere in the system.

"No."

"No."

"No," the man replies, to one question after another.

Finally: "Are you afraid to return to Haiti?"

The credible fear question.

The man sits up, his shackles clanking.

"Yes, yes, I am. My mother died in the hurricane in 2016, my cousin also. I'm afraid that if I went back, I would also die, be displaced in a storm or an earthquake. I am afraid to return to Haiti."

You can see Boston Harbor, placid and icy out the window of the courtroom, it's one of those dazzlingly bright and bitterly cold March days. Boats slowly glide past, bare branches have a greenish glow to them that indicate that before long, there will be leaves again.

Asylum, a legal category of migrant created in the aftermath of the Holocaust, is granted because an applicant is afraid that they will be the subject of violence from either the government or a group the government is unwilling or unable to stop, on the basis of race, religion, nationality, political opinion, or belonging to a particular social group. Even though the government of Haiti, and any number of other small nations that have been or will be ravaged by climate change are unable to stop the wind and the waves, and even though those most affected by the violence of the natural world are those who are poor, those who live in countries discarded as secondary, fear of the rising sea does not make a successful asylum claim.

Qui pro domina justitia sequitur, the motto of the United States Department of Justice, can be translated as "They who prosecute on behalf of justice." The man who prosecutes on behalf of justice does not tell the man in front of him that he is not eligible for asylum for fear of the elements. Instead, the judge tells this tall man to look for a lawyer, to come back at his next appointment, set for a month out, to see if perhaps one of the other forms of cancellation of removal might be available to him.

The man stands and shuffles his way back down the aisle between our two rows of pews, shoulders hunched from the chains at his ankles, and the transportation officer from the prison shuffles him down the aisle and out the door of the courtroom, back to the detention center for another month until his next court date.

THE DIFFERENCE BETWEEN "TE QUIERO" and "te amo." The intimacy of "tutear" or the curdle away from sweetness of an "empalago." The difference in weight between a hielera and an icebox.

Translation loss is said to occur when an element in the source language—an assonance, a joke, a double entendre—doesn't transfer over to the target language. Take hielera and icebox, for example.

"Hielera" comes from hielo, ice. "Hielera" in one context means a U.S. Customs and Border Protection detention center, a holding pen for recently apprehended people at the border that is allegedly kept at an internal temperature of around sixty-eight degrees, although migrants report uncomfortably cold conditions—claims that CBP's distribution of mylar blankets both reinforce and mock. "Hielera" in any other context would suggest a picnic or a 1950s kitchen, when in-home refrigeration was a novelty—pleasure-filled, sleek, modern in a kitschy, chrome-y kind of way. Sixty-eight degrees in any other context is a pool that makes you gasp when you jump into it, the kind of day with weather that makes you never want to go indoors, a turn in the air. In hieleras, as in translation, context is everything.

Migrants who have spent extended periods of time in hieleras report blue fingertips and cracked lips, fevers and vomiting and shaking. Part of it is down to the temperature, the other part down to the inhumane conditions: no showering, little water—none of it clean—and less food, overcrowding. The agents say the temperature is low so that they can be comfortable in the stations while wearing boots, socks, bulletproof vests, jackets, tactical gear, an environment suited only to their needs. It seems important to point out here that the vast number of people that they encounter in the desert are the furthest thing from being armed, and those who have had the energy or foresight to bring a sweatshirt or a jacket have these articles taken from them as they are processed into the hielera.

In secret Facebook groups, Border Patrol agents have been seen making disdainful jokes about the kind of humanitarian care they are required to perform as part of their jobs. The way they see themselves, they should be chasing down narcos and shooting human smugglers on sight; instead, they're charged with offering first aid, hydration, and care to families at the very edge of desperation. Many of the posts take on a sneering tone, a disbelief in having to care for fellow humans.

I'm not sure whether "hielera" or "icebox" came first, linguistically. When journalists are explaining hieleras in tweet threads, they emphasize that this is the language used by people to describe the architecture they're encountering. A new kind of jail, a new kind of dehumanization. In English though, "icebox" works a little differently, perhaps a little better, in that it brings more meaning with it. Hielera doesn't just become icebox, it becomes an ICE box.

The U.S. Immigration and Customs Enforcement is the police/paramilitary branch of what used to be Immigration and Naturalization Services, now housed under the Department of Homeland Security. ICE was formed and given its own mission in 2003, explicitly as a response to 9/11 and perhaps intentionally envisioned as a sort of anti-terrorism squad—there to dig up prayer rugs from the desert and track down Al-Qaeda in the caravans or some such nonsense—they are now largely in the business of inserting themselves into public life, looking for the "wrong" kind of immigrant. ICE breaks down the doors of family homes, shoehorns into routine traffic stops. They conduct massive raids at workplaces, wait in courtrooms for women literally wrapping up cases related to their own trafficking, get to drive tanks down New York City streets and occasionally shoot people with impunity. Despite not having jurisdiction or the legal right to do so, many of their arrests come from asking random citizens for their papers. A large part of their job ends up being racial profiling—looking for the brown, the Black, the poor. Occasionally they fuck up and put citizens and legal permanent residents into deportation proceedings, largely for not walking around with their drivers license, passport, social security cards or whatever other paperwork a law enforcement official has decided to ask for that day.

So, when I translate "hielera" into "icebox," into ICE box, I bring all of that with me. Not just the cold temperatures, the cold storage of living bodies, but the midnight knocks on the door, the assumptions that brownness and Blackness is equal to criminality, all of it. When I translate it back from icebox into hielera, though, all of that still comes along. The specificity of Immigrations and Customs Enforcement doesn't, but the terror and white supremacy of all of it does, because how can it not? A hielera has this within it because it is the language used by the vast majority of its occupants, because the word came about to describe a kind of cruelty that otherwise had no words.

There's a loss there that predates any translation of it, the dehumanization of ICE present whether or not you write it out.

45

WHEN THE EXPANSION OF THE border wall was announced, much of
the hubbub that might have been spread along miles and miles of national
parks and state monuments ended up centering around the fate of a single
butterfly sanctuary along the southern border of Texas. I have to imagine
that the visual was just too good: De repente, these gorgeous, non-threatening
migrants, made of painted silk and on their way to survival, to a reproduc-
tion in a way that people found nice and lovely, would azote into a rusty
steel behemoth.

Just outside of Mission, an hour and a half's drive west from coastal
Brownsville, the National Butterfly Center found that a strip of land, no
more than 200 or so feet across, would be seized by eminent domain in
order to construct a 40-foot concrete and steel bollard wall, with a 150-foot

clear-cut enforcement zone, paved and floodlit. In an op-ed in *The Washington Post*, the center's outreach coordinator, a Trump supporter, bemoaned the wall as a symbol of the Republican party's abandonment of conservative values: small government, low spending, and of the utmost importance, a deep respect for private property, in this case particularly, his employers'.

Thanks to a media firestorm, the butterfly center became a symbol of all that might be lost, all that was at risk with the border wall: views, a kind of virgin landscape that might, for all anyone knows, stretch into eternity, an unbounded, borderless American wilderness, ready to be laid claim to. The butterfly center is, of course, already laid claim to, and left purposely untouched, a monument to a specific idea of what nature ought to be and look like.

The wall, once built, will sever the southernmost 70 acres of the butterfly preserve from the rest of it, disrupt animal migration patterns—not just butterflies, but the birds that feed on them, and the creatures of prey that feed on the birds, and the herbivores attracted by the scrub brushes, and the plentiful water stored inside the paddle of a nopal.

There's also the Organ Pipe Cactus National Monument out west in Arizona, home to ancient cacti and unique life forms, and Big Bend National Park, just where the Texan panhandle dips southward along the Rio Grande, all bisected by this rusting behemoth and state-of-the-art technology watching, waiting, attending not to the nowhere-else-on-Earth wildlife, not to the vast expanses of strange and beautiful desert, but to the people moving through it.

All of this technological detritus and physical disruption is somehow less visible in some of the discourse than the detritus left behind by those moving through the desert, making the imagined purity of these landscapes part of the argument for keeping migrants out. As people cross the desert, they leave things behind: water bottles, rosaries, energy bar wrappers, bags of supplies too heavy to carry any farther. In 2019, four volunteers from the group No More Deaths were found guilty of littering in Cabeza Prieta National Wildlife Refuge for leaving water in the desert to ease the passage of migrants through the hostile terrain. These volunteers hiked out into the remotest parts of the park and dropped supplies, usually gallon jugs of water Sharpied with encouraging slogans. The idea of a pure, unspoiled wilderness, waiting for a wall to cross it with its path of destruction became more important than the lives of those given no other option but to traverse it.

The same people that argue that migrant treks despoil the desert, argue that in order to prevent the unspoiled wildernesses of North America from becoming overrun, exploited, dirty, we need to close our borders. This, of course, ignores the natural gas pipelines inching ever closer to national parks in the southwest, the cattle ranchers allowing herds to roam through public lands in the west, the rising tides and shifting weather patterns of climate change that present a much clearer and present danger than a population increase.

One of these arguments, put forward by eco-anarchist and nature writer Edward Abbey, is that immigrants bring with them an "alien mode of life," and that the "squalor, cruelty, and corruption of Latin America" stands in direct opposition to the possibility of the "open, spacious, uncrowded, and beautiful—yes, beautiful!—society," that most Americans wanted for themselves and their families. Abbey found it convenient to ignore that much of the openness of the United States was made possible by the "squalor" of Latin America, that the long arm of colonialism made it possible to export some of our smelliest, least lovely industries (a great deal of agriculture, oil, and manufacturing) to make room for the wide open skies and lovely homes on the range of his fantasies.

I read Abbey's most famous book, *Desert Solitaire,* shortly after President Trump announced that he had ordered ICE to conduct massive raids in "sanctuary cities" across America. In his book, Abbey describes his year of living as a park ranger in the area that would eventually become Arches

National Park. It's a ruggedly beautiful book, full of animal encounters and dangerous canoeing trips through deep river canyons that speaks over and over again to the beauty of landscape, of the necessity of wild places. Abbey suggests public lands as the place from which a new democracy might be born—that an armed insurrection against an increasingly totalitarian government might be mounted from the rocks and hills and trees of Arches or Yosemite or Yellowstone. I looked up from my book, jostling home on an over-packed subway after spending a long day making easily readable graphics to inform people of their rights if ICE were to come knocking at their doors, reminding people it was best to put in place emergency custody plans for their children in the case of their detention. It was foolish of Abbey to think that totalitarianism, if it came, would not come like this, and for these people first—the immigrants, the poor, the Black and brown. Despite knowing better, despite having seen it over and over again, it was once again surprising to me that someone who could see the beauty and promise of nature so clearly could be so blind to so much else.

When Abbey died in 1989, he was buried secretly, possibly illegally, in his trusty blue sleeping bag by a group of friends in the Cabeza Prieta Wildlife Refuge, the same stretch of land in Pima County, Arizona, that now makes up one of the most commonly used immigration corridors for those seeking to cross while evading detection from the authorities.

In Mexico, butterfly-laden pine trees shake their branches.

THE KINDS OF arguments Abbey put forward—that immigrants specifically are responsible for overpopulation and environmental degradation—are better known as ecofascism, and the ecofascist movement is growing in power and destructive tendencies as it becomes conflated and combined with other white supremacist theories like the Great Replacement Theory, arguing that immigrants and people of color are set to "replace" white people in Western countries and change the values and culture.

I understand being scared. I have also been alive on this planet of late, have also felt each summer get hotter than the last, have watched the floods and storms and fires on TV, have wondered about the moment my own corner of the world will become threatening, worry about my future children and the world they will live in. I've seen forests clear-cut in the Pacific Northwest, the blinding lights and gas flare fires of oil refineries outside of Houston, the weird uniformity of crop fields across the country, and wondered about the corners we have chased nature down into.

Where I stop understanding, though, is that the reaction of ecofascists is not conservation or preservation or the creation of alternative resources, but instead, destruction. In August 2019, a shooter gunned down twenty-three mostly Latino families doing back-to-school shopping in an El Paso Walmart. The manifesto he left behind spoke of decreasing the number of people drawing on dwindling resources in order to protect a future for white Americans, never mind that many of the brown people in this country are here precisely for the resources that white Americans took from their countries of origin. In May 2022, a shooter entered a grocery store in a largely Black neighborhood in Buffalo on a Sunday after church and killed ten Black elders. Across the planet, a gunman in Christchurch, New Zealand, killed fifty-one worshippers at a mosque in March of 2019, leaving behind a manifesto that would go on to inspire the perpetrators of both the El Paso and Buffalo shootings. And these are just the deaths caused by overt acts of violence.

THERE ARE SOME stretches of desert so inhospitable that a wall isn't needed. For these sections of the border, the United States government counts on a policy known as "Prevention Through Deterrence" rather than 20 feet of reinforced steel. Let me translate: The United States government knows they do not need a fence because people will not survive crossing the desert, the only fence needed is that which funnels people into inhospitable terrain to die.

During the 2022 fiscal year, 853 deaths were confirmed along the U.S.–Mexico border. The bodies of women, of fathers and their daughters, of men and boys and families. People resting under trees in one last attempt to find shade, or who stumbled on their way up a hill and were too weak to stand up, people who got lost and wandered the desert until they could no longer do so, people who drowned while crossing the Rio Grande, people who were injured and unable to continue walking to safety. Fifty-three people died of suffocation in an abandoned truck trailer. The 853 deaths are just those that could be confirmed by officials: The heat, harsh winds, and prevalence of scavenging creatures means that bodies are claimed by desert winds within a matter of days, and the wildness and severity of the terrain means that there are hundreds of square miles that are not regularly traversed by people. While 2022 has been the deadliest year on record due in part to high numbers of border crossings while official ports of entry remain closed to asylum seekers along with record droughts and heatwaves in the southwestern deserts, every year the number of deaths rises into the hundreds.

Every day, a migrant's body is discovered by someone—ranchers or Border Patrol agents or water hikers out in the desert. The body is then transported to a local coroner, who, if they are unable to identify the person before them, contact an organization, Colibrí Center, that has a staff of volunteer forensic anthropologists who can help put a name to the body by matching it to missing persons reports filed by families anxiously awaiting news back home—some trinket in a nearly decayed pocket, a family bible found nearby, dental prints when they're available, or a tattoo on a remaining fragment of skin. Colibrí Center houses the remains of twelve hundred of the nameless dead, and the case files, submitted by worried families, of an additional four thousand missing.

A colibrí in English is a hummingbird, and the center is named after a specific bird, small and green and reminiscent of a distant home, found dead in the pocket of a man who also died in the desert, far from where he lived.

Here, again, we think about holy relics, the bones of the saints gilded and revered for their suffering. While there's something still awful about valorizing the pain of the martyrs, there's also a beauty in sanctifying the bones of those that have died for a more beautiful life, and in recognizing the power that those bones hold, unnamed though they may be.

We fight for a world in which no one has to die in the desert, but until that day, we hold our dead sacred, try to find their names.

THERE IS A WIKIPEDIA PAGE: "List of names for the biblical nameless."
From it, we learn that the name of Lot's wife is Edith. Edith means "prosperous in war," but like many in wartime, Edith was chased out of Sodom,
the city of her birth, under the darkness of night, violent men at her heels.
We know Edith less as a wife and more as a monument—mid-flight, God
turned her into a pillar of salt. The reasons for Edith's punishment are as
varied as the extracanonical texts that mention her: Was her glance back to
Sodom an indication of her unwillingness to leave her evil lifestyle behind?
Was her sin asking a neighbor to borrow some salt, setting off a chain of
events that ended with a howling pack of bloodthirsty men beating down
her door? Or was her only sin seeing God, coming down from the clouds
to level a city, her city, and so she turned to a pillar of salt, her only sin that
she witnessed God in His own sin of wrathfulness?

Today, in the desert along the shores of the Dead Sea, a salt formation rises out of the ground. There's a Jewish prayer to be said over the crystallized body, but Lot's wife has been looking out over the ruins of her home for centuries now.

The story of Edith's flight, the way that Christianity, and Catholicism especially, has taken hold in Latin America is at least some of the reason that people migrate. In a Catholic interpretation of the Bible, the men at Edith's door were demanding access to her angelic house guests to rape them, and God burns down the city in the wake of the evilness of their demand. This interpretation comes down to a translation debate—the men ask to "know" Lot's guests, and whether this refers to carnal knowledge or an interrogation is a mystery hidden in the complexities of ancient Hebrew that have been lost to time.

When conquistadores and Spanish missionaries brought this interpretation of the Bible with them to the New World, they also brought with them condemnation of homosexuality as a particularly despicable sin. Today, trans and queer people band together to travel to the United States, a place that is seen as a haven from the constant violence, shaming, and threats associated with their identities in their largely Catholic home countries.

When the big, headline-grabbing caravan came north at the end of 2018, a group of about eighty queer migrants arrived in Tijuana days ahead of the rest of the walkers, having split off from the larger caravan because their needs and safety were overlooked by the collective. Although queer asylum seekers generally have higher rates of asylum acceptance—much of the violence they face is directly related to their personal and political identities, as is required by contemporary asylum laws—they also face abuse and violence from within the very system they are petitioning for help.

A judge's lack of understanding of trans identity might mean that someone stays incarcerated for months longer than they otherwise might, or that their case is outright denied. Time spent in detention centers is fraught with risk, including violence from guards and other detainees. In May of 2018, Roxsana Hernandez, a trans woman detained at Cibola's infamous "trans pod" died, reportedly of dehydration and complications from HIV. After her death, the Transgender Law Center published an investigation that revealed that she had been subject to beatings with batons while handcuffed, and that other migrants detained with her had begged officials to get her medical help. Instead, ICE withheld the medications she needed to keep her HIV under control, and she was left to suffer in detention until the last possible moment, when she was sent to a hospital and discharged days before her death, so ICE might avoid counting her as part of their official tally of people that died under their custody. In interviews with family members and people who traveled with her, Roxana is described as being open—ready to share her own struggles with the queer people she traveled with, to share some of her carefully curated and selected makeup. In the U.S., she wanted to get married, have a blue-collar job, settle down somewhere with a quiet life.

The trans pod at Cibola, especially in the years after Roxsana's death, was also the site of some of the most vibrant organizing and political speeches to come out of the detention centers. It held at least two of the people with some of the longest detention records—Kelly, a twenty-three-year old who was held by ICE for three years, and Sza Sza, who is in her fifties but has spent at least seven years in immigration detention. Because of these long stays, these women have an institutional memory that goes back years, hardwon knowledge of how detention operates, and a deep community. In 2019, a group of women wrote an open letter, published in LGBTQ+ media, to protest the conditions in the detention center—focusing especially on the lack of adequate medical care, the bad food, and discrimination from guards.

"Tenemos miedo a las represalias, pero más al miedo de estar en esta situación."

ICE had staged a photo shoot of the women gardening, in the detention center's salon, eating fresh-looking food, and playing basketball.

A week later, the women replied with another letter to the media. The garden it showed them tending? A few tree branches stuck in the soil for the photo op. The salon was opened especially for the photos and was otherwise closed. Expeditions to the rec yard were only permitted if the guards were in a good mood that day and didn't lock them up early.

"Les preguntamos, ¿por qué no hablan o fotografían la realidad?"

The second part of that letter again details the reality of living in a detention center: women locked up in solitary confinement, sometimes for months, for minor infractions, badly treated cases of HIV and skin infections, uniforms stinking after being washed alongside dirty mops, blankets full of holes, drinking water only available from the toilet tank drinking fountains that seem to be a particularly cruel staple of ICE detention.

Trans womens' voices have been among the clearest in speaking out about the dangers and degradations of living under detention, attempting to improve conditions for themselves and everyone else living in their circumstances.

Each of the open letters released by the women of the Cibola County Correctional Center's "Transgender Women's Pod" is signed by a dozen people—Kelly and Alejandra and Shakira and Melisa neatly lined up against the left margin. Everything to the right of those first names is a concession to the government that holds them: Dead names, still present on government forms, are written out alongside the numbers assigned to them by the Federal government. These women name themselves, even as it has cost them their homes and their freedom. They set down their names even though they fear retaliation because they fear their situation more. They name the ways they are mistreated, name the entities that mistreat them, name the entities they ask for help. Their power lies in the naming.

47

IN THE BOSTON COURTROOM, THE next case is called.

The detainees from Suffolk County have already been led out of the room by the warden, and everyone else waiting on the benches is either with the same organization I am, or obviously a lawyer in a rumpled suit with shined shoes. An enormous screen on one side of the room flickers to life, the cinderblock walls of a detention center are in view. Someone leans into the frame, a severe woman with a ponytail, and as the judge reads the next name, she opens the door visible at the back of the room, waves someone in, and steps out herself.

This man is appearing via video screen from Bristol County House of Corrections in southern Massachusetts, close to the old whaling town of New Bedford. A lawyer I met the week before described it as a dismal place, worse than Suffolk County, another county jail turning a profit by taking federal money to hold ICE detainees. This man is older, and white, with a grizzled black-and-white buzz cut and the kind of deeply lined face that speaks to time spent outdoors through bright sun and stinging winds.

The judge goes through his preamble, turning away from the man on the screen and towards his computer so he can read out the name and the date and the location again, the time stamp has ticked forward. He turns to the man and asks: "I see here you have Georgian on your file, do you want a translator?" The man nods, and the judge says, "Alright, one moment."

The sound of a phone ringing fills the courtroom, piped in over speakers embedded in the ceiling. "Hello, this is Language Line, a translation and interpretation service. What language are you looking for today?"

"Georgian," the judge intones.

"Please wait one moment."

The tinny sound of hold music plays, crackling and garbling over the loudspeakers for a few seconds, until a young man's voice comes over the line. "Hello, I am Viktor, I will be your interpreter today!"

The judge introduces himself, and asks Viktor's chirpy, disembodied voice to introduce himself to the man on the screen, to make sure they can understand each other. The man's face on the screen, which has worn a drawn look of concern, relaxes a little when the first sounds of Georgian come through first the speakers in the ceiling of the courtroom to be picked up by the microphones on the monitor he is displayed on, and conveyed some 60 miles south to the speakers on whatever computer he's peering into. He nods, says hello back, tilts his head forwards and turns, angling an ear towards the speakers.

This hearing proceeds, much as the previous one, judge and translator and the man all talking over each other, in a jumble of decorum and a faltering script, or leaving huge gaps in the conversation, each waiting for the other to speak. All the while, the man on the screen moves his ear closer and closer to the speakers. I don't know how well the judge can see his face from where he's sitting, or whether there's a camera angled towards him or just out the window of the courtroom and into Boston Harbor. In the end, the result is this: The judge is explaining very patiently to a disembodied voice, which is explaining to a collection of pixels on a screen he cannot see, that it is unlikely that he will be able to stay in the country. That information is being received, far away somewhere, by a man in a prison, leaning forward to catch an electronic garble that sounds like home from a computer's speaker, almost unable to believe that this is how fate comes down to touch him.

FRENCH PHILOSOPHER EMMANUEL LEVINAS TALKS about the moment in which we encounter the face of the other as a moment of disruption, as an intrusion by an Other—one that is not ourselves—that calls us into "giving and serving" the Other.

For Levinas, a European Jewish survivor of World War II, the face represents a vulnerability, a reminder of shared humanity, a link between the space you are occupying and your own particular mind and the fact of the existence of another mind, occupying space also.

A friend of mine, in her first month of medical school, told me about her first time dissecting a cadaver, the bodies that people had donated to science so that a new generation of doctors, her included, might learn to save lives. She told me about the first cut they made, from the nape of the neck downwards to uncover the gleaming whiteness of the spine. As she did so, she reached her own hand back to touch the knob of bone at the base of her neck, the cervical vertebrae.

She said that the bodies had been draped—fabric covering head, hands, and torso—in part to obscure at least some of the horror of slipping a scalpel into them. She said it worked, mostly, except that in life, the woman in front of her had a tiny tattoo of a hummingbird fluttering on her hip, and in death, the hummingbird was still there, and through it called a whole life into the cold body of the woman in front of her.

This is not to say that Levinas is wrong, but rather that he was more right than even he wrote, that the Other does not come in at just the eyes, or in the hunch of the shoulders and the movement of a living body, but in the smallest lines of the hand, in the traces of the skin. Our physical presence reminds us, time and time again, that we are in trust to one another, that this hand, this elbow, this child's skinned knee or woman's ankle eased from a too-tight shoe, that these faces and bodies and breaths are things we are responsible for.

AND THAT'S WHERE the other joke that my father tells comes in.

"Between, between, drink a chair for the water zero is coming!" A "better" translation for the original Spanish phrase ("entre, entre, tome una silla, viene el aguacero!") is this: "Come in, come in, take a seat, because the downpour is coming!" You can almost see it, a woman flinging open her front door to pull her friend, caught umbrella-less in an increasingly vicious wind, inside by the wrist, convincing her to stay despite an unfilled shopping list or an unmet appointment. It's a phrase that might also be communicated by a not particularly elegant set of pantomimes: a beckoning wave in, a gesture at your warm and cozy house, a jab at the ominous sky above. And honestly, that bit of it is mostly what matters. Even if you end up telling someone to drink a chair, they're still going to sit in it gratefully instead. The important thing is that you stuck your head out the front door and made a little noise, and ultimately kept someone out of the rain.

This is the reason that it feels like translation matters: that you, for one minute, get to throw open the doors of your language, wave someone new into the conversation, make space where there wasn't before.

I'm not trying to say that translation will save us all, as much as I'd like to believe that this thing that I've poured my life into is some kind of salvific key, the thing capable of brushing away the mess of borders and political units we have made of the world, the stepping stone to a harmonious future. I'm sure there are cases where some UN translator has saved a delicate negotiation through their understanding of nuances in the language, or cases when a hastily translated message arriving just in time has prevented tragedy. I know there are people who have gotten asylum because their story was made intelligible to an officer of the United States Citizenship and Immigration Services, but even so, these days when I translate, I translate towards power—towards the English-speaker used to being met on their own language, towards a government that has proven time and time again to be uncaring at best and malicious at worst.

On the worst days, my translation feels a little like a dilettante's exercise, pointless in the face of great suffering in the same way all art sometimes does. But I can't help but shake the feeling that it *matters*, both as a political reality and as a gesture—an invitation you don't have to accept but made anyways, a door flung open in an upcoming storm. Come in, come in, there are people here also, we've saved you a spot.

THE MAJORITY OF THE CASES I observe in Boston's immigration court are remote, just like the man from Georgia. A man, or very occasionally a woman, grainy on the screen, a disembodied voice coming over the loud-speakers or whispered by a woman with a headset who is in the room with us, increasingly snappy in her Spanish as the person she is translating for asks questions, the judge, on a bench higher than the rest of them, only made faintly ridiculous by his robes when he walks in and out of the room.

I spend a lot of Wednesday mornings, the only day I don't have class, in court. I do this for a month or two, and watch people rotate in and out of the same cell across the three or four prisons within the court's jurisdiction. When I go home, I read about telecourt, I pay closer attention to the ways that my phone's speakers crackle and garble words the next time I

FaceTime with a friend, I stop just short of asking my friend to conference call someone in, to play a song from their room's speakers.

One of the days I am in court, the connection to one of the jails does not work, so we move smoothly on to the next prison on the docket. Each location takes an hour or two to run through all their cases, their matching scripted questions and individual answers, and even so, the transition to the next prison is seamless. Later, I find out that this is because even if your call is late in the afternoon, you're taken from your bunk early in the morning and made to wait in a cramped holding cell with everyone else that has a hearing that day. The call never goes through on the first prison, and so everyone on that docket is reassigned a court date, a month out, and must stay in detention until then.

The video calls supposedly are meant to cut taxpayer costs and help free up space in the horrifically backlogged immigration system, but there's no evidence that this is true. I read an article that says that those who receive trial-by-video are less likely to win cases, more likely to be misunderstood or waved off. Immigration judges who meet their defendants in person often find them much more compelling, much more trustworthy in person than over a grainy video. The weird, pixelated distancing enforced by these video calls is nothing more than dehumanization, and through that a means for detention centers, for the immigration system, to extract just as much profit out of an individual as they can before deportation.

EVERY TIME SOMETHING new comes out about detention centers, everyone is surprised and outraged for a few days.

The moldy food, the rotten chicken, the fifty-five-degree temperature. The sick people crammed fifty to a cell with a capacity of twelve, or in weeks-long stretches of solitary confinement for no real reason. The chain-linked parking lots full of white canvas tents full of hundreds of children made to stay outdoors in 105-degree weather or thunderstorms. The foil blankets and the taking away of medications and the denial of medical care. The commissary and phone call costs that make it impossible for anyone to call home or to call a lawyer or even hope to get out. The converted Walmarts and Japanese internment camps brought back into use in the middle of the windblown high desert.

Each time a report, a photo, an eyewitness account, an audio recording of children crying for their parents while a Border Patrolman says, "Well we've got an orchestra here," is released, it gets shared widely. They become inescapable online.

"Don't look away."

"This is America."

And then, just as quickly as it flared up, it goes out, at least until the next report, the next set of pictures.

It is hard to write about detention in any way other than a list, hard to show the scope in any way other than tiny little bullet points that bounce off of any true understanding.

"Don't look away" is hard when not all of it can fit inside your field of vision, when, in fact, it is hidden from you on purpose. Most detention centers are located far from the places where people actually live. Journalists write about how difficult it is for them to get permission to go inside, to get photographs, proof of the things that people report when they're picked up from Greyhound stations days or weeks later. It is a hell reserved only for those that have been in it.

Detention centers are black boxes, stuck in the blank spaces of our maps, and the people in them are meant to be forgotten, meant to be disappeared. News of ten-year-old Darlyn Valle's death while in United States custody wasn't reported until eight months after she died following complications from a surgery that happened under the care of the Office of Refugee Resettlement, which cares for all unaccompanied children. The very ill are regularly released from detention if ICE believes they are close to death, so they don't need to report it in their official numbers.

Back in Tijuana, at El Chaparral, a man I had chatted with for a few days in a row joked about having a big breakfast on the day he thought his number might be called.

"Unos huevos, un chorizito, una conchita, el pan dulce, un café, yo creo que con eso sí aguanto mis dos o tres días." Then he got serious. "Solo van a ser dos o tres días, ¿no? Lo que sea lo aguanto por dos o tres días."

I didn't know how to answer him.

50

WHEN I LEFT GRAD SCHOOL, I got a full-time job in immigration advocacy, doing communications work for a nonprofit made up of mostly lawyers offering direct services and litigators and policy experts working on broader systemic changes. Occasionally, my primary task is to comb through thousand-page PDF files that are the results of Freedom of Information Act requests, peel apart individual ICE detention center inspection reports, one by one, upload them to a site, and annotate them, putting a digital yellow flag on any box labeled "Does Not Meet Standards," then highlight any other salient information that made it past the redactors.

Most days, this task feels standard, a little boring or nitpicky in a way I'm not good at—cover letters floating free from inspection reports three hundred pages later in the document, the fact that York County Prison is different from York County Detention Center, and pages from the two inspections are interspersed with each other. When you're wading through ICE paperwork, it's sometimes hard to tell if what you're dealing with is active malice or just a staggering amount of ineptitude.

Reading the reports, though, there is no question. Phones that don't work, food prepared in unsanitary conditions, hundreds of grievances, inadequate medical checks, dozens of "unsubstantiated" allegations of sexual assault, all in the same facility.

The Nakamoto Group, the main federal contractor used for Enforcement and Removal Operations (ERO) inspections, has routinely come under fire by the Department of Homeland Security's Office of Inspector General for cutting corners, overlooking braided bed sheets hanging from the ceiling of cells, glossing over negative interviews with detainees that mentioned lack of rec time, verbal and physical abuse from guards, and glitchy payment systems that swallowed up the hard-won money families sent for phone calls to family and attorneys and edible food from commissary.

The owner and founder, Jennifer Nakamoto, has the tendency to defend her practices by speaking out about her own family's history of incarceration in internment camps during World War II, and argues that her company has made life in detention better for hundreds of immigrants. I cannot imagine the lines that connect the Nakamotos, stepping into dusty barracks eighty years ago to Jennifer Nakamoto, striding through a detention center, clipboard in hand, eyes glancing off the whitewashed cinderblock, cannot imagine the dinner conversations that made these thousands of pages of reports possible from a child of survivors of a place just like this. And still they reel off my computer screen, hundreds of boxes filled out one after another, just another bureaucratic paper shuffle in the way of actual justice.

AT THE END of 2019, my boss and I drive in a rental car across hundreds of miles of cotton fields. I can see long, thin filaments of it blowing off of telephone wires, and hawks circling lazily overhead or perching on the tops of poles, watching the traffic go by. We are on our way to a detention facility deep in the rural South, in a small town a three-hour drive through cotton fields from the nearest city, to conduct our own kind of inspection.

The organizer of our trip, an attorney from a different organization, sent over the questionnaire we would be asking the men in the detention center, the observations we were asked to make. I recognized several of them from the ERO inspection reports: schedules and maps and phone numbers hung in a visible location, a law library, rec yard, food, laundry schedules. The bare, federally mandated minimums. Because I had read inspection reports, I thought I knew what I was going to walk into, thought I knew the kinds of things that lay unspoken under the surface of even a "Meets Standards" rating.

As we pull up to the prison, there is a tiny sign announcing the town line, and just behind it, an enormous sign with the name of the correctional facility, as if to make it clear that it is the only game in town.

First, there is the corporate lawyer who drove from the second-nearest big city to be here, fresh faced and clipping through the endless miles of halls in heels, and the warden, who is from the same part of Texas as I am. I recognize the kind of good old boy swagger that spits dip into empty sweet tea bottles, getting away with having the silty brown liquid where he shouldn't, and is jovial and jokey until he isn't. Every time anyone from the group asks a question that someone doesn't have memorized, they tell us to consult the handbook, tell us that's a matter of policy and the policy can be found in the handbook. When one of the lawyers clarifies that they're trying to determine the ways in which practice might differ from policy, they make it clear it's none of our business. They refuse to answer any questions about numbers or anything to do with the things that have gone wrong. In the debrief afterwards, one of the lawyers who was there with us jokes that it felt like a deposition.

Then we walk into a dorm. It's as big as two high school gyms side-by side, with ceilings as high, and no windows except in the top 3 feet, narrow and small. Metal bunkbeds with mattresses so thin they're folded in half in unoccupied cots line two walls, the other wall is shower facilities I have an unobstructed view of from the guard station which takes up the rest of the wall with the door. I keep myself glued to the guard station, unwilling to step further into the room. Men are milling around in dusty green uniforms, sitting on tables with attached chairs, looking over their shoulders at us when we walk in. One of them is mopping up a mess on the floor. Darren Aronofsky's *Noah* is playing on one of the TVs, Emma Watson gives birth in prehistoric Israel, and there's a History Channel Western on the other, two mustachioed men bouncing around in a carriage, guns held just out of frame. No one is watching either movie.

Some of the other attorneys who have done this kind of site visit before immediately walk into the room, walk up to tables, start chatting with men, asking them questions. This is their second facility inspection this week alone, they'll end up visiting half a dozen for this report. I, on the other hand, don't know where to stand, don't know where to put my eyes that doesn't feel like gawking, that doesn't feel like adding on to what is essentially already a huge, ongoing, continual invasion of privacy. I examine the bulletin boards for visitation schedules, watch the floor that the man is mopping. The men mostly ignore us—we find out later that they were told we were ICE representatives, that speaking to us would be a fast track to deportation or transfer to another detention center, even farther and more remote, that we were journalists trying to publish a story at any cost, including their safety.

We're shuffled from one section of the prison to another, down nearly identical hallways with spare and strange murals: a huge span of wall announcing that the company that owns this particular detention center cares(!), spangled with stars and an American flag. After a few stops: the medical center where surly staff barely answer questions about mandatory fourteen-day checkups or procedures if someone gets sick or whether they have translators on staff, an empty rec gym and barren, dry rec yard that gets "hotter n' hell" in the summer, according to the warden. As we're presented with dorm after dorm, as rules and regulations are rattled off, as we're told time and time again to consult the manual, the horror of a detention center becomes embodied, real. The lights come on at four in the morning and go off at eleven at night, people are served the meals that they are served at the hours they are served, are allowed outside when they are allowed outside, can communicate with their medical care providers or can't, can communicate with other people in their blocks or can't, can afford phone calls or good food or can't. Either way, it is no skin off of anyone's nose, things are just the way they are because this is how some corporation has decided is the cheapest way to house the most people for as long as they can, each day charging the government some seventy dollars and a few cents to do it per person.

The high-security dorm means that the men who live there, unlike all of the other detainees, have been arrested for crimes other than simply crossing the border, that there are priors somewhere along the line—a DUI, some shoplifting, domestic violence, or drug possession. It doesn't have to be violent to count, but the other detainees in low-security refer to them as "the bad ones." Still, high security means that these men get cells, which, while they provide more privacy than the open dorms of low-security, also means that they can be confined to these 8 x 10 rooms for hours at a time on the whims of the warden or the guards. There's also only one TV, but their day room has the dimensions of an actual room and not a warehouse for people.

The warden invites us to look into an empty cell, and I crouch down to look at the wall by the bottom bunk. It's traced over with thin ballpoint pen doodles, words scrawled onto the walls at some point in a stay that might have stretched on for weeks or months.

Dios Padre Dame Fuerza

Flores Comayagua Honduras Dios
JESÚS EL DÍA EN QUE CLAMÉ ME RESPONDISTE Y AUMEN-
TASTE LA FUERZA

All the handwriting is either just like my cousins', a kind of over-rounded hand that is seemingly taught by every nun in Mexico, or the kind of square handwriting familiar from every middle school's desk graffiti. By the bed, right next to where your head might be if you spent hour after hour laying in this bunk, someone has drawn a calendar, a few months, with days crossed out, a careful accounting of incarceration:

Hielera 27 y 28
Valverde del 29 al 11
Peatisse 11 y 12
Mississippi del 13 al

THE CRIMINAL JUSTICE SYSTEM TEACHES us that first comes jail, then comes court, then comes judgment: freedom or prison. Prison is either punishment or rehabilitation, depending on who you talk to. In any case, it constitutes a debt that must be paid—either in a changed heart or time served apart from society. The immigration system builds on this pattern: First comes detention, then comes judgment, then comes deportation, sometimes to death.

Many people are in detention because they have already been through the criminal justice system. Many of the men in the Boston courtroom had not recently traveled from the border. Instead, they were picked up by the local police for crimes like weed or DUI or small thefts, and were sentenced—sometimes asked to plead guilty to avoid the expense of a trial.

Most of them did not realize that it meant that, after they had served their time, as soon as the sally ports closed behind them and opened ahead, that ICE agents would be waiting to pick them up. Some people in the immigration system are in essence serving double time for a double punishment, and sometimes, immigration detention outlasts and outstrips the time they have served for whatever their initial offense was. In addition, those that have previously been convicted of a crime are ineligible for bond in immigration detention, meaning that they are incarcerated until the terrible backlog of cases winds its way to their own.

The arguments for pre-hearing detention are similar to those in criminal court: These people might be unstable, unsafe, and it constitutes a public threat to expose the general American population to them. An oft-cited statistic is that 90 percent of undocumented people do not go to their assigned immigration court hearing dates, instead disappearing into the general population, untraceable, slipping in among everyday Americans to steal jobs, opportunities, money.

This statistic is not accurate—the Department of Justice itself gives us a number that is closer to 40 percent of absentee immigrants, and only about 6 to 11 percent of asylum seekers are ordered deported *in absentia*— while they were absent from court to defend their cases. Court appearance rates are also much higher for those with attorneys, and not only because those who have attorneys presumably have more invested in the process (money, the time it takes to call a thousand organizations and clinics and programs to find an attorney), they are able to better navigate systems. Having an attorney means that if someone moves between their initial court date, which is maybe set for a border court, and later ones, probably in New York or Chicago or Atlanta because that's where their family is, an attorney can file a motion for a change of venue, or if an emergency comes up, the attorney is there to communicate with the court and let them know that someone is in the hospital or sick, or can at least serve as one more safeguard between a person and the grinding teeth of deportation court. Deportation court, and all the forms and motions and tiny minutiae that feel overwhelming even for someone who speaks English, sometimes feels like it has been specifically designed to make it difficult to proceed—deportation by bureaucracy.

There was maybe a point in my life in which I thought a detention center might be an excusable evil—a necessary caution, a proper safeguard for some of the reasons outlined above. I no longer believe this. Detention—which is not detention, it is incarceration, it is imprisonment, it is the strategic and systematic stripping of all freedom from an individual until their spirit breaks—is simply cruel for cruelty's sake, a reminder as soon as you get in the door that you are worth nothing, *nothing*, and that no one is coming to find you.

Asylum seekers and immigrants in detention centers are political prisoners. They are held against their wills for a political belief, manifested into action: that they deserve life, that they deserve safety, that they deserve freedom and the ability to breathe easy, and that they should be allowed to immigrate to find these things.

I have heard people ask to be deported to get out of detention centers, have met people who have tried to die to escape the confines of the prison. Formerly detained men, real tough guys, have admitted to me that they have "a little trauma," after describing seeing people go into diabetic shock from poor diet and medical neglect, after spending time in solitary confinement, after missing the births of their children, and after seeing their families lose their homes.

All the larger ICE detention centers are run by private corporations, so this warehousing of human bodies on an enormous scale serves not actually to protect "American lives" (of course not) or "American jobs," but to enrich stockholders and companies and the congresspeople whose pockets they line. There's a version of immigration in which we welcome asylum seekers, set them up with language classes and within communities that are ready to welcome them. (I wonder all the time about those yard signs in bougie neighborhoods, IMMIGRANTS WELCOME HERE, and what it would actually look like if there was affordable housing, and community centers and partner programs where families with children of similar ages could get guidance on navigating the school system, if people were more open to hearing languages that weren't English as they went through their day-to-day lives.) This is, of course, a future in which the average $133.99 a day it cost in fiscal year 2018 to keep a single immigrant in ICE detention is instead spent in the communities where immigrants live, alongside the rest of the 7.5 billion dollars in ICE's budget, and the 16.4 billion dollars in CBP's budget. A future with health-care services, schools, housing, job training. Most days, this future feels so, so far away—a goalpost receding towards the horizon in an age, in a country, where the concept of family detention centers exists.

52

IN THE COURTROOM, A NEW man's face flickers onto the screen. He's middle aged, with a buzzed head that still shows a receding hairline. The judge reads out his name, goes through the whole script. Country of origin: Mexico. Date of crossing: 1997. Married to a green card holder, U.S. citizen kids, but none of them are seriously sick or disabled to the extent of needing full-time care, thank goodness, but also not a reason to allow him to stay. The man rattles through his answers as fast as he can, but as soon as the judge asks him if he's been able to get representation, he breaks in.

"Please, sir, can I just be deported? It's too expensive for me to be in here, my wife can't pay for me to be in here any longer. I can't afford phone calls or any of it. If I get deported, I can at least go back to Mexico, get a job, send some money back here for them. My wife, my kids, they're having a really tough time, sir, and it would just be a lot easier if I got deported."

The judge frowns. "Have you looked for a lawyer? Did you call the numbers on the list?"

The list is one required by law to be hung near the phones in every immigration detention center, and it usually lists between six and ten *pro bono* legal service providers. The numbers on the list represent organizations that are horrifically overburdened; calling to see if they will take your case is like calling to see if you won the lottery. This is, in part, because getting an attorney means you are eleven times more likely to pursue relief from deportation, and twice as likely to receive it, allowing you to stay permanently in the country. Finding an attorney outside of the lists is possible—many organizations aren't represented on them, dozens of corporations allow their attorneys to take on *pro bono* immigration cases because immigration case law rarely conflicts with high-paying clients' interests—but finding these orgs and individuals requires people on the outside doing legwork, calling numbers, asking neighbors for advice, something difficult to do for people who work, for mothers with small children, for people who pay by the minute on phone calls, who get paid by the hour at jobs that don't pay enough to begin with, and often whose primary breadwinners are in detention. This is why only 37 percent of all immigrants and 14 percent of detained immigrants go to court with lawyers on their side.

"I don't have money for that, sir, I can't afford to be making calls. Sir, please, I'm just asking, it would be so much easier for me, for my family if you could just deport me, sir, as fast as possible."

The judge frowns, glances at his screen, glances at the screen where the man appears, brow furrowed in anxiety. "I'm going to reschedule this hearing for four weeks from now, to give you time to look for an attorney, okay?"

"—No, sir, please."

The judge bangs his gavel, and the man's face flickers off the screen.

WHEN PEOPLE SAY things like "Don't Look Away," they generally mean not until the problem is fixed, until children are no longer in cages, or until things are just . . . better, generally. No one has any idea what that might actually look like—borders closed to all immigration is an acceptable enough nativist dream that executive orders around it have been put into action multiple times, including during my lifetime, and been threatened many more times before that, but the concept of open borders is discarded as a fantasy, an impractical hippie pipe dream right alongside a world free of war or prisons.

The truth is that prior to the Trump administration, most people were more than comfortable looking away. Looking away as the Clinton administration made a laundry list of misdemeanors including shoplifting, some kinds of gambling, and low-level drug offenses punishable by deportation even for green card holders. Looking away as the W. Bush administration created ICE and gave them a mandate so broad and nebulous that today they surveil, monitor, and terrorize communities across the country. Looking away as the Obama administration deported more people than any other administration before or since and took a historic influx of unaccompanied minors and turned it into an excuse for "rocket dockets"; expedited deportation hearings that didn't allow sufficient time for finding representation, securing evidence, preparing anything close to a defense from deportation; and instead put children on a fast track to deportation. It wasn't until the beginning of an administration headed by a man, by men, that people found morally and aesthetically repugnant that the protests really kicked off, that people suddenly wanted a way to get involved, to fight back, to #resist. The kind of anger immigration has garnered during the Trump administration isn't the kind of anger that lasts past a change of power, past a president that's even a little more dignified or easily palatable to those with "good taste."

To wit: The Biden administration, despite campaigning on a platform of decency, of making promises to undo the immigration horrors of the Trump years, has dragged its feet on changing even one of those rules. Title 42, the policy that closed the border to immigrants during the pandemic, remained in place even past the president's declaration of the end of the crisis. Migrant Protection Protocols, aka "Return to Mexico," which sent people back into Mexico to await asylum hearings was still in place months after the Supreme Court overturned an injunction that kept it in place.

Before long, it'll be easier to forget about the people literally on the margins of the country—some program like Deferred Action for Child-hood Arrivals (DACA) will pass again, ensuring the youngest, healthiest, most charismatic and photographable, the most easily assimilable, best positioned to achieve easily understandable measures of success will have one meager line of protection from deportation. And it'll be easier to turn our backs on everyone else for being too old, too lazy, for living in a way that is not only incomprehensible but actually invisible to those with normative middle- and upper-class perspectives.

When was the last time you knew the name of one of the hundreds of people deported in a single day by the United States government? When was the last time you saw a name or a face set to be deported in the newspaper, saw them surrounded by their family? When did you last really let it sink into you what detention, what deportation really mean, and how they can shape the course of a life?

Family separation and the Zero Tolerance policy were bad in a loud and obvious way—audio clips of children crying, the children who didn't recognize parents after months of separation—but detention and deportation, ICE raids and check ins are quieter, more pernicious means to the same ends. Children in cages are obviously bad, these same children's parents in cages while the children are disappeared into the foster care system, adopted into white families, and stripped of their culture—these things are also bad, if more easily ignored.

I don't want to exempt myself. Before the Trump administration, I had cared about immigration, in the same kind of abstract way you care about the environment when you recycle or switch off a light when you leave the room—it was a little out of being conscientious, a little out of self-interest. And once the Trump administration began, it took the children of Valeria Luiselli's *Tell Me How It Ends,* who I imagined as big-eyed, silent versions of my younger cousins, it took the specter of roving gangs of ICE agents pulling my little sibling off the streets and disappearing them into a detention center somewhere that got me into the streets, that got me into that church basement as an interpreter for the first time.

It took deep involvement in the movement, took listening and interviewing people whose lives had been directly touched, it took and continues to take so much goddamn work to understand the full scope of the problem, to continue to look it in its ugly face, time and time again.

Let me give you an example that is also a confession: When I walked into the correctional center and saw ICE detainees dressed in prison scrubs, I knew in my head that they were innocent by every definition of the word. These were men whose only offense had been asking for a right they legally had and, beyond that, had crossed a border in search of a better life, just like every mythical first-generation forefather of every huge Italian-Irish-German family that has been here since the 1800s. Even so, something about a room of men who were obviously prisoners, men who were guarded and monitored and counted and made to stand in lines and wear identical clothes, a room of Black and brown men who were treated like they were threats, meant that somewhere in my mind, I believed these men had to have done something to deserve this treatment, that they were in some way criminal, or unsafe, or threatening. Walking into a dorm and seeing how people were made to live, I wasn't just ashamed, but a little afraid. I mention this not to suggest that it is in any way true, or to excuse this line of thinking, or rhetoric based on it, but to show how deeply this thinking is entrenched, how far we have to come. I believe wholeheartedly in a post-carceral future, I have interviewed hundreds of people caught up in this system and spend many of my days thinking about the ways that the system is unjust and designed to criminalize and harm those who have committed no crimes, and even so, this was my gut reaction: If they're in jail, they *must* have done something bad. It took an active intervention, a conscious thought that cut into the low background murmur of the perceptions I've been educated into and silenced it, to be able to take in the full injustice of a detention center: None of these men did anything wrong, and further: Nothing they could have done would have made them deserve to be deprived of their freedom in this way for any length of time.

It is so much easier to let that murmur drone on, much easier to allow myself to continue to believe that the things I have been taught about the world are true—that people who are in jail belong there, that prison is a kind of debt you have to pay for your wrongdoings, that there is some kind of justice at work in the world—than to cut off that voice and replace it with a constant thrumming awareness that all of the systems I was raised to believe were just, simply because they spared my family, are actually horrifically, tragically broken across a far wider field than I had originally believed.

It continually surprises me all the ways in which immigration is connected to every other problem of the modern world: droughts or agritech forcing farmers to abandon the fields that have fed their families and communities for generations; the sprawling prison system designed to replicate systems of Black enslavement and which readily provided the infrastructure and profit system to reap the rewards of incarcerating migrants; the homophobia, transphobia, misogyny and anti-Blackness that put specific people at risk because of unalterable characteristics. It took and continues to take peeling myself away from narratives that are easily prepackaged, nearly second nature to remind myself that borders are a modern invention, that everyone deserves a safe place to live, that, for all I've invested into thinking about current legal apparatuses for immigration, like asylum, that people have the right to migrate and move for reasons beyond political persecution, that no one deserves or should be in detention.

Thinking about immigration, daydreaming about how to pick apart the Gordian knot we've gotten ourselves into makes it quickly apparent that all of these problems are deeply interconnected, that there is no solving one thing without entirely dismantling the oppressive systems of the world. It's all held together by the same kind of logic that takes only a small amount of questioning before it falls apart, the kind of reasoning that is in place because it always has been in place.

Some activists speak of "the right to remain"—the right not just to migrate, but to ensure that home is a place that is safe to remain. This means ensuring that countries devastated by colonialism and the economic reach of the global north have the conditions they need to be livable. Drinkable water, clean air, safe streets, protections for the most vulnerable. Of course, these are also conditions that many lack, regardless of where they live.

I think what I am saying is there is no easy way out. There is no way to sweep under the rug a problem that needs to be fixed in the same way it was built up: law by law, misconception by misconception—life by life.

53

IN MEXICO, THERE WAS ONCE a man who was known as the guardian of the butterflies. He would appear in videos he tweeted out, wrapped in a shimmering, frenetic haze of butterflies. As he spoke about the need for conservation, the need to save Mexico's wild forests, a few butterflies rested quietly on his body as he moved his loggers' hands slowly and deliberately.

Homero Gómez González spent his life arguing that attention to conservation would not impoverish his community but strengthen it, that unlike logging, preserving the butterflies would not slowly siphon away the few resources available to locals. Homero, named after a storyteller and descended from a logging family, told a story of a different kind of Michoacán—one full of wonder and beauty, one full of jobs that would be easier on the body, a place where people would come to find something rather than try to leave for the promise of bigger cities or opportunities across the border. In service of his dream, he took on political positions, vocally opposed lumber companies trying to make a profit from the land and politicians trying to make a profit from the lumber companies, fought hard for his vision of a different way of life for his community.

In the first month of 2020, Homero Gómez González was found face down at the bottom of an irrigation pond. His body showed signs of blunt force trauma, of asphyxiation, and two weeks later, one of the guides he employed at his sanctuary was also found dead.

While the exact details behind their murders remains a mystery, there isn't that much of a question as to what happened, or whose interests were served by the death of a man who had dedicated his life to protecting lives that seemed small and fragile and without thought, but were actually resilient and full of mystery. He joins people like Berta Cáceres, a Lenca woman from Honduras murdered because of her opposition to a dam across a sacred river, the five Garifuna men disappeared from their community by armed men after they fought to ensure their community's right to its land, and the protesters at Standing Rock, pressure hosed by the United States federal government, and countless other Indigenous land and water protectors who have given their lives, their health, their freedom to making their homes habitable, sacred, beautiful, before being bulldozed over by the relentless wheels of capitalism.

OUR TOUR OF the detention center finishes in the visitation room, where a sign on the wall tells us that photos are five dollars apiece, payable at the commissary, and a huge mural of Mickey, Minnie, Donald, and Daisy with little fairytale houses on the Mississippi spans the wall opposite, likely to make the room less austere for the county inmates' visiting children. While the prison holds overflow inmates from the prison systems of Puerto Rico, Wyoming and a handful of other states, along with those in the custody of the federal marshals and ICE, no one but the men in county lockup really have visitors all that often, given how remote the jail is.

The other volunteers and I eat a quick lunch that we assembled in the hotel lobby that morning: thin, cold cut sandwiches and granola bars and a large bag of sweet BBQ chips the guards had opened and made us pour into a plastic grocery bag for some reason.

When we finish our food (or finish eating, since we had packed enough trail mix and beef jerky for a trip to the arctic rather than a daylong trip to a detention center), one of the organizers hands out questionnaires, reminds us of the protocols and our goals in interviewing, and before we're even done, men are led in in groups, according to their cell blocks. Since I am one of the few Spanish speakers present, I mostly interview men who only speak Spanish. Since this place is really only a temporary processing center, most of the men I interview have been sent over almost directly from the border processing centers, and only stay for a week or two before being shipped to another neighboring state to await either deportation or their court date. ICE field offices and immigration courts in this part of the country are brutal. The New Orleans field office under the Trump administration is notorious for not giving parole—in 2018, 98 percent of cases were denied. This rate of denial means that the men who are lucky enough to receive asylum court dates may be in detention for years before it rolls around, only to face some of the harshest immigration judges in the country. Immigration judges associated with the New Orleans field office only grant between 12 and 19 percent of asylum cases they hear, in comparison to the national average of 33 percent. I interviewed several men that day, one after the other, following the same rote form, so the edges of one interview bleed into the next in my memory.

"Are you fighting your immigration case? How long has it been? What is the status of your case?"

"What impact has detention had on your family?"

"Do you believe the facility is overcrowded?"

"How is the food? Has anyone ever gotten sick from the food? Are there any bugs/rats in the food? Is the food spoiled?"

"Have you ever experienced verbal abuse from corrections officers?"

Sixteen pages of questions and one by one, men across the table from me answering them, some of them joking that they were just glad to be alive, but wished they got pizza instead of the bland food served by the detention center, others looked like they were still chased by lack of sleep, wary of the other detainees they were surrounded by. All of them indignant at being shackled on the long bus ride here from the border, all of them knowing, declaring that they weren't criminals, so why were they being treated like one?

One interview, though, stood out from the rest, the conversation brightly defined around the edges. He was a small man: His prison-issue denim jacket, a few sizes too big for his wiry frame, was wrapped around him protectively, shoulders hunched down. I almost want to remember him as wearing a cowboy hat with a brim he would try to use to shield himself from my gaze, but obviously that wasn't possible in the detention center—he was bareheaded, like everyone else, with close cut salt-and-pepper hair, and big ears. If I'm being honest, he reminded me of my grandfather—quiet and unassuming, but fiercely funny and irreverent under his breath.

As we began the interview, he told me he didn't speak Spanish, or not that well—his mother tongue was an Indigenous language, a branch of Mayan spoken by a few hundred thousand people who mostly live in the isthmus that makes up the meeting point of Mexico and Central America, people in small towns tucked in the mountains and rainforests, little communities that had held on to their own language even as Spanish had crept in around the edges, eventually flooding over the country. I had never heard of the language, couldn't understand his heavy-grained voice very well, and so after my repeated questions on how to write it or what it was called, he spelled it out with one blunt finger on the table, clearly frustrated with me.

I ran through the questionnaire, pausing to make sure he understood questions—mimed washing my hands or brushing my teeth when I asked about access to hygiene products, explained bond hearings and Credible Fear Interviews in simple words as well as I could without ever having been in one. Yes to the CFI, but in Spanish and he hadn't really understood or been able to explain himself; no to the bond hearing. No one had had a bond hearing. He answered my questions in the same way: He had been a farmer back in his home country—he mimed tilling a field. He was a little cold most of the time, he said, shivering and clutching his jacket around his shoulders and drawing them up around his ears. There were worms in the beans, he said, grinning at me. At first I thought it was a joke until I realized he was looking me in the eyes, the first time in the interview.

Going through the list of questions about medical care, I made a joke in the last few interviews and said the questionnaire—developed for immigration centers that also held women—asked if he was pregnant. I mimed a rounded belly with my hands, and he looked up at me, surprised: "Me? No!" When he saw my grin, laughed with me.

"Usted cree que hay demasiada gente aquí en la cárcel?" I asked.

"Sí, sí," he nodded emphatically.

By objective standards, it wasn't. There were empty cots in each dorm, enough seating for everyone, the wardens had told us the population had been some two hundred people more just a few months ago.

"¿Por qué cree eso?" I asked.

"Mucho ruido," he said, his hands exploding like fireworks next to his ears, moving closer and closer. "Todo el día, y en la noche, ruido ruido ruido ruido."

I thought about the farm that he came from, warm earth and starry skies, the kind of silence, or the kind of ambient noise that you might hear as you worked the earth and as you closed your eyes at the end of the day, tired to your bones, the kinds of stars you might see up in the mountains or in a valley miles and miles away from everything. And seeping into that,

I could hear the sounds of the prison: industrial fans working day and night to pump cold air in, the heavy sounds of doors opening and closing, far away, the humming whine of fluorescent lights, the ambient sounds of one hundred men trying to get through another day in a federal detention center, conversations and prayers and rustling and crying, none of them in his language. And I saw his hands moving around his head, closer and closer as the sounds worked their way in.

54

STRETCHING ACROSS TWO LANGUAGES DOESN'T make it any better or any easier to say the thing you mean, to build up a whole, to arrive at just the right thing to say. I know this for a fact, and I know it from experience.

I have spent a lot of time thinking about finding a pure place to stand. This place, mythological and imaginary, can only exist when I've explained myself so utterly well that there's no more hidden biases, no motivating idea that hasn't been dragged out into the light and unpacked to show all its linty, photophobic insides. I want this place to exist because I want to say something unimpeachably true, something that can't be argued against or given a caveat I haven't spelled out myself. This is why I exist in this book, why instead of a journalism account you have me, leading you through the pages: because making my fingerprints obvious seems more honest than trying to hide them, because a pure place to stand, if it exists, is my own.

Cicero, the ancient Roman orator, and author of some of the first texts of translation theory, saw translators as invading generals, setting out to capture new lands for an army—a language advancing across a bloody field. St. Jerome, the first translator of the entire Bible into Latin, describes the act of translation similarly: full of horses and swords and prisoners of war, brought back in glory. Both were working in Latin, language of empire and conquest, language of inscriptions that have been found from Britain to North Africa to Turkey, carried there by war and violence.

English, too, can be found around the world, and for similar reasons, although today those reasons are cloaked in lessons for schoolchildren about "competition in a world economy." That makes this language as weighty, as strange and as laden as Latin, as implicated in webs of power and oppression. No matter how much I explain myself, how much shame or justification or history I bring out for examination, I still have to do it in a language, and when I do it in English, I do it in a language that is colonial, that circumscribes what I recognize as kin through its objectification of the natural world, that is the lingua franca of global systems of capital, whose speakers expect to be met and accommodated within this language. A language forced onto some of its speakers through violence and kidnapping and coercion, and onto others through sheer economic necessity. The language itself is contaminated by its dirty histories.

Even if I were to write this book in Spanish, some of that bloodshed would still be inevitable. It, too, is a historical language of dominion and colonization. Whenever any word or neologism was in doubt, my dad would haul out a volume of his Diccionario de la Real Academia Española and look up "sirope" or "parquear" or "troca," words we brought home sometimes and he'd see as possible contaminations of a pure language. He'd look them up, his index finger running down the pages and rows of words approved by committee in a country that had claimed the one he was born in as an extension of itself, full of resources. Castilian Spanish came to Latin America on Columbus' and Hernán Cortés' ships, with the soldiers fresh off the Reconquista of Spain and with the priests setting up missions that hid unpaid labor under the guise of evangelization.

But maybe purity of position, of anything, really, is how we got into this whole mess in the first place. The desire for a pure homeland, for a pure language, for a single people and language stretching across the globe seems as good a place as any to pinpoint the start of our problems.

Maybe there is something to be said instead, for making myself a porous body. Something to be said for allowing myself to be colonized by a specific language—not Spanish or English, but *his* Spanish or *her* English—by letting someone else's language filter into me like mushroom spores and then explode out of me to float in the breeze.

THERE'S A KIND of accepted wisdom that exists in both advocacy and translation that you're not supposed to get too involved, emotionally. You're supposed to hold yourself at arms' distance, to do objective good for the text, for the person in front of you, without letting something so messy or strange as your emotions get in the way.

Lately, translators have begun arguing for their right to fall in love with a text, to dive into it. I love the idea, love the acknowledgment that for any project as big and as intimate as a translation, our messy human feelings are going to get in the way, are going to be a part of the conversation. This, of course, gets more complicated in the realm of translating within advocacy and activism.

It feels inappropriate to claim I've "fallen in love" with any of the people I've interpreted for—a little too much like a single white, blonde person surrounded by Black children, claiming that her mission trip in Africa, like, totally changed her life. Being *reminded* of love, however, also feels like a different kind of rhetorical issue, a way of cheapening the work or making my support of any one-person contingent on my own selfish whims. There's this idea that because the way someone speaks Spanish reminds me of my mother, that because a young man across the table from me pushes up his glasses in the exact same way as my brother does, that my desire to help them, to see them safe is not so pure, not so altruistic—that by allowing love, or some kind of messy self-identification into the mix, I'm putting myself where I don't belong, or confusing the issue, or limiting the help I give in some critical way.

As much as it is nearly unimaginable for my actual sibling, my actual mother, my sister, my father to have to flee across borders with very few resources, for members of my family to be imprisoned or ill or relying on the help of strangers—in part because of the money and the networks of support my family has, and in part because all of these things are unimaginable for the people you love until they're not, because your mind protects you from it—as much as all these things are nearly unimaginable, there are few people I sit across from who don't bring my family to mind in some way. And with that reminder comes a whole host of associations, imaginations, possibilities, not just for my family but for the people in front of me. Their first Christmas in the States, in a dark and kind of shitty apartment like my parents' student housing, but still some kind of festive lights, everyone's face aglow with relief and the promise of a new year. That same Christmas table a few years down the line, a generation in, sounding that much more like my family's now—a mix of languages and registers and voices, a river returning to its wellspring. The gradual way a family roots down into a new place, shakes out branches, becomes part of a new kind of community, finds itself capable of a new way of growing in new soil.

I translate and I interview people and I care about immigration because for my whole life I've spoken two languages as if they were secret from one another, as if my family was an island in a sea of monolingualism, and when I was able to fill out a form for someone for the first time, or interview someone about the conditions in which patriotism kept them, it was a way of throwing open the door into the warm, safe world of my relationships held in Spanish, of waving them in, even if for a moment, of providing a shelter from the storm. Spanish is the language of my mother and grandmother, of long sobremesas, and half of my dad's terrible jokes; it's the language in which my family loves one another. English is the language of school, and learning, and most of my friends; it's the language I write in, the language and context of my politics and my ideas. When I translate for someone, I make both intelligible to myself: This is the way that belonging might be broader than a fistful of people, this is the way a country or a family might expand its welcome beyond its borders, this is the way that all my fight and all my love might coexist in one strange project.

Translation and immigration advocacy—because for me, one does not exist without the other—are a way of allowing me to read myself in a way that is new and strange, to put myself in a context where suddenly and somehow the fragmentation of growing up in two languages has had a purpose and a beauty beyond itself all along. Most importantly, the braided work of the two allows me to clear out a space, to sweep a path, even though it might be ever so narrow, for someone else to make the same realizations, to carry the same steps that I've taken, to take the same realizations that I have even further and in doing so to figure out a new way to allow the language of home and the language of the world to be in conversation with each other, for the walls between the two to come down.

BUT MAYBE THIS is all optimistic, privilege-blinded drivel. By helping families come into the United States, the only things I'm guaranteeing are their need to learn another language, not because of the richness or textures that bilingualism brings, but because it's nearly impossible to survive in a capitalist America without it.

Outcomes like the one my family had—three kids, all college graduates, all employed in fashionably low-paying industries (nonprofits, sciences, publishing), all flying across the country just to share a holiday meal—are improbable if not downright impossible without the kind of financial resources my family has. America may be safer in some ways—a lower murder rate, less tolerance of organized crime, a more effective police force for some but not all Americans—but in many others, it allows the violence of poverty and capitalism to go unchecked. The first time someone in the family gets sick enough to require a trip to the doctor, with or without insurance, and they get an unimaginable, dizzyingly high bill. When predatory landlords or utility companies or sleazy back-alley immigration attorneys swindle them out of hard-earned cash and there is no one they can go to for help. When they realize the cost of even a single semester of college, even with scholarships, and they multiply that by all four or eight semesters, subtract the aid they might have gotten if they had their papers and guess at the money they might be able to earn after leaving, divide that by the number of mouths to feed, calculate the kind of resources that are needed right away against taking a loss for the vaguest possibility for future growth.

And that's just the financial side of things, the realities that will hit even if you're a straight white cisgendered immigrant from a country that's considered "desirable" as a point of origin. Trans people, queer people, Black immigrants, immigrants from the global south—all of them come to America because it's been shown to them as a beacon, a city on a hill where a better life is possible. Instead, trans women, especially those of color, continue to be subject to incredibly high rates of violence and assault. Black people are regularly murdered by police officers and civilians who go unprosecuted. Levels of trust in police departments are low and murders frequently go unsolved in communities of color. Up until recently, it was legal in many states to discriminate and fire employees for being gay or trans, and some states are doing everything they can to bring back the criminalization of queerness. Coming to the United States for freedom and safety is a promise that goes so largely unfilled for so many families, and yet is still better than what many of them left behind. However, before they can even settle into new communities and lives, the government poses its own kind of test, much more difficult than the Credible Fear Interview—what is harder, what you left behind, or what we will do to you here?—before letting you in.

The kind of trauma that the government has enacted on generations of families crossing the border to escape violence is the kind of trauma that becomes encoded in your genes, that changes the trajectory of family trees. A two-year-old who was separated from his mother by the United States government will have the emotional memory of that fact long after he has forgotten the historical truth of it. Even if the kind of enforcement that ends in separated families stopped tomorrow, even if we welcomed those stranded across the border waiting and then waiting again for their number to be called into communities, held acclimatization programs, ushered new immigrants into a robust net of social support and into a society that has rid itself of racial and class inequalities that actively shorten people's lifespans, there is damage that has been done already that will echo for generations.

I have read the affidavits from parents and children separated at the border: eight-year-olds who can't sleep through the night, four-year-olds who have regressed from the thousand and one insistent questions about the world into endless frightened silence, mothers who thought they would be forced onto a plane while their children were adopted by shining blonde families.

In Tijuana, I met a woman who was eight-and-a-half months pregnant who had stopped feeling her baby move in the last few days, after she had a high fever. No hospitals in Mexico would admit her because she was Black, because she didn't speak Spanish, and when someone offered to intercede on her behalf with Grupos Beta, she shook her head, told the French speaker in the group that she heard that in the detention centers, they would cut your baby out of you and kill it. I opened my mouth to say it was a myth, that it couldn't be true, and she would be safe, and I closed it because I realized I had no way to prove that.

We cannot take the night terrors away from the eight-year-old, cannot return trust in the world to the four-year-old, cannot, in any real way, prove to these mothers that we will never try to take their children again, have no moral standing for outrage when it is suggested that we are performing medical monstrosities on innocent people who arrive on our border, looking for a better life.

Even now, having seen it, I can't finish fitting it in my head that this exists, that there's a giant engine just dedicated to the regular and steady dehumanization of people, for no other reason than the sheer authoritarian, bureaucratic pleasure of it. This strangeness is largely the product of who I am and where I was raised—for so many others, the experience of dehumanization by organizations and institutions is hardly noteworthy, but the scale here felt both brand new and breathtaking to me.

I was at a talk with Valeria Luiselli, one of the first writers to look squarely at the way the United States government was treating the youngest and most vulnerable of those who came here asking for help. The talk was in Boston, and her interlocutor, a mustached white man from the local public radio station, asked her what she could tell us, so far from the border and presumably removed from its problems, about the conditions there, asked her to make it real for this audience of well-educated Bostonians who presumably had never beheld such barbarity and lawlessness as the Sonoran Desert. She held up her hands to the auditorium, to the space around us, and reminded us that ICE had jurisdiction 100 miles from any border, including our coastlines. ICE agents could burst into the room right now, if they wanted, demand identification, round us up. She pointed out that there was an immigration detention center probably no further than 30 miles from where we sat. Suffolk County House of Corrections, just over 3 miles away, was then in the midst of a hunger strike by detainees asking for an end to abuse and inhumane conditions.

She didn't mean it as a dig against her interviewer, or against anyone in the audience, but it was true. Even in San Diego, the wide streets and sprawling suburban malls where I slept every night felt miles away from the gates of San Ysidro, and further still from Tijuana.

Maintaining object permanence for systems of cruelty is difficult and overwhelming. That week in Tijuana, I met one week's worth of people who were going across, but people go across every day, day after day, and will continue to do so, and they will continue to get numbers, to get in vans, to get chewed up and spit out at some dismal Greyhound station on some midnight in January or February or June. It is happening now, it will be happening tomorrow, and the day after that.

THIS IS WHAT I mean by "el azote"—you can be wandering along, doing all the good you can with all the strength you can, thinking you understand the problem, when all of a sudden you slam into a new facet of this reality, a new way in which your ability to make the material conditions of even one person's life better are limited and hampered. You forgot to open your little alitas, or worse still, your alitas are powerless in the face of a 20-foot steel wall.

Even though I find so much of the "Don't Look Away" discourse so empty and devoid of actual meaning or action or solutions, there's something there, a hard little kernel of reality or difficulty that you might grab hold of and turn into something newer and more beautiful.

French mystic and theologian Simone Weil wrote an essay that moves nimbly from a teacher's order in front of a classroom ("Pay attention!") to prayer to the bedsides of the ill and aggrieved. Her argument hinges around attention. She alchemizes it from the kind of attention a schoolchild turns to a tricky Latin translation or a mathematical proof—unfocused, somewhat unrewarding, aware of one's own shortfalls and failings—into the kind of attention that is turned towards God in prayer, and towards the suffering other. This attention becomes a kind of negative capability that leaves you open to the encounter, but not straining towards it or pulling away.

I think about this essay all the time because sometimes it feels like the only way to survive in a world that is full of problems so large and entrenched that any individual human feels tiny and insignificant and unable to leave the narrow path etched out for them. The attention Weil asks for in this essay sometimes feels like the only way to wake up each morning and put my shoulder to dismantling a Sisyphean boulder of systematic, widespread brutality. So much of the narrative around justice work is that of the hero—your Erin Brockovichs, your Martin Luther Kings, your Dolores Huertas and Cesar Chavezes righting wrongs and upending systems as they go. In reality, and as I think all these people might be able to tell me, the work of justice is slow and painstaking and full of spreadsheets and phone calls and Post-its, full of, like so much else in life, little bullshit administrative tasks that at the end of the day feel not so much liberatory as oppressive. Yes, to me, personally, but also sometimes it feels like the thing we are most fighting for is a world without so much bureaucracy—a world where you might say "I need help" and then receive that help, without having to index and cross-index three separate forms with fourteen affidavits of proof, a world where massive index funds and ten thousand ways to hide money and all their accompanying paperwork just . . . don't exist.

Every morning I wake up and I log onto my computer for work, and I copy-paste a dozen or so links on how utterly broken and destructive our immigration system is into an email and send it to a hundred people that are extremely busy helping one person through this system at a time, and I write a little press release about an unjust policy, or I format something on the website, or scroll through thousands of pages of FOIA requested detention center inspection reports to make them legible for journalists, or do any of the other ten thousand tasks that are a part of modern office work. The whole time, I am paying attention to detail, and toggling over links to look at the HTML behind the website to ensure the formatting isn't weird or the link won't break, and CTRL+I and CTRL+U-ing things to ensure that they're legible and look nice, and getting frustrated when I accidentally erase my own work or slightly resentful of having emails in my inbox, or whatever. And the whole time any or all of this is going on, there's this knowledge of all of the injustice in the world, which I have very carefully copy-and-pasted into an email earlier that day just screaming and howling on the other side of the screen, and I, sitting there, at a desk in Chicago, can do absolutely nothing about it except what I am doing, which is to say, making note of it, and moving around paperwork about it that needs to be moved. But this is, of course, where Weil helps.

In the essay, Weil speaks of this kind of attention as an experimental certainty. If you continue to pay attention, and are certain that this attention can change things, change will happen. You'll get better at math, or after ten thousand hours of good faith prayer that results in silence, you'll hear the whisper of the divine, or maybe, just maybe, by showing up and paying attention and doing your job every day, no matter how rote or how insignificant-feeling, your shoulder, next to everyone else's on the millstone, will eventually bend the arc of history really, truly, decisively towards justice.

Of course, attention alone is not enough, not really—the documents still need to be cut and pasted, rallies still need to be attended, the work still needs to be done, but when you've got an eye on the rest of it, all the little administrative tasks can feel like a byproduct of that attention, the least you could do for the people on the other side of the screen, for the work that you're helping along, however minutely.

So, no, don't look away, mark the injustices, bear witness to the detention centers and the courtrooms and the articles and cover-ups and the damage done, to the horrible expediency of the court system while it also slowly grinds its horrific gears—but that attention must be reinforced, undergirded, held aloft by busy hands and continued work, even when that work is hard or boring or seemingly pointless.

And who knows what good you're doing along the way, almost by accident? Sitting in court can feel like this. In Boston, I worked with a network of faith leaders and lay volunteers to show up and witness for people who had requested it. Faith leaders are among the only people who can go into detention centers without having a specific detainee to visit, so when they go in, they take down the names and numbers of those who would like accompaniment and witnesses for their day in court, and the rest of us get a weekly email where we sign up for shifts, or to take notes on a particular case.

But because of the way cases click along, one after another, like beads on a string, and are only scheduled in large blocks of time, we end up listening to far more cases than have asked for our presence. We are usually the only support in a courtroom—occasionally family will be able to make it, but because ICE relies on a system of transferring detainees to meet quotas at privately-owned detention centers around the country, the odds of being detained near your support system are low. Everyone else is either another detainee, or an attorney, and as the cases go by, the courtroom gets emptier and emptier, people drifting out into the hall.

Court is often deeply boring as an observer—the same script, repeated case after case, the mix of highly stylized legal language and the deadpan, rote recitation given to it by the judge; the uncomfortable, stiff-backed pews reminiscent of church; the early morning sunlight streaming into the room;

the way that most hearings only really serve to push back a date, or to set another a month or two in the future. You have to be paying close attention to catch any kind of humanity or story in the details. Someone who is twenty years old, but has been here since 1999, someone just asking for the judge to actually explain the forms to him while the judge hustles him along, repeating the same instruction to just fill it out, until he can switch the system over to the next case, a man already detained for over a year getting his date pushed back another three months, and the helpless way he agrees to it because there really isn't anything he can do.

It's important to note that most of the men passing through the court, unlike the people I encountered at the border, or in a church basement, or even in the detention center, are people who have been in the United States for some time. It's hard to get statistics on undocumented populations, for obvious reasons, but many of the people in court are living out the worst nightmare of five, ten, thirty years in the country—thirty years spent setting down roots and establishing a life and networks and communities, five years of kids in school, ten years at a job or three with their own small business after ten years learning the trade. Years in which children were born (with U.S. citizenship), in which friends were made, partners were met in business and in love and in life. This is not to say that those at the border have any less to lose—a life without a certain kind of fear, a place in which to start over—but that for these people in the courtroom today the loss is differently textured.

These are not stories that are often covered in the news or, when they are, their most heart-wrenching versions are presented in local papers—the mother deported away from adult children and infant grandchildren, the son trying to be there for his sick father only to be caught up in ICE detention. Those featured are often "model" immigrants—no criminal history, put on ICE's radar by a traffic stop or happenstance. Not everyone at court, most people at court, in fact, don't fit this model. They're regular people—guys in their mid-twenties working whatever kind of job they could get, an older sister who babysat siblings and cousins, day laborers and health-care workers and restaurant workers and couriers and delivery boys and people who were out of a job just then. I met a man once who had been in the United States for fifty-odd years, so long that his English was colored with the sounds of the Louisiana bayous. He had, by his own account, lived a colorful life, but here, at the end of it, after decades working in American industries for low wages, after a lifetime paying into social supports like Medicare and Social Security, after a lifetime of building community and capital and an accent as if he had sprung fully formed from the heart of New Orleans, we were preparing to toss him out to a country he hadn't been to in half a century.

Being an American is not a privilege you get to earn, unless you do—I was born here, and no amount of shoplifting or speeding or even murder can get me deported, can bar me from the place I've lived my entire life, but for any one of these people, even the smallest mistake, or no mistake at all, is enough to get them removed from the country, barred from returning for years.

ONE OF THE mornings in court, a judge asks an attorney what a reasonable but not onerous bail would be, given the family's income levels. "I want Mr. Rodriguez to be able to pay bail, but I want it to be an amount that is nevertheless significant to the family, to serve bail's function and compel the client to return for later court dates," she explains.

The attorney nods and gives a number on the low end of the range, and the judge agrees to it, bangs her gavel. Bail is set.

Another one of the volunteers leans over to whisper in my ear: "This judge is usually pretty tough, she's a Trump appointee. I think she only gave reasonable bail because we're here, you know?"

I don't know that I agree with her at first—this client has an attorney, a family lined up against one of the walls, a sister that slaps the back and shakes hands with the young lawyer after bail is set—but when the judge does it again for someone later in the day, someone without attorney or family, and looks over at us, it seems suddenly possible that my presence for a long, slow day in court might have actually made a difference.

I can't get over how utterly stupid it is, to have such a tremendous difference made in someone's life based on whether or not I am watching, that something as utterly banal as immigration court can absolutely alter the course of someone's life, that a stupid webcam malfunction could mean the difference between getting out next week and getting out next month, the difference between eating enough of ICE's food that you get pre-diabetes or not having to worry about that, to have this stupid, stupid system be the thing that removes all agency from people, that keeps them trapped, both literally and otherwise, in cycles of fear and anger and exhaustion.

55

WHEN YOU ARE TRANSLATING, YOU are constrained by what you can
see on the page—if you miss the way that two words flow sibilantly into
one another, or don't know the meaning of an aphorism or maxim, then
they don't turn up in what you create. A sentence carefully crafted for the
way it sounds read aloud falls flat, the sky literally begins to rain cats and
dogs. This kind of mistake is invisible to most readers who will never read
both the original and the translation, who probably don't know enough of
the source language to clock a sloppily translated axiom, but this is also the
kind of mistake that might keep a translator up at night—what injustice
did you do to the original, what nuances in the text does your audience have
no hope of grasping because they flew over your ignorant head entirely?

The same thing happens with writing, which is, after all, translating the real world into language. I can't write something I haven't seen, can't transmit the entirety of reality to you on the page because I can't see it all. This kind of misreading or blindness also keeps me up at night—am I doing the stories I tell justice? Am I missing content and context that then you will also miss? As with the men in prison, it is so easy to lean on simple stories to avoid doing the work and making sure I am saying what I want to say, getting across the important thing. The stories we tell ourselves, the stories we receive, culturally, also work as blinders, giving us quick mental shortcuts to a misconception or letting us take the way out of the story that makes us feel the least bad. We prefer to gloss over complexity in preference of a simple story, easy to tell, and understand, and respond to. They're the equivalent of a word-for-word translation, getting the skeletal facts down but otherwise oddly constructed and ungainly, easily misunderstood. They fall apart under any kind of closer scrutiny.

So much of our current immigration system—the stories in the media, the laws that are written, are meant to be like these word-for-word translations. They supply us with the easy stories, the "bad hombres" or the "children in cages" and through them legions of other stories are erased, thousands of other contexts and individual lives papered over or omitted from the record in favor of the easy story, the digestible one. It is easy to be moved to emotion and action by these stories—to anger, to grief or fear, to protest—but it is just as important to keep paying attention even as the big stories run out, even as the narrative unspools into a gray area. The very existence of the immigration laws we have today are proof of this.

Our immigration laws, specifically, were created to respond to a single story, and for narratives outside of that, the aid we can offer is hamstrung by the laws we are governed by. Our asylum laws are based on ideas about religious and ethnic persecution that began during the Holocaust, and are narrowly crafted to prevent another state-organized genocide, and only that. During the Second World War, national immigration quotas—based themselves on a story about other nations overrunning the United States with floods of immigrants—kept the MS *St. Louis*, full of German Jewish refugees who couldn't claim a formal kind of immigration assistance, floating off the coast of the United States, so close they could hear the music from Miami nightclubs. The *St. Louis* eventually turned around and docked again in Europe, resulting in the deaths of about a quarter of its passengers in German prison camps. In response to great horror, we have expanded our story once, and need to expand it again today.

Our immigration laws, and the story that has inspired them since the 1950s, keep us from helping the man from Haiti who is legitimately afraid of returning home because of rising sea levels and a lack of local infrastructure. The United Nations predicted that by 2050, between 25 million and a billion people worldwide will be climate refugees, displaced by droughts, floods, fires, and rising seas. Our immigration laws force us to treat the man with a possession charge who has been in the United States for all but the first year of his life differently than the man with a possession charge who was born here. Both get a few months or a year in prison, but at the end of that time, we tell one of them he has "paid his debt to society" and can go home while the other is incarcerated for even longer, separated from his family and community and sent to a strange country he barely knows. Today's immigration laws ask us to pretend that border cities are safe places for people to wait to enter the country even as the State Department issues travel advisories warning U.S. Citizens to stay away, ask us to ignore violence against people unless it happens under deeply specific circumstances, ask us to formulaically and easily refuse to help those who, were we to actually listen, we would extend ourselves for.

I know, even as I'm writing this, that there are those for whom any one of the stories I've told throughout this book are accounts of people attempting to use sob stories to subvert systems set in place to protect "ordinary Americans," who see immigration not as something fundamentally broken but as a last safeguard against the hordes of Spanish speakers willing to take badly paying jobs out of the hands of their children. I don't know what to do with that kind of interpretation of people's lives, but I want to acknowledge that it's out there, that people who believe these things are in charge of our nations' immigration policies, that again, we come up against a hard wall if we believe that mere listening is enough to change hearts and minds.

You make a personal politics the same way you translate a text, the same way you write a book: You look at the world around you, and there are things that you notice and there are things that you don't. If you're lucky, you read the words of other people who have looked out on the world before you, who have caught other things you didn't, you change your mind, change your actions, start seeing things you had been blind to before. There are many things that, because of the family, the place in society that I was born into, I had the luxury of learning slowly, of learning only intellectually and never emotionally until someone who had learned them the hard way was kind enough to show me. There are other things, other experiences I know people to be blind to that I've felt down to my bones.

This book is about immigration, but it's also about reading and rereading—going over passages in your life, poring over someone else's words until you find your own life irrevocably altered. I can't go back to the person I was before that church basement in New York, before el Chaparral, before the Boston courtroom or the prison along the Mississippi. I can't un-become my parents' daughter, can't unlearn Spanish or unteach myself English, and so I'm left to return to these things and places, over and over, to draw strength from them to see the world more clearly, to think of them not as the facts of a biography but as tools to dismantle walls, tools to fling open doors and beckon people in, gentle hands to guide butterflies on their way.

I ALSO WANT TO GESTURE at another idea, want to leave a door open at the end of this text: I want to say that translation is also, is primarily, an activity dedicated to the future. Not just because readers of a translation are always future readers, not just because we translate texts of the past into the language of the future, not just because the most starry-eyed of translation proponents seem to be gesturing towards building a utopian future in which we all share a sort of global-Esperanto-language-literature-culture in which all things are held equal, but because translation is a way of life that corresponds to a mode of living that exists now, and will exist even more in the future. "*Un lenguaje que corresponde a un modo de vivir.*"

The mere presence of a translation does not make the world a broader or a better place—reading a text that has been carried across from one language to another will not change your mind on its own, but I believe that the act of doing the carrying yourself changes something. Translation as a practice forces you to step outside the structure of your sentences, the shapes that your languages are accustomed to taking. Translation is an encounter, an embrace of another mind, willingly ceding the egotism of your own words to amplify another. As Simone Weil points out, a lot of times it underscores your mediocrity—reading a first draft of a translation is an exercise in humility, I've translated I-don't-know-how-many semi-legal documents and advisories and I have to look up the word "parole" every time, keep inventing new workarounds for "law enforcement." Translation also teaches you to be creative, to be flexible, to walk yourself around a word you don't know the 1-to-1 equivalence for. Translation gives you a second way of talking about a thing, a language that will feel, despite your best attempts, like a different kind of register—more intimate or louder or sharper or funnier, a different kind of personality. My parents even claim that my voice in Spanish is softer, less strident than when I'm speaking in English.

There are millions of kids who have grown up as tiny professional translators, helping their parents shuttle meaning from one language to another, figuring out the shape of their own rooms within language, and they know these lessons by heart already. There are adults, painstakingly finding their footing in a second language through necessity or adding a third or fourth to a list already shaped by colonialism and global forces. For them, translation is not an expansion, it is not anything special, it is just the way that life is lived, day after day, because there's no other way to bridge their worlds. Switching languages is not a matter of a specialized skill being flexed, or specialty, it's a matter of survival. But this survival brings along with it all of the lessons above—the openness, the willingness to meet on someone else's ground, the knowledge of worldviews beyond your own, encoded in languages you've never heard spoken. They're lessons learned not out of curiosity but out of necessity, but they're there.

Translanguaging is a linguist's term for speaking with your entire semantic range: all your words in all your multiple languages, set out before you like a feast you might sample from. What a linguist calls translanguaging, my mother calls hablar pocho—there's this idea that it's maleducado, that it's because you didn't learn either language right and so you're just stuck there, in the middle of it all instead, without a home on either side. This assumption falls short of what actually happens when someone is translanguaging.

There are entire generations of linguistic innovators, figuring out that they can stand in the middle of the river sometimes, can ask for and expect meaning to flash by on both banks. Have you ever heard a kid actually speaking Spanglish? Like, deep in the flow of it? It's like a fly fisher or a stork, as if the middle of the river was exactly where they belonged, as if there were no land at all and just an expanse of swirling water, as if the delta of the river was the most fertile, plentiful place to be.

Ancient cultures sprang up along river deltas, entire civilizations rising along the banks of the Nile— the meeting points of the Tigris and the Euphrates—at rivermouths around the world. By the time the river meets the sea, it is laden heavy with the soil of all the places it has traveled before arriving here. When it overruns its banks, the land beneath the floodwater is enriched, transformed, filled up with nutrients and the knowledge of distant land. Translation, translanguaging in the rivermouth is not the building of a flimsy bridge or a second-best option, it's an invitation to step into the river, to embrace all the wild possibilities swirling around your ankles, to let yourself be enriched by all the places your words have been before you have taken them up.

Afterword

I WAS GIVEN MY LANGUAGES in the same way I was given my citizenship— as a birthright, a motherland and a mother tongue at once. In my interactions with people that were working towards both Americanness and English, I came to see the outlines of both as artificial. In contexts where everything was being done to divide me politically from the people I was speaking to, it was our shared language that allowed us to find shared ground. I wanted to explore this territory—solidarity and its limits between the privileged daughter of wealthy immigrants and asylum seekers fleeing to this country with little in the way of material resources.

For me, as part of that privileged group of Latinx who could count themselves as white, or wealthy, highly educated, or with citizenship or permanent residence, or an easy ability with English, the 2016 election was a moment of unfamiliar politicization. The language we spoke with our mothers at the grocery store checkout line became an even more distinct mark of otherness. I felt a prickly refusal, a sense that it didn't, couldn't possibly apply to *me*, felt that familiar immigrant desire to prove myself in the face of discrimination.

It was in the midst of this discomfort that I showed up at that church basement in New York—caught somewhere between my guilt at feeling targeted by policies that wouldn't ultimately affect me and anger that the President's words were actually aimed at people who had far less recourse than I did. It was in doing the work, in the translation, and the interpretation, but most importantly, the listening, that my world shifted. The political, moral, emotional category that encompassed me and my family and the people I loved grew and expanded not just in name or in ideals but in actual fact. It was in sitting across from Mayra on that winter day in 2017, pen poised over a government form, that I took the first step in writing this book.

That step, in turn, was born from another book. I started my translation work, and with it, working in the immigration world, after reading Valeria Luiselli's *Tell Me How It Ends*. After her immigration attorney passed her case on to a colleague because they were wrapped up in representing minors on the Expedited Removal Docket, Luiselli herself got involved, translating for child asylum seekers. I credit that book, more than anything else with getting me out of my seat and into the streets—of New York, of Tijuana, into a Boston courtroom and a Chicago legal service provider and a prison in the deep South. My entire life has been radically transformed by that text, and while I won't delude myself into thinking that my own writing, or even my day job will make any kind of systemic difference, I do hope it invites people into the movement in the same way I was invited. This is the way change happens: through the tiny accretion of more and more people who care more and more, and not just about immigration, or language, or stories.

As I delved further into translation—both within the context of immigration and as a literary translator, I began to understand that just as translation allows me to help someone tell their own story of immigration and movement, translation theory could illuminate and allow me to elucidate the power structures that undergirded the stories we tell about immigration.

Translation for asylum seekers was the thing that finished transforming my tongue into a political actor, finished bridging the divide between the Spanish inside my head and the Spanish in the rest of the world. Spanish, the language of my family, allowed me to feel my way into a kind of intimacy with people I knew very little about, allowed me to be useful in a way I didn't know how to imagine. It allowed me to take a thing—a language, a vocabulary, a way of speaking—that was the province of my safe childhood and to try to extend it, as a protective mantle, over people who wanted the same for their own children. The intimacy of translation, when combined with the intimacy of Spanish in my own biography, changed my life, my politics, the way I speak.

It's this work, and this group of people—the language learners and the translators and those caught between two languages, bilingües of all varieties—that this book is for and about. Mayra's is the first of dozens of stories I will translate from Spanish to English, from someone's stammering words to a box on a form, from personal to legal; and the other volunteer interpreters scattered around the clinic are the first of dozens of people I will meet who are engaged in the same work I am doing.

Encountering people as they moved through the immigration system, though, meant watching them encounter English and prepare themselves for a monolingual society. After only three weeks in the country, Mayra had already enrolled in English lessons at a local community center. At the border, I met children who wanted to practice their English on me, shouting "How are YOU, miss?" in my general direction as they zoomed around a nonprofit's office space while their parents spoke to attorneys. I also heard those who had passed through and into English over the course of their immigration: the deeply accented Louisiana-bayou English of a man who had lived in the U.S. for forty years and was now in deportation proceedings, the formerly deported women who were gearing up for another entry into the States by dusting off their old English phrases, grinning as they said "My English is . . . un poco shit, yes?" More than anything, on both sides of the language divide, I saw people gesture and concentrate and scowl and apologize and smile their way around language, all in an attempt to talk to one another.

IMMIGRANTS COME TO the United States for a million reasons—an uneven distribution of resources, global warming, violence, sickness, to be reunited with family or to flee domestic abusers—only to encounter similar situations here. Karla Cornejo Villavicencio outlines these issues in her fantastic book, *The Undocumented Americans,* where she interviews cancer riddled men subcontracted to clear out Ground Zero who now have no health insurance, and undocumented families in Flint unable to get onto government programs for clean water, and housecleaners who face down sexual assault unprotected in Miami. All of the stories she tells place undocumented people at the center of American tragedies—9/11, yes, but also our miserable lack of healthcare, the crumbling infrastructure and lack of investment in largely Black communities that means that they end up with lead-filled water, and our national inability to take sexual assault and harassment at any level seriously.

The year 2020 was supposed to be the year of perfect vision—and in a way, it was. COVID-19 has shown the cracks in our system, all the ways in which our fates are dependent on one another, in which our wellnesses are intertwined. We are in trust to one another, our lives bound up and inseparable. Part of this is the result of living in a globalized economy, of being able to be on the other side of the world within a matter of hours or days if we needed to, but another part is just the result of living.

Since the laws governing the immigration system move so quickly, particularly during the years in which I have been working on this book, no single part of the system as I described it is necessarily what it looks like today, no individual policy or regulation I describe may necessarily be what's happening to people on the ground as you're reading these words. In many cases, at least as of publication, it's gotten worse, although maybe by the time you're reading this, it will be somewhat better. It's my hope, however, that by describing these individual laws, policies, and procedures as I witnessed them, a general picture of the disdain and cruelty of the U.S. immigration system has made itself clear to readers who have not experienced this system themselves.

I AM NOT a policy expert—the little I know I have learned from my day job, and while much of the work we do would make conditions better for immigrants, it's also often a day-by-day response to conditions as they exist now, when what is needed is a radical reimagining. For a model of activism, I look to the prison and policing abolition movement, which has spent the last several years both pointing out the problem—that prisons and policing are vastly overfunded and largely ineffective at keeping people safe, and instead reinforce systems of oppression already present within society—and invite people not to a specific solution, but rather to collaboratively dream together and imagine a better future from which policy proposals should spring. I feel like the immigration movement is in a similar place: Pointing out that the system as it exists is a problem, not just in egregious individual cases or under certain conditions but always, universally, unquestionably. This book invites you to look at that problem, and begin to imagine a future in which those arriving in this country to seek refuge are treated as individual people first and foremost.

This book is born of the thousands of words I have ferried over from one language into another, of the hundreds of people I've met engaged in the precarious process of ferrying themselves into a new life. In it, I've tried to explore the tensions inherent in translation in the immigration space. Sometimes, it is a violent act, mutilating stories it has forced out of people into narratives that are easier to digest by an overburdened legal system. And other times, it's an act of radical power and acceptance that gives voice to new ways of thinking. Translation allows an immigrant to tell her own story in her own words, to a much larger audience in her new country. It allows her to shake off the narratives prescribed to her, to amplify the voices of those otherwise silenced as a means of liberation, of decolonizing the stories and narratives we are given.

Fixing the immigration system means fixing everything else in this country that is tired of living up to its promises or never did, means transforming this country, and the reach it has across the world, into one that does not take resources—including people—rapaciously for capital while leaving those it considers disposable by the wayside. Any work you do to improve the world is work that can be done to improve it for everyone. Whether your call is to fight global warming, or to divest your university or organization from for-profit prisons or the petroleum industry, to ensure fair housing, to create art or make it accessible, to reimagine how disabled people fit into our society, to advocate for a racially just world or a dismantling of dangerous prisons and policing, all of these make the world a safer, more beautiful place for everyone.

Endnotes

PREFACE

1. **One attorney general after another**—Guttentag, Lucas. "Immigration Policy Tracking Project." Last modified January 9, 2023. immpolicytracking.org.

2. **Deployed into too-welcoming sanctuary cities**—Miroff, Nick, and Devlin Barrett. "ICE Preparing Targeted Arrests in 'Sanctuary Cities,' Amplifying President's Campaign Theme." *Washington Post*, September 29, 2020.
   The premise of birthright citizenship will be questioned—Cook, Nancy. "Trump's Immigration Push Is Stephen Miller's Dream Come True." *Politico*, October 31, 2018.
   Tent cities to house migrants will be erected in the desert—Delgado, Edwin. "US Builds Migrant Tent City in Texas as Trump Likens Influx to 'Disneyland.'" *The Guardian*, April 29, 2019.
   Eventually pushed back across the border—Coronado, Acacia. "Conditions Deteriorating at Makeshift Camp on the Rio Grande Where Thousands Await U.S. Asylum." *Texas Tribune*, October 25, 2019.
   Ground sacred to the Indigenous—Connolly, Colleen. "Border Wall Desecrates Native American Lands in Southern California and Arizona." *The American Prospect*, October 12, 2020.

3. **Can sometimes feel like reliving it**—Rothschild, Babette. *The Body Remembers: The Psychophysiology of Trauma and Trauma Treatment*. New York: W.W. Norton & Company, 2000.

7. **New Sanctuary Coalition**—NSC has since closed its doors, but you can find a brief history of the organization here: Judson Memorial Church. "Immigrant Rights." January 3, 2023. judsonclassic.org/ImmigrantRights.

PART 1

CHAPTER 1.

13. **Generations of mystics and monks**—Merton, Thomas. *The Wisdom of the Desert*. New York: New Directions, 1970.

14. **Artist Nicole Antebi**—Antebi, Nicole. "Between Texas and Mexico, a Restless Border Defies the Map." *Bloomberg*, August 16, 2019.
    You can also see more of the meander map and read more about Nicole's wide-ranging, multidisciplinary work at nicoleantebi.com.

CHAPTER 3.

18. **An organization I had worked with in New York**—New Sanctuary Coalition started the Sanctuary Caravan project in November 2018 to meet the caravan from Central America. They maintained a presence in Tijuana through approximately March 2019.

CHAPTER 4.

20. **Translation is something we do with our bodies.**—Robinson, Douglas. *The Translator's Turn*. Baltimore: Johns Hopkins University Press, 1991.

21. **Walter Benjamin describes**—Benjamin, Walter. "The Task of the Translator." In *Illuminations*, 59–68. Translated by Harry Zohn. New York: Knopf, 1968.

CHAPTER 5.

24. **The Credible Fear Interview**—Glass, Ira, and Aviva DeKornfeld, Molly O'Toole and Emily Green. "The Out Crowd," November 15, 2019 in *This American Life* produced by Ira Glass.
    Or, if you prefer print media: O'Toole, Molly. "Asylum Officers Rebel Against Trump Policies They Say Are Immoral and Illegal." *Los Angeles Times*, November 15, 2019.

CHAPTER 6.

29. **seeking asylum**—Washington, John. *The Dispossessed: A Story of Asylum at the US-Mexican Border and Beyond*. New York: Verso Books, 2020.
    United Nation's Universal Declaration of Human Rights—"Universal Declaration of Human Rights: Article 14." United Nations, December 10, 1948.

United States' own laws—Immigration and Nationality Act. 8 U.S.C. § 1158 (1952).

31. **Al Otro Lado**—Al Otro Lado, alotrolado.org.

CHAPTER 7.

33. **The handlers of the notebook**—Semple, Kirk. "What is 'La Lista,' Which Controls Migrants' Fates in Tijuana?" *New York Times*, November 30, 2018.

34. **Elegiac newspaper articles**—Smith, James F. "Mexico's Grupo Beta Tries To Make Life Safer for Migrants." *Los Angeles Times*, June 17, 2001.
    Reject people's identity documents—Stanton, Jill. "Part 2: La Lista, a near impossible hurdle in the migrant search of asylum." *El Tecolote*, October 10, 2019.
    Deport groups of migrants—Isacson, Adam, Maureen Meyer, and Hannah Smith. "Increased Enforcement at Mexico's Southern Border: An Update on Security, Migration, and U.S. Assistance." WOLA, November 9, 2015.

35. **First-hand accounts**—Kinosian, Sarah. "How to Organize Thousands of Asylum-Seekers in Tijuana." *Washington Post*, November 28, 2018.
    The list itself is illegal—Spagat, Elliot. "Judge Says Forcing Waits in Mexico to Seek Asylum Is Illegal." *AP News*, September 2, 2021.

36. **Metering was implemented at moments of high traffic**—Frederick, James. "'Metering' at the Border." *NPR*, July 29, 2019.

37. **These prosecutions**—Dickerson, Caitlin. "The Secret History of the U.S. Government's Family-Separation Policy." *The Atlantic*, August 7, 2022.
    Years-long, expensive class action suits—"Challenging Customs and Border Protection's Unlawful Practice of Turning Away Asylum Seekers." American Immigration Council. 4 January 2023.

38. **A humanitarian crisis on the Mexican side**—Spagat, Elliot, Nomaan Merchant, and Patricio Espinoza. "For Thousands of Asylum Seekers, All They Can Do Is Wait." *AP News*, May 9, 2019.
    Compounded by the Remain in Mexico policy—Gonzales, Richard. "Trump Administration Begins 'Remain in Mexico' Policy, Sending Asylum-Seekers Back." *NPR*, January 29, 2019.

39. **His photo is published in the paper**—Arias, Guillermo. *Carlos Catarlo Gomez*. Photograph. Getty Images. January 29, 2019.

CHAPTER 8.

41. **Around 7,000 members strong**—Correal, Annie, and Megan Specia. "The Migrant Caravan: What to Know About the Thousands Traveling North." *New York Times*, October 26, 2018.
    2,300 children—UNICEF. "An Estimated 2,300 Children Traveling With Migrant Caravan in Mexico Need Protection and Essential Services." Press release, October 26, 2018. unicef.org/press-releases /estimated-2300-children-traveling-migrant-caravan-mexico-need-protection-and.
    Families escaping famine—Hayden, Sally. *The Fourth Time, We Drowned: Seeking Refuge on the World's Deadliest Migration Route*. New York: Melville House, 2022.
    wet foot, dry foot—Campisi, Elizabeth. *Escape to Miami: An Oral History of the Cuban Rafter Crisis*. Oxford: Oxford University Press, 2016.
    Recently in danger of being deported—Hayoun, Massoud. "Some Fear That Vietnamese Americans Could Be at Greater Risk for Deportation." *Pacific Standard Magazine*, November 1, 2017.
    Rapid, seaborne escape—Tran, Ham, dir. *Journey From the Fall*. 2007. ImaginAsian Pictures.

43. **They released a consensus statement**—Rodriguez, Jesús A. "How the Migrant Caravan Built Its Own Democracy." *Politico*, December 12, 2018.

44. **"Caminante no hay camino,"**—Machado, Antonio. "Proverbios y Cantares." In *Campos de Castilla*. Madrid: Renacimiento, 1912.

CHAPTER 10.

48. **Poet and theorist Gloria Anzaldúa**—Anzaldúa, Gloria. *Borderlands/La Frontera: The New Mestiza*. San Francisco: Aunt Lute Books, 1987.
    Lynchings in the 1800s—Romero, Simon. "Lynch Mobs Killed Latinos Across the West. The Fight to Remember These Atrocities Is Just Starting." *New York Times*, March 2, 2019.
    Border Patrol agents destroy water stations—"Death and Disappearance on the U.S.-Mexico Border Part Two: Interference with Humanitarian Aid." No More Deaths, January 20, 2018.

CHAPTER 14.

66. **Men who cross with children aren't detained as long**—Hennessy-Fiske, Molly. "Immigration: Are Male Detainees Treated Differently Than Women?" *Los Angeles Times*, August 31, 2015.

CHAPTER 15.

69. **17th century poet and nun Sor Juana Inés de la Cruz**—de la Cruz, Sor Juana Inés. *Sor Juana Inés de la Cruz: Selected Works*. Translated by Edith Grossman. New York: W. W. Norton & Company, 2015.

There's also a fabulous bilingual chapbook of her riddles, which is out of print, but fun if you can find a copy: de la Cruz, Sor Juana Inés. *Enigmas*. Translated by Stalina Emmanuelle Villareal. Brooklyn, NY: Ugly Duckling Presse, 2015.

70. **The language of Malintzin**—Glantz, Margo, ed. *Malintzin, Sus Padres, y Sus Hijos*. Mexico City, Mexico: Taurus, 2001.

Language is made up of the personal and the cumulative—This theory of language is somewhat cribbed from Wilfred Cantwell Smith's theory of personal faith versus cumulative tradition.

Cantwell Smith, Wilfred, ed. "The Cumulative Tradition." In *The Meaning and End of Religion*. Minneapolis: 1517 Media, 1991.

76. **Writer and theologian Simone Weil**—Weil, Simone. "Reflections on the Right Use of School Studies with a View to the Love of God." In *Waiting for God*. Translated by Emma Craufurd. Jenkintown, PA: Capricorn Books, 1959.

CHAPTER 16.

78. **The Lord's Prayer**—Matthew 6:9–13.

The Jesus Prayer—Anonymous. *The Way of the Pilgrim and the Pilgrim Continues His Way*. Translated by Helen Bacovcin. New York: Image Books, 1985.

79. **Known as "El Camino"**—Carson, Anne. *Plainwater: Essays and Poetry*. New York: Vintage Books, 2000.

80. **There's a church service here every Sunday**—The Border Church / La Iglesia Fronteriza, borderchurch.org.

82. **Annie Dillard writes**—Dillard, Annie. *For the Time Being*. New York: Vintage Books, 2000.

CHAPTER 18.

89. **The term "wetback"**—Hernández, Kelly Lytle. *Migra! A History of the U.S. Border Patrol*. Berkeley: University of California Press, 2010.

90. **Stories of deported DREAMers**—Freed Wessler, Seth. "Phone Home: No Place Like Home," March 14, 2014 in *This American Life* produced by Ira Glass, podcast.

91. **ICE's detention locator**—"Online Detainee Locator System." U.S. Immigrations and Customs Enforcement, locator.ice.gov.

92. **Small county jails**—You can find a full list of immigration detention centers, including county jails and locations with 287(g) police-immigration collaboration agreements at freedomforimmigrants.org/map.

CHAPTER 19.

95. **When the world is sick**—Thee Silver Mt. Zion Memorial Orchestra. 2005. "God Bless Our Dead Marines." Track 1 on *Horses in the Sky*. Constellation Records.

96. **San Isidro the Laborer**—If you want to know anything about any saint, Butler's *Lives of the Saints* (originally published 1756) is really the way to go. Different editions have different saints, and there are 300-page individual paperback condensed editions with well-known saints that you can get at any large bookstore; multiple-volume leather-bound sets full of the holy and obscure are probably best consulted at a library.

97. **Minimum occupancy quotas**—"The Issues: Detention Quotas." *Detention Watch Network*.

98. **A watch list of journalists**—Devereaux, Ryan. "Journalists, Lawyers, and Activists Working on the Border Face Coordinated Harassment from U.S. and Mexican Authorities." *The Intercept*, February 8, 2019.

Devereaux, Ryan. "Faith Under Fire: A Pastor's Legal Fight Against CPB Exposes a Reckless Surveillance Operation." *The Intercept*, March 6, 2022.

CHAPTER 21.

104. **The Society of Saint John the Evangelist**—Society of Saint John the Evangelist. ssje.org.

105. **Second-hand trauma**—van Dernoot Lipsky, Laura, with Connie Burk. *Trauma Stewardship: An Everyday Guide to Caring for Self While Caring for Others*. Oakland: Berrett-Koehler Publishers, 2009.

106. **The LGBTQ+ caravan**—Flores, Adolfo. "LGBT Members of the Caravan Went Ahead First to Dodge Danger and Discrimination." *BuzzFeed News*, November 14, 2018.

109. **Allowing ICE to destroy records**—Cachero, Paulina. "ICE Says It Plans to Destroy a Trove of Detention Records, Including Numbers on Detainee Deaths and Sexual Assaults." *Insider*, February 19, 2020.

111. **Dozens of other translators and interpreters**—Mounzer, Lina. "War in Translation: Giving Voice to the Women of Syria." In *Kitchen Table Translation: An Aster(ix) Anthology*, edited by Madu H. Kaza, 134-151. Pittsburgh: Blue Sketch Press, 2017.

PART 2
CHAPTER 24.

126. **A traitor**—Polizzotti, Mark. *Sympathy for the Traitor: A Translation Manifesto.* Cambridge, MA: The MIT Press, 2018.

127. **The origin of languages**—Genesis 11:1–9.

129. **Dismantling a wall**—Gansel, Mireille. *Translation as Transhumance.* Translated by Ros Schwartz. New York: The Feminist Press at CUNY, 2017.

CHAPTER 25.

130. **"I want to be clear"**—The White House. 2021. "Remarks by Vice President Harris and President Giammattei of Guatemala in Joint Press Conference." Last modified June 7, 2021.

Statue of Liberty—Goldman, Emma. "The New Colossus." *Berfrois,* January 21, 2014.

Melting Pot—Unknown. *Melting Pot Ceremony at Ford English School, July 4, 1917.* Photograph. The Henry Ford Museum of American Innovation.

Cher Horowitz—Heckerling, Amy, dir. *Clueless.* 1995. Los Angeles, CA: Paramount.

131. **The United States**—Grandin, Greg. *Empire's Workshop: Latin America, the United States, and the Rise of the New Imperialism.* New York: Metropolitan Books, 2006.

In large part by Indigenous and Latinx workers—The National Center for Farmworker Health keeps detailed statistics on the demographics and trajectories of farmworkers in the United States at ncfh.org.

Spanish Missions in the 1800s—Dunbar-Ortiz, Roxanne. *An Indigenous Peoples' History of the United States.* Boston: Beacon Press, 2014.

CHAPTER 26.

136. **Walking up the continent**—Zamora, Javier. *Solito: A Memoir.* New York: Hogarth Books, 2022.

Riding atop speeding trains—Martínez, Oscar. *The Beast: Riding the Rails and Dodging Narcos on the Migrant Trail.* Translated by Daniela Maria Ugaz. New York: Verso, 2014.

CHAPTER 27.

140. **Kate Briggs, in her book**—Briggs, Kate. *This Little Art.* London, UK: Fitzcarraldo Editions, 2017.

Robinson Crusoe—Defoe, Daniel. *Robinson Crusoe.* New York: Signet Classics, 2008.

141. **John tells us**—John 13–17

Matthew tells us—Matthew 26:17–30

Mark about—Mark 14:12–26

Luke recounts—Luke 22:7–38

"This is my body"—Matthew 26:26–29, Mark 14:22–24, Luke 22:19–20. The exact quote in the book is taken from Luke, *New King James Version.*

CHAPTER 28.

143. **When the United Fruit Company**—Chapman, Peter. *Bananas: How the United Fruit Company Shaped the World.* Edinburgh, UK: Canongate, 2008.

This book is a fantastic history of UFCO and goes far, far more into depth about many of the incidents and individuals mentioned in this chapter.

145. **In *One Hundred Years of Solitude***—García Márquez, Gabriel. *One Hundred Years of Solitude.* Translated by Gregory Rabassa. New York: Harper & Row, 1970.

CHAPTER 29.

149. **An Octavio Paz poem**—Paz, Octavio. *The Poems of Octavio Paz.* Edited and Translated by Eliot Weinberger. New York: New Directions, 2012.

"And it so happened that I'm here with you."—Szymborska, Wisława. *Map: Collected and Last Poems.* Translated by Clare Cavanagh and Stanisław Barańczak. New York: Mariner Books, 2016. The poem in question is untitled, and appears on p. 191. An appearance in the July 10, 2014 issue of *The New York Review of Books* credits the translation of this particular poem to Cavanagh.

CHAPTER 31.

154. **Photographer Sid Avery**—Eldridge, Fred. "Helping Hands from Mexico." *Saturday Evening Post,* August 10, 1957. Rothman, Lily. "Long-Lost Photos Reveal Life of Mexican Migrant Workers in 1950s America." *Time,* April 11, 2017.

155. **This isn't necessarily how the program worked.**—Galarza, Ernesto. *Merchants of Labor: The Mexican Bracero Story: An Account of the Managed Migration of Mexican Farm Workers in California 1942–1960.* Santa Barbara: McNally & Loftin, 1964.

Galarza's account stands out for being one of the few contemporary in-depth examinations of the injustices of the Bracero Program.

Filmmakers set out to capture some of these testimonies—Gonzalez, Gilbert, and Vivian Price, dirs. *Harvest of Loneliness: The Bracero Program [Cosecha Triste: El Programa Bracero]*. 2010.

The full film is available on YouTube.

156. **If they themselves organized**—Akers Chacón, Justin, and Mike Davis. *No One Is Illegal: Fighting Racism and State Violence of the U.S.-Mexico Border*. Chicago: Haymarket Books, 2006.

Ten percent of all bracero earnings—Buff, Rachel Ida. *A Is for Asylum Seeker: Words for People on the Move / A de Asilo: Palabras para Personas en Movimiento*. Translated by Alejandra Oliva. New York: Fordham University Press, 2020.

I first found out about this bracero wage theft when translating Rachel Ida Buff's *A Is for Asylum Seeker* for the bilingual edition. Even though I'm somewhat biased because I was involved in the creation of this book, it's a comprehensive, easy-to-read, quick tour through immigration history and vocabulary.

157. **Passage of the North American Free Trade Agreement**—Gálvez, Alyshia. *Eating NAFTA: Trade, Food Policies, and the Destruction of Mexico*. Berkeley: University of California Press, 2018.

Every piece of produce you pick up—Holmes, Seth M. *Fresh Fruit, Broken Bodies: Migrant Farmworkers in the United States*. Berkeley: University of California Press, 2013.

Holmes' excellent book, which has him working alongside and experiencing life with a Triqui farmworker family, contains this vital reminder.

CHAPTER 32.

159. **It's the feast of the Pentecost**—Acts 2:1–13. Many thanks to Dr. Chance Bonar for reading this chapter and providing feedback on ancient languages.

CHAPTER 33.

165. **Eighty to ninety percent of all asylum applicants**—The Transactional Records Access Clearinghouse (TRAC), run by Syracuse University researchers, is a database of information collected from all the major federal agencies, including immigration agencies and the Department of Homeland Security, often obtained as part of Freedom of Information Act requests as well as required reporting. This and many of the other statistics in this book are pulled from TRAC analysis at trac.syr.edu/immigration.

CHAPTER 34.

169. **Their lives on the actual line**—Reporter Alice Driver has written a number of articles on individuals at the intersection of meat processing, immigration, and COVID-19. While she has a book on this forthcoming, you can read her reporting now.

Driver, Alice. "Their Lives on the Line." *The New York Review of Books*, April 27, 2021.

Driver, Alice. "Working in Their Sleep." *The New York Review of Books*, December 23, 2022.

Sent a memo—Philpott, Tom. "Workers Churning Out America's Favorite Meat Fear for Their Safety." *Mother Jones*, April 14, 2020.

One of the largest employers of undocumented people in the Brazos Valley—Press, Eyal. *Dirty Work: Essential Jobs and the Hidden Toll of Inequality in America*. New York: Farrar, Straus and Giroux, 2021.

In 2014—NRLB Case #16-CA-124053

In 2018—Bellow, Noelle. "Activists Protest for Sanderson Farms Workers Claiming Inhumane Working Conditions at Bryan Plant." *KBTX*, October 1, 2018.

In 2019—Mehrtens, Savannah. "Advocacy Groups Call for Humane Work Environment at Sanderson Farms in Bryan." *The Battalion*, February 18, 2019.

170. **Bored work-from-home white collar workers**—Thrasher, Steven W. *The Viral Underclass: The Human Toll When Inequality and Disease Collide*. New York: Celadon Books, 2022.

171. **Peracetic acid**—Philpott, Tom. "Workers Churning Out America's Favorite Meat Fear for Their Safety," *Mother Jones*, April 14, 2020.

Found betting—Wamsley, Laurel. "Tyson Foods Fires 7 Plant Managers Over Betting Ring On Workers Getting COVID-19." *NPR*, December 16, 2020.

Thanks to a Presidential Executive Order—Grabell, Michael. "The Plot to Keep Meatpacking Plants Open During COVID-19." *ProPublica*, May 13, 2022.

CHAPTER 35.

174. **The Catholic Worker movement**—Day, Dorothy. *The Long Loneliness*. San Francisco: Harper & Row Publishers, 1952.

I would recommend reading this alongside a biography of Dorothy Day, but it's among the best books on providing direct services to people in need.

178. **Roberto Tijerina had predicted exactly this**—Tijerina, Roberto. "What Did They Say? Interpreting for Social Justice: An Introductory Curriculum." Curriculum. The Highlander Research and Education Center, 2009.

CHAPTER 36.

181. **Cicero and the ancient Romans**—Friedrich, Hugo. "On the Art of Translation." In *Theories of Translation: From Dryden to Derrida*, edited by Rainer Schulte and John Biguenet. Translated by Ranier Schulte and John Biguenet. Chicago: University of Chicago Press, 1992.

CHAPTER 37.

183. **The *Florentine Codex***—de Sagahún, Fray Bernardo. *General History of the Things of New Spain by Fray Bernardino de Sahagún: The Florentine Codex*. World Digital Library, Library of Congress, 2012.
The codex was written in Nahuatl, but if you'd like an English translation anthropologist Charles E. Dibble and Arthur J.O. Anderson completed a translation in 2002. The twelve-volume set was published by the University of Utah Press.

184. **Fees to the drug cartels**—Rainsford, Cat. "Mexico's Cartels Fighting It Out for Control of Avocado Business." *InSight Crime*, September 30, 2019.

CHAPTER 38.

189. **Do not have the benefit of court-appointed representation**—The Vera Institute of Justice, along with the Center for Popular Democracy and the National Immigration Law Center, have put together a toolkit about why universal representation is particularly important for those facing deportation cases from the detention system. You can find that here: vera.org/advancing-universal-representation-toolkit.
Scammers and notarios—Moreno, Nereida. "Scam Artists Target Immigrant Communities, Promising Legal Status for Cash." *Chicago Tribune*, May 30, 2017.

CHAPTER 40.

194. **The task of reviving a text**—Benjamin, Walter. "The Task of the Translator."
The warehouse where all the asylum applications must exist—Office of Inspector General, Department of Homeland Security. *USCIS Faces Challenges in Modernizing Information Technology*. Transactional Records Access Clearinghouse, September 2005.
This report includes several photos of USCIS's information storage—that is to say, a lot of actual banker's boxes and card catalogs. More contemporary pictures can be found here: Moore, John. *Millions of U.S. Citizenship Applications Processed at Texas USCIS Center*. Photograph. Getty. August 22, 2016.
Around 60 percent of all asylum applications are rejected—This number varies greatly across years and presidential administrations as well as from one geographic area to another. Current or more local information can be found on TRAC: trac.syr.edu.

195. **We get news of someone being murdered**—Stillman, Sarah. "When Deportation Is a Death Sentence." *The New Yorker*, January 15, 2018.

CHAPTER 41.

196. **Ultimately biblical translation theory**—Robinson, *The Translator's Turn*.
197. **Like no one else ever has or will again**—Antena. *A Manifesto for Ultratranslation*. Houston, TX: Antena Books / Libros Antena, 2013.
While God spits out enigmas—Job 38–42
Paul, in his second letter to the Corinthians—2 Corinthians 11:24–33
Christ's sufferings—2 Corinthians 12:9–10
Blessings of suffering—St. Teresa of Ávila. *The Life of St. Teresa of Ávila by Herself.* Translated by J.M. Cohen. New York: Penguin Classics, 1957.

PART 3

CHAPTER 42.

204. **Let's talk maripositas.**—Slee, Mike, dir. *Flight of the Butterflies*. 2012. Toronto, Ontario: SK Films.
Reserva de la Biósfera Santuario Mariposa Monarca—Aridjis, Homero. "A Una Mariposa Monarca / To a Monarch Butterfly." Audio Exhibition. New York: New York Public Library. 10 January 2023.
Aridjis was a major proponent for the creation and preservation of the Reserva.

205. **Decreasing the numbers of monarchs**—"Migratory Monarch Butterfly Now Endangered - IUCN Red List." International Union for Conservation of Nature. July 21, 2022.
The southern border of Mexico—Jaffe, Alexandra. "Mexico, Honduras, Guatemala Deploy Troops to Lower Migration." *AP News*, April 12, 2021.
The southern border of the United States—Grandin, Greg. "The Militarization of the Southern Border Is a Long-Standing American Tradition." *The Nation*, January 14, 2019.

206. **Writer Karla Cornejo Villavicencio**—Cornejo Villavicencio, Karla. *The Undocumented Americans*. New York: One World, 2020.

CHAPTER 43.

207. **Volunteer court observers**—We were there with BIJAN, the Boston Immigration Justice Accompaniment Network, an outreach program of the Beyond Bond & Legal Defense Fund: beyondbondboston.org.
210. **A legal category of migrant**—Immigration and Nationality Act. U.S.C. § 1158 (1952).
Created in the aftermath of the Holocaust—The United Nations created the Convention Relating to the Status of Refugees in 1951, which established much of the language, rights, and responsibilities that are present in the U.S. Code today. However, the U.S. did not adopt this language until the 1980 Refugee Act.
United States Holocaust Memorial Museum. "United States Immigration and Refugee Law, 1921–1980." Holocaust Encyclopedia. 10 January 2023.

CHAPTER 44.

211. **"Hielera" in one context**—Human Rights Watch. "In the Freezer: Abusive Conditions for Women and Children in U.S. Immigration Holding Cells." Human Rights Watch Website, February 28, 2018.
212. **In secret Facebook groups**—Thompson, A.C. "Inside the Secret Border Patrol Facebook Group Where Agents Joke About Migrant Deaths and Post Sexist Memes." *ProPublica*, July 1, 2019.
213. **Breaks down the doors of family homes**—Lopez, William D. *Separated: Family and Community in the Aftermath of an Immigration Raid*. Baltimore: Johns Hopkins University Press, 2019.
Routine traffic stops—"ICE pulled over my car! What are my rights?" Infographic. Immigrant Legal Defense Project. April 2020.
Massive raids at workplaces—Jordan, Miriam. "ICE Came for a Tennessee Town's Immigrants. The Town Fought Back." *New York Times*, June 11, 2018.
Wait in courtrooms—Coll, Stephen. "When a Day in Court Is a Trap for Immigrants." *The New Yorker*, November 8, 2017.
Drive tanks down New York City streets—Offenhartz, Jake. "Armored ICE Vehicle Sparks Panic in Queens During Firearms Bust." *Gothamist*, November 7, 2019.
Shoot people with impunity—McDonnell Nieto del Rio, Giulia. "Two Years After ICE Shoots Unarmed Man, His Family Still Waits for Justice." *Documented*, February 14, 2022.
Put citizens and legal permanent residents into deportation proceedings—Finnegan, William. "The Deportation Machine." *The New Yorker*, April 22, 2013.
Statistics on the numbers of ICE detainers issued for U.S. citizens and legal permanent residents are also kept by TRAC.

CHAPTER 45.

214. **The fate of a single butterfly sanctuary**—Meyer, Will. "The Weather and the Wall." *Longreads*, January 23, 2019.
The National Butterfly Center—National Butterfly Center. nationalbutterflycenter.org.
215. **In an op-ed**—Guerra, Luciano. "I Voted for Trump. Now His Wall May Destroy My Butterfly Paradise." *Washington Post*, December 17, 2018.
What nature ought to be and look like—Cronon, William, ed. "The Trouble with Wilderness; or, Getting Back to the Wrong Nature." In *Uncommon Ground: Rethinking the Human Place in Nature*. New York: W. W. Norton & Company, 1995.
Organ Pipe Cactus National Monument—Romero, Simon. "Tribal Nation Condemns 'Desecration' to Build Border Wall." *New York Times*, February 26, 2020.
Big Bend National Park—Tempest Williams, Terry. *The Hour of Land: A Personal Topography of America's National Parks*. New York: Sarah Crichton Books, 2016.
They leave things behind—Baker, Peter C. "A Janitor Preserves the Seized Belongings of Migrants." *The New Yorker*, March 12, 2017.
216. **No More Deaths**—No More Deaths. nomoredeaths.org.
Found guilty of littering—Ludden, Nicole. "4 No More Deaths Volunteers Found Guilty of Entering Refuge, Abandoning Property." *Cronkite News/Arizona PBS*, January 17, 2019.
"Alien mode of life"—Abbey, Edward. *One Life at a Time, Please*. New York: Henry Holt and Company, 1978.
Abbey's most famous book—Abbey, Edward. *Desert Solitaire: A Season in the Wilderness*. New York: Touchstone Books, 1968.
217. **Buried secretly, possibly illegally**—Dungan, Ron. "Burying Edward Abbey: The Last Act of Defiance." *AZ Central*, April 17, 2015.
Known as ecofascism—Guidi, Ruxandra. "Eco-Fascism, Uncovered." *Sierra*, December 27, 2022.

Great Replacement Theory—Confessore, Nicholas, and Karen Yourish. "A Fringe Conspiracy Theory, Fostered Online, Is Refashioned by the G.O.P." *New York Times,* May 15, 2022.

218. **In August 2019**—Guidi, "Eco-Fascism, Uncovered," *Sierra.*

In May 2022—Aronoff, Kate. "The Buffalo Shooter and the Rise of Ecofascist Extremists." *The New Republic,* May 17, 2022.

Black elders—Glass, Ira and Brittany Luce, Bim Adewunmi, Eve L. Ewing, Kiese Laymon, B.A. Parker, Damon Young, and Michael Harriot. "Name. Age. Detail," August 12, 2022 in *This American Life* produced by Ira Glass, podcast.

Across the planet—Gilsinan, Kathy. "How White-Supremacist Violence Echoes Other Forms of Terrorism." *The Atlantic,* March 15, 2019.

"Prevention Through Deterrence"—De León, Jason. *Land of Open Graves: Living and Dying on the Migrant Trail.* Berkeley: University of California Press, 2015.

People will not survive crossing the desert—Urrea, Luis Alberto. *The Devil's Highway: A True Story.* New York: Little Brown, 2004.

219. **853 deaths**—Montoya-Galvez, Camilo. "At Least 853 Migrants Died Crossing the U.S.-Mexico border in past 12 months—a Record High." *CBS News,* October 28, 2022.

An abandoned truck trailer—Martínez, Delmer, Sonia Pérez D., and Christopher Sherman. "Migrants in Texas Trailer Tragedy Died Seeking Better Lives." *AP News,* June 30, 2022.

Colibrí Center—Colibrí Center for Human Rights. colibricenter.org.

CHAPTER 46.

221. **God turned her into a pillar of salt**—Genesis 19:26

222. **A translation debate**—Boswell, John. *Christianity, Social Tolerance, and Homosexuality: Gay People in Western Europe From the Beginning of the Christian Era to the Fourteenth Century.* Chicago: University of Chicago Press, 1980.

Brought with them condemnation of homosexuality—Karp, Sky. "Why Are There So Many LGBT Asylum Seekers? A Brief History." National Immigrant Justice Center (blog), June 29, 2022.

Bowles, David O. "Mexican X Part XII: Xochihuah and Queer Aztecs." *Medium,* February 10, 2019.

Band together to travel to the United States—Pérez D., Sonia. "In Mexico Caravan, LGBTQ Migrants Stick Together for Safety." *AP News,* November 12, 2018.

Eighty queer migrants arrived in Tijuana—Flores, "LGBT Members of the Caravan Went Ahead," *BuzzFeed News.*

Note that there's currently no data kept on asylum grants to LGBTQ+ applicants.

223. **Roxsana Hernandez**—Garcia, Sandra E. "Independent Autopsy of Transgender Asylum Seeker Who Died in ICE Custody Shows Signs of Abuse." *New York Times,* November 27, 2018.

Kelly—#FreeKelly Campaign Team."After 1,051 Days in Detention, Kelly Was Released!" National Immigrant Justice Center (blog), July 14, 2020.

Sza Sza—Vasquez, Tina. "What Life Is Like Caught in Crimmigration's Web: How a Black Trans Asylum-seeker Is Fighting for Her Freedom." *ZORA Mag,* October 16, 2019.

Wrote an open letter—Critchfield, Hannah. "Migrants Inside ICE's Only Transgender Unit Decry Conditions." *Phoenix New Times,* July 12, 2019.

224. **Open letters**—Oliva, Alejandra. "Trans Women Condemn Conditions at Cibola ICE Jail as Federal Legal Action Seeks to #FreeAlejandra." National Immigrant Justice Center (blog), July 18, 2019.

Alejandra—Oztaskin, Murat. "The Harrowing, Two-Year Detention of a Transgender Asylum Seeker." *The New Yorker,* October 31, 2019.

CHAPTER 47.

226. **Language Line**—Jaafari, Joseph Darius. "Immigration Courts Getting Lost in Translation." *The Marshall Project,* March 20, 2019.

CHAPTER 48.

228. **French philosopher Emmanuel Levinas**—Cohen, Richard A., ed. *Face to Face with Levinas.* Albany, NY: SUNY Press, 1986.

The first full essay in this, "Dialogue with Emmanuel Levinas," has one of the clearest explanations of his theory.

229. **These faces and bodies and breaths**—Butler, Judith. *Precarious Life: The Powers of Mourning and Justice.* New York: Verso, 2004.

CHAPTER 49.

232. **Those who receive trial-by-video are less likely to win cases**—Franklin, Stephen, Miriam Annenberg, and Ankur Singh. "Video Hearings In Immigration Court Are Harming Immigrants' Cases." *Pacific Standard Magazine,* July 2, 2019.

Detention centers—Pitzer, Andrea. *One Long Night: A Global History of Concentration Camps.* New York: Little, Brown and Company, 2017.

The moldy food, the rotten chicken—Sachetti, Maria. "Watchdog Report Finds Moldy Food, Mistreatment in Immigrant Detention Centers." *Washington Post,* December 17, 2017.

Weeks-long stretches of solitary—Urbina, Ian. "The Capricious Use of Solitary Confinement Against Detained Immigrants." *The Atlantic,* September 6, 2019.

White canvas tents full of hundreds of children—Misra, Tanvi. "CityLab Daily: The Life and Death of an American Tent City." *Bloomberg,* January 15, 2019.

233. **The denial of medical care**—Aleaziz, Hamed. "A Secret Report Exposes Healthcare for Jailed Migrants." *BuzzFeed News,* December 12, 2019.

The commissary and phone call costs—Conlin, Michelle, and Kristina Cooke. "$11 toothpaste: Immigrants Pay Big for Basics at Private ICE Lock-ups." *Reuters,* January 18, 2019.

Najmabadi, Shannon. "Detained Migrant Parents Have to Pay to Call Their Family Members. Some Can't Afford To." *Texas Tribune,* July 3, 2018.

The converted Walmarts—Fernandez, Manny. "Inside the Former Walmart That Is Now a Shelter for Almost 1,500 Migrant Children." *New York Times,* June 14, 2018.

Japanese internment camps—Shimoda, Brandon. "We Have Been Here Before." *The Nation,* August 21, 2019.

"Well, we've got an orchestra here"—Thompson, Ginger. "Listen to Children Who've Just Been Separated From Their Parents at the Border." *ProPublica,* June 18, 2018.

For a comprehensive history of family separation and child incarceration during the Trump administration read: Sobroff, Jacob. *Separated: Inside an American Family Tragedy.* New York: Custom House, 2020.

Far from the places where people actually live—Wilson Gilmore, Ruth. *Golden Gulag: Prisons, Surplus, Crisis, and Opposition in Globalizing California.* Berkeley: University of California Press, 2007.

While Wilson Gilmore's book covers a specific set of circumstances and ideas, her theories about prison location in rural, remote areas and the difficulties it raises for the loved ones of those detained ring true to prison detention systems.

Darlyn Valle—Morales Rocketto, Jess. "Opinion: Seven Children Have Died in Immigration Custody. Remember Their Names." *BuzzFeed News,* September 30, 2019.

234. **Regularly released from detention**—Castillo, Andrea and Jie Jenny Zou. "ICE Rushed to Release a Sick Woman, Avoiding Responsibility for Her Death. She Isn't Alone." *Los Angeles Times.* 13 May 2022.

CHAPTER 50.

235. **Upload them to a site**—More of these facility inspections and contracts can be found at the National Immigrant Justice Center's website: immigrantjustice.org/transparencyandhumanrights/.

236. **Come under fire**—Feltz, Reneé. "Private Contractor Defends Detention Inspections Deemed 'Useless' by ICE Staff." *Truthout,* September 28, 2019.

Her own family's history—Densho, a nonprofit dedicated to preserving the stories of Japanese internment camp survivors fighting for justice, has issued an open letter to Jennifer Nakamoto.

Densho Staff. "An Open Letter to Detention Profiteer Jennifer Nakamoto." *Densho,* September 26, 2019.

240. **Peatisse**—Note that there is no detention center as far as I know called "Peatisse," but this is copied directly from my notes taken during the visit.

CHAPTER 51.

241. **Plead guilty**—Ballesteros, Carlos. "Cook County Aims to Disrupt the Conviction-to-deportation Pipeline." *Injustice Watch,* March 31, 2021.

242. **Double punishment**—Deng, Grace. "Immigrants and Refugees Are Spending Decades in Prison Only to Be Released into ICE Custody." *Prism,* March 10, 2022.

An oft-cited statistic—Rizzo, Salvador. "How Many Migrants Show Up for Immigration Court Hearings?" *Washington Post,* June 26, 2019.

243. **Enrich stockholders**—Ross, Michaela, Madi Alexander, and Paul Murphy. "Immigration Spending Surges as White House Calls for More Funds." *Bloomberg Government,* January 25, 2019.

244. **$133.99 a day**—Urbi, Jaden. "This Is How Much It Costs to Detain an Immigrant in the US." *CNBC,* June 20, 2018.

7.5 billion dollars…16.4 billion dollars—"Fact Sheet: The Cost of Immigration Enforcement and Border Security." American Immigration Council, January 20, 2021.

CHAPTER 52.

246. **Eleven times more likely to pursue relief**—Eagly, Ingrid, and Steven Shafer. "Access to Counsel in Immigration Court." Special Report. American Immigration Council, September 28, 2016.
All stats in this paragraph come from this report.

247. **The Clinton administration**—Lind, Dara. "The Disastrous, Forgotten 1996 Law that Created Today's Immigration Problem." *Vox*, April 28, 2016.
The W. Bush administration—Timmons, Heather. "No One Really Knows What ICE Is Supposed to Be. Politicians Love That." *Quartz*, July 7, 2018.
Deported more people—Thompson, Ginger, and Sarah Cohen. "More Deportations Follow Minor Crimes, Records Show." *New York Times*, April 6, 2014.
"Rocket dockets"—Semple, Kirk. "In Court, Immigrant Children Are Moved to Head of Line." *New York Times*, August 14, 2014.

248. **Hundreds of people**—These numbers are pulled from TRAC's yearly deportation number. The lowest average daily deportation was 2003, the year of ICE's creation, with 147 people deported daily. The highest was in 2014, with an average of 558 people deported every single day.

249. *Tell Me How It Ends*—Luiselli, Valeria. *Tell Me How It Ends: An Essay in Forty Questions*. Minneapolis: Coffee House Press, 2017.

251. **"The right to remain"**—Bacon, David. *The Right to Stay Home: How US Policy Drives Mexican Migration*. Boston: Beacon Press, 2013.

CHAPTER 53.

252. **Videos he tweeted out**—You can still find many of them on Gómez González's Twitter account, his handle is @homerogomez_g.
Homero Gómez González—Sieff, Kevin. "He Told Me of His Battle to Save the Monarch Butterfly From Illegal Loggers. Now He's Missing." *Washington Post*, January 23, 2020.

253. **In the first month of 2020**—Wamsley, Laurel. "Sadness and Worry After 2 Men Connected to Butterfly Sanctuary Are Found Dead." *NPR*, February 3, 2020.
Berta Cáceres—Lakhani, Nina. *Who Killed Berta Cáceres? Dams, Death Squads, and an Indigenous Defender's Battle for the Planet*. New York: Verso Books, 2020.
Five Garifuna men—Lakhani, Nina. "Fears Growing for Five Indigenous Garifuna Men Abducted in Honduras." *The Guardian*, July 23, 2020.
Protesters at Standing Rock—Estes, Nick. *Our History Is the Future: Standing Rock Versus the Dakota Access Pipeline, and the Long Tradition of Indigenous Resistance*. New York: Verso, 2019.
Our tour of the detention center—The report that came of our research trip: Cho, Eunice Hyunhye, Tara Tidwell Cullen, and Clara Long. "Justice-Free Zones: U.S. Immigration Detention Under the Trump Administration." Report. American Civil Liberties Union, 2020.

254. **Notorious for not giving parole**—Cho et al., "Justice-Free Zones," ACLU.

255. **He didn't speak Spanish**—For more on the particular struggles of Indigenous language speakers in the U.S. immigration system, particularly those that are perceived to be Latinx by officials: Nolan, Rachel. "A Translation Crisis at the Border." *The New Yorker*, December 30, 2019.

CHAPTER 54.

259. **Language of empire and conquest**—Hugo, "On the Art of Translation," *Theories of Translation*.
Webs of power and oppression—Akbar, Kaveh. "Crushed Glass and Medusa's Veil: Exploring the Revelatory Break." Lecture at Warren Wilson College, Swannanoa, NC, January 2020. This is available for purchase and download from Warren Wilson College's website.
Objectification of the natural world—Kimmerer, Robin. "Speaking of Nature." *Orion Magazine*, June 12, 2017.
Diccionario de la Real Academia Española—Zentella, Ana Celia. "'Limpia, Fija, y Da Esplendor': Challenging the Symbolic Violence of the Royal Spanish Academy." *Chiricú Journal: Latina/o Literatures, Arts, and Cultures* 1, no. 2 (Spring 2017): 21–42.

260. **Right to fall in love with a text**—Briggs' *This Little Art* is basically a book-length argument for this on behalf of literary translators.

264. **Encoded in your genes**—Carey, Benedict. "Can We Really Inherit Trauma?" *New York Times*, December 10, 2018.
The emotional memory of that fact—Khazan, Olga. "Separating Kids From Their Families Can Permanently Damage Their Brains." *The Atlantic*, June 22, 2018.

Affidavits from parents and children—*C.M. et. al. v. United States, et. al.* (United States District Court for the District of Arizona, complaint filed September 19, 2019). The affidavits and personal accounts of the events begin on page 27, paragraph 70.

265. Valeria Luiselli—Luiselli has written two books on unaccompanied minors traveling to the U.S., a work of nonfiction titled *Tell Me How it Ends* (Coffee House Press, 2017) and the novel *Lost Children Archive* (Knopf, 2019).

100 miles from any border—Small, Andrew. "CityLab Daily: Inside the Massive U.S. 'Border Zone.'" *Bloomberg*, May 14, 2018.

266. A hunger strike by detainees—"ICE Detainees in Boston Jail Refuse Meals." *WBUR*, February 17, 2019.

Empty and devoid of meaning—Merton, Thomas. *Raids on the Unspeakable.* New York: New Directions, 1961.

French mystic and theologian—Weil, *Waiting for God.*

268. Next to everyone else's—For more on hope through work in hard times, there's truly no one better than St. Oscar Romero.

Romero, Oscar. *The Scandal of Redemption: When God Liberates the Poor, Saves Sinners, and Heals Nations.* Edited by Carolyn Kurtz. Walden, NY: Plough Publishing House, 2018.

269. The people on the other side of the screen—Buff, Rachel Ida. "The Opposite of Loneliness." Translated by Alejandra Oliva. *Thinking C21,* 2022.

CHAPTER 55.

275. The MS *St. Louis*—Ogilvie, Sarah A., and Scott Miller. *Refuge Denied: The St. Louis Passengers and the Holocaust.* Madison: University of Wisconsin Press, 2006.

A billion people—"Ecological Threat Register 2020." Institute for Economics & Peace, 2020.

Climate refugees—Vince, Gaia. *Nomad Century: How Climate Migration Will Reshape Our World.* New York: Flatiron Books, 2022.

CHAPTER 56.

278. Translanguaging—Vogel, Sarah, and Ofelia García. "Translanguaging." *Oxford Research Encyclopedia of Education,* December 19, 2017.

AFTERWORD

282. Born from another book—Luiselli, *Tell Me How It Ends.*

284. Her fantastic book—Cornejo Villavicencio, *The Undocumented Americans.*

285. Prison and policing abolition movement—Kaba, Mariame. *We Do This 'Til We Free Us: Abolitionist Organizing and Transforming Justice.* Chicago: Haymarket Books, 2021.

Purnell, Derecka. *Becoming Abolitionists: Police, Protests, and the Pursuit of Freedom.* New York: Astra House Books, 2021.

Discussion Questions

1. In the Preface, Alejandra writes: "This book is unapologetically bilingual. It is written for an audience of largely English speakers because that is where the power and the fault in much of our immigration system lies." Why does she focus her attention on these readers? What does this focus suggest about the author's view of power as it relates to the act of translation?

2. Early on in the book, Alejandra discusses her relationship to the U.S.– Mexico border and to translation as practice—as a third generation Mexican American and as interpreter for migrants seeking asylum. How does Oliva's background affect her analysis of the conditions at the border?

3. In describing the conditions migrants face entering the U.S. via "legal" means, Oliva writes about "la lista," a notebook containing the names of every migrant in Tijuana who has declared that they want to cross the border "the right way," a process that obliges migrants to "cross, get detained for an indefinite period of time, and, during that detention, ask for, demand, insist on a Credible Fear Interview." How does the anonymous nature of "la lista" affect the options migrants are offered to cross the border? And what is the value of entering "the right way" in a system Oliva describes as "a veritable mountain of xenophobic laws, rules, and regulations"?

4. In Part II, Oliva introduces the term "sobremesa"—the conversations and space held over a dining table, the tending to matters following a meal, idle chat, and chores. How does the idea of "sobremesa" work as a metaphor for the work Oliva does at the border, interpreting the stories of people preparing for a Credible Fear Interview?

5. Alejandra shows how the exploitation of migrant farm workers serves as the basis of U.S. food production. How does American consumption force the reality of the conditions at the border?

6. In revealing the working conditions during the COVID pandemic at Sanderson Farms, the third-largest poultry processor in the U.S., Oliva shares the contents of a memo sent by the president of the company to his employees that read: "If people like you and me stop coming to work every day, people will go hungry. . . . We call upon you to look at this crisis as an opportunity to serve." What might this company's expectations about the necessity of the labor of its migrant workers suggest about the relationship between the U.S. and countries south of the border, where much of this labor is extracted from?

7. Throughout the book, Oliva looks at the act of translation through the lens of biblical theory. As she suggests, "even when you're not necessarily talking about the word of God, the original is held as a bright, inviolable light that the translator must struggle to approach, much less replicate." How does her understanding of biblical translation theory factor into her position that translation is an act of transferring power, and what impact might Christian theology have on the way immigration policy is determined and enacted in the United States?

8. After 39 people died in a fire in an immigration detention and processing center in Ciudad Juárez, Mexico, in March 2023, Oliva wrote in an op-ed: "These migrants may have died just outside the borders of our country while under the custody of the Mexican government, but their deaths were caused by the policies, practices, and biases of the U.S. government." In what ways has she proven this argument in *Rivermouth*? What are some potential policy alternatives that might alleviate the conditions described in the book?

Q&A with Alejandra

Q: When did you realize that this was the book you needed to write? Was it an idea that grew over time or was there a specific moment when you just knew?

A: It was definitely an idea that grew over time. The very first versions of what I thought might be a book were some five or so essays on food, ritual, translation, and immigration that I had written for various classes in divinity school. There was an essay on Virginia Woolf's novel *The Waves*, one on the concept of sobremesa and the eucharist, one on translation and ritual. I kind of realized that they all fit together alongside my interest in immigration and translation, and from there, the book both concentrated and expanded into what it is now!

Q: You are bilingual and one of the central themes of the book are the power dynamics in language. What was it like for you writing the book primarily in English? How and why did you make the decision to keep parts of the text in Spanish?

A: In spite of my parents' best efforts, I'm primarily an English speaker—I speak really good Spanish, I'm comfortable translating and reading and holding a conversation, but I think that if I want to be really artful or deliberate, English is the language I'm going to reach for first. That being said, and as I write in the book, Spanish for me is this language of family and homecoming and safety. I know that there are millions of Spanish speakers around the world, but it still feels like this special family language to me. I wanted to both give Spanish-speaking readers that little spark of recognition and monolingual English speakers a sense of what it might feel like to not have a book or a space cater completely to their linguistic needs.

Q: People often have strong personal views around immigration, migration, and asylum. Sometimes these views are tied to personal experiences, sometimes they are tied to false beliefs about economics and society. What would you say should be the core principles that shape our views on the issue?

A: I want to also base this answer on personal experience. My family and I had a very different experience with immigration, one ensconced in privilege and economic plenty, and so for a long time, immigration inequality and asylum were all issues that pertained to other people. What changed that was talking to people who had firsthand experiences within the immigration system. People who had left their homes in search of peace, who had traveled across a landscape that was hostile to their presence, who had encountered the militarized, dangerous U.S. border, who affirmed the justness of their presence in the United States and who spoke clearly and powerfully about the injustices they had encountered along the way. Other issues that are often linked to immigration in public discourse—questions of allocation of resources, jobs, safety, and society—are often either extremely thinly disguised white supremacist rhetoric (looking at you, Great Replacement Theory) or questions of economic injustice in which it's easy to scapegoat immigrants rather than talk about the actual systemic inequalities at the heart of the problem. In short, I think the core principles that should shape our views on the issue of immigration are questions of justice, humanitarianism, and generosity as we strive to build a better country and world for everyone to live in, regardless of their nation of origin.

Q: You spent time in 2019 translating at the border crossing in San Ysidro—the largest land border crossing in the world—where 90,000 people pass through daily, by foot or by car. This made the border a vivid, real place. For many (most) people, the border is a vague mostly political concept: what do you want people most to understand about the border as a place?

A: San Ysidro—and on the other side of the border, Tijuana—is a place where you can see all the contradictions of what the border is. You have all this military surveillance apparatus—the barbed wire, the armed guards, the security cameras, the tall fences—but you also have people moving through it. And they're not just the concept of people but they're real, specific people who, as they're crossing the border, are bringing with them all these hopes and ideals and fears and Minnie Mouse luggage and idiosyncrasies. The people at the border are in this very loaded, very intense place both geographically and often emotionally but they're also just people, trying to get by, trying to make the best choices they can.

Q: Faith is another strong throughline in this book, from your own belief system to religion as it relates to immigration and language/interpretation. Can you explain how these things are related?

A: Immigration stories are everywhere in the Bible, the book of the faith tradition I was raised in. From the 40 days and 40 nights wandering the desert, to the flight from Egypt, migration is this extremely old story that has echoes in these stories we tell as central parts of our culture. A lot of my adult journey has been taking this faith I was raised in and often chafed against and both coming to terms with the fact that it did have a profound effect on me as a person, and the values I live by, but also that there are ways to live into those values that aren't necessarily the same kind of conservative, self-isolating and self-centered church I was raised in—and one of the first ways I saw people doing that was in the immigration rights movement. From providing sanctuary in church spaces for immigrants with deportation orders to accompanying people as they encounter the bureaucratic mess of the immigration system to attending to people in immigration detention, religious groups are a huge part of the immigration justice movement, and for many individuals, fighting for justice is a part of their religious practice. When it comes to language and translation—a lot of the oldest translation theory in the West comes from people talking about how or whether to translate the Bible, where the holiness resided in a text written by God and whether it would remain holy if you translated it. Many of the conversations we have today about translation that really venerate the original as this kind of sacred text that we clumsy translators can't help but mutilate as we pass it into another language echo and reflect those early theories. When I was working with asylum seekers' accounts of the violence they had faced, I witnessed how these original "texts" often created through great hardship and effort in remembering and reliving trauma—they were cut and shaped into a very specific narrative and format to fit an immigration form. This process kind of raised my hackles as a translator, and it was through that discomfort that I started thinking about a lot of the questions that led to the more language theory parts of the book—questions about how we value stories, and how we change them through translating or interpreting them.

Q: The difficulties and dangers of migration are often in the news and the scale can feel overwhelming for the layperson. What process

would you recommend for your readers who want to contribute and support their local immigrant communities?

A: First of all, the border is everywhere. There's this really pervasive idea that the border is this very specific place where all these issues are isolated, but the truth is that many large U.S. cities have an ICE field office and/ or an immigration court where people go to regular check-ins, attend hearings, and the like, and there are immigration detention facilities in just about every state (a few, including my home state of Illinois, have banned immigration detention, but that simply shifts the problem to other states). There are also immigrants in just about every community in the U.S., from the huge cities to tiny farm or factory towns in rural areas. I can also almost guarantee that there's someone already doing the work in your community—providing services, working to ensure that resources are available in the correct languages, delivering on any one of a dozen things that people who are just trying to set up their lives in a new country might need. If you're willing to volunteer, I'd recommend seeking these places out and figuring out how you can help. That sometimes looks like direct services, but can also look like emailing people, translating documents, setting up spreadsheets, soliciting donations. If you're already volunteering or involved in your community in some way, it can also be a good practice to figure out how or whether that organization is engaging with the local immigrant community, and working to make that better. Are you offering services, events, or literature in different languages? Are you making it clear that people from all immigration statuses are welcome or eligible for your services? Finally, there are times when the border comes to us really clearly and directly—there's an ICE raid in our neighborhood or workplace, local officials announce that they're in talks to build an immigration detention facility in your town or county. Being prepared for those moments—finding bystander trainings, getting involved in a local site fight—is critical. So much of the most vibrant and critical activism I've seen is through people looking out for their neighbors in this way.

Q: There are also clearly huge issues at the systemic and policy levels. What are three concrete steps that would lead to a more humane and effective approach to the asylum process?

A: I think the three concrete steps we need to take on a systemic, federal level, all center on the idea of making the system less punitive for those who are forced to engage in it. The first and most urgent step is completely ending immigration detention—there's absolutely no reason anyone should be in prison for exerting their human right to migration. The medical neglect in immigration detention is rampant, and has been known to kill and disable people. The second is to demilitarize the border and end the policy of "deterrence," which basically involves making crossing the border dangerous in the hopes that people stop coming. We know that this isn't a policy that works—people are still arriving at the border all the time, and hundreds of people die each year attempting to cross. That leads me to the third step: in not spending the billions of dollars we currently do on both detention and militarization. These funds can be far better used in helping support new arrivals—language classes, helping secure job permits, integration into communities, all kinds of things that have benefit not just for immigrant communities or new arrivals, but all of us.

Q: What was the big takeaway for you in the experience of writing this book? What do you hope your readers discover in these pages that will stay with them when they finish reading?

A: More than in the writing of the book but in researching it, living the events that came to take place in the book, it is the lesson that getting involved in your community is absolutely worth it. It's almost always going to put you into contact with hard things, things you're not able to fix or even get your arms around. It's still worth it to put your shoulder in, to try to change things for the better. I have to believe in a world where collective action can make a difference, where mutual aid matters to the health of individual people and our communities. For me, the road into this kind of understanding of the world was through immigration, but I've seen it over and over again in all kinds of places and situations.

Selected National
Immigration Organizations

American Immigration Council | americanimmigrationcouncil.org

Asian Americans Advancing Justice | advancingjustice-aajc.org

Asylum Seekers Advocacy Project | asylumadvocacy.org

CAIR | cair.org

Catholic Charities | catholiccharitiesusa.org

Freedom for Immigrants | freedomforimmigrants.org

Immigration Advocates Network | immigrationadvocates.org

Immigration Equality | immigrationequality.org

Movimiento Cosecha | lahuelga.com

National Bail Fund Network | nbfn.org

National Immigrant Justice Center | immigrantjustice.org

Never Again Action | neveragainaction.com

Southern Border Communities Coalition | southernborder.org

United We Dream | unitedwedream.org

Acknowledgments

There are approximately one thousand people whose work, dedication, time, and talent came together to make this book, and approximately another thousand whose patience, care, and love enabled me to write it. It would be impossible to thank them all, so here's an attempt.

Thank you first of all to my brilliant agent, Dana Murphy, who asked all the right questions throughout this process and worked with me throughout the long first months of a global pandemic to get this book ready.

Thanks to my editor Danny Vazquez who saw more in this book than I would dare to dream. And thanks to the entire team who has worked on *Rivermouth*, both inside and outside of Astra House—Rola Harb and Alessandra Bastagli on the editorial side; Rachael Small in publicity along with Emily Lavelle; marketing and sales geniuses Tiffany Gonzalez, Jack W. Perry, and Sarah Christensen Fu; Rodrigo Corral and Paola de la Calle for making the outside of this book beautiful and Richard Oriolo for making the inside match; Lisa Taylor, Alisa Trager, Elizabeth Koehler, and Olivia Dontsov for keeping me on track and on time with the production; and Jenn Baker for a careful, insightful copyedit that means this book has far fewer run-on sentences for the reader to bang their head against. Working with this team meant that I got to work with people whose values and hopes for *Rivermouth* aligned with my own in a way I could have never imagined.

Thank you to the organizations and individuals who gave critical financial and logistical support while I worked on this book. Harvard Divinity School's Experiential Learning Fund and Susan Shallcross Swartz funded my trip to Tijuana in January 2019. Aspen Words gave me an emerging writer fellowship that changed the trajectory of my writing career. Yale's Whitney Humanities Center and Mr. and Mrs. Richard and Barbara Franke gave me a six-month Franke Visiting Fellowship and the space and resources I needed as I finished the first draft of this book. Alice Kaplan and Diane Berrett Brown welcomed me into the community they built at the Whitney Center so beautifully, even amid unexpected waves of COVID-19. The Whiting Foundation's support in the form of the Creative Nonfiction Grant brought the book home. The National Immigrant Justice Center employed me during the majority of the writing of this book and not only paid me a salary; provided health insurance; and taught me a thousand things about immigration, policy, and what it looks like to do good work; but they were also incredibly supportive, flexible employers as I balanced working for them and writing a book.

This book would not have been born without my time at Harvard Divinity School. As such, I owe its existence to a number of the faculty there—Matt Potts, whose class on the sacramental imagination planted the very first seed that would become this book; Amy Hollywood, who read translation theory alongside me and helped me think more deeply about archives; Stephanie Paulsell, who let me write essays about anything and everything in her classes and helped me secure funding to go to Tijuana in January 2019; and Terry Tempest Williams, who gave me so many gifts and so much time it would be impossible to enumerate here. Amy, Stephanie, and Terry also read early, early drafts and provided some much needed encouragement and critique.

Thanks to early readers/good friends Madeline Vosch, Iuscely Flores, and Gia Kagan-Trenchard, whose insights, questions, and challenges made the book better.

Thanks to the people I've met along the way while doing research and writing this book. To the New Sanctuary Fam: Sara, Gia, Kitty, Ravi, Juan Carlos, and everyone else at the clinics week after week, both friends and volunteers. In Tijuana: Libby Garland, Rachel Ida Buff, and Katie Freeman, short-term residents of the best little Airbnb in Chula Vista, as well as Sara and her family, who were kind enough to let me share their story. In Chicago(ish): my coworkers and colleagues at the National Immigrant Justice Center, especially comms team members Tara Tidwell Cullen, Julia Toepfer, and Jordyn Rozensky; executive director Mary Meg McCarthy; policy team members Heidi Altman, Nayna Gupta, Jesse Franzblau, Azadeh Erfani, and Nubia Fimbres, as well as Kate Ramos and Libby Kalmbach Clark. It's worth noting that all the opinions in this book are my own, but were shaped and molded by working and learning alongside this team.

Thanks especially to anyone who has taken the time in the last few years to share their story of encountering the U.S. immigration system with me. I'm incredibly honored to have spent time with each of you, and the trust you placed in me by talking to me and spending time answering my questions is a gift.

And at last, and most of all, to my friends, family, and community.

Missy and Haley, I could not have finished this without our group chat, your endless support, and screaming together on our respective couches when time and geography permitted.

To the Didiers—I love you all so much. Joan, getting to know you and your many sisters is the unexpected bonus to my marriage. Tim, I'm eternally grateful to have known you, and will miss you so much. Matt, you're absolutely the best.

My grandparents—Enriqueta, who I did not get to meet but I hear I take after; David, who is so missed; Rogelio, who called me Señorita Pulitzer from when I was ten years old and who I miss so much; Dolores, the best Ima a girl could ask for.

My parents, Rogelio and Susana: I am so, so grateful for everything. You gave me two languages—sometimes against my best efforts—love of books, and a home that felt worth sharing. My siblings, Bettie and Rojas: I'm so glad we've gotten to live near each other as grown-ups. I love you all.

And finally, to Jason. None of this would have been possible without your support—logistical, emotional, practical, all of it. I am a better version of myself when I'm with you, and this book is a better version of itself for having been discussed, debated, and written alongside you. All my love, always.

PHOTO BY ANNA LONGWORTH

ABOUT THE AUTHOR

Alejandra Oliva is an essayist, translator, immigrant justice advocate, and embroiderer. She is a recipient of the 2022 Creative Nonfiction Whiting Grant. Her writing has been included in *Best American Travel Writing* 2020 and was nominated for a Pushcart prize. She was honored with an Aspen Words Emerging Writers Fellowship and was the Franke Fellow at the Yale Whitney Humanities Center in spring 2022. Read more at olivalejandra.com.